T0414093

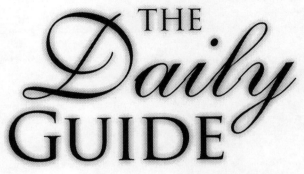

THE Daily GUIDE

Prayers, Readings and Devotionals

Atarah Shalom

WESTBOW
PRESS®
A DIVISION OF THOMAS NELSON
& ZONDERVAN

Copyright © 2017 Atarah Shalom.

All rights reserved. No part of this book may be used or reproduced by any means, graphic, electronic, or mechanical, including photocopying, recording, taping or by any information storage retrieval system without the written permission of the author except in the case of brief quotations embodied in critical articles and reviews.

Scripture quotations marked (KJV) are from the King James Version.

This book is a work of non-fiction. Unless otherwise noted, the author and the publisher make no explicit guarantees as to the accuracy of the information contained in this book and in some cases, names of people and places have been altered to protect their privacy.

WestBow Press books may be ordered through booksellers or by contacting:

WestBow Press
A Division of Thomas Nelson & Zondervan
1663 Liberty Drive
Bloomington, IN 47403
www.westbowpress.com
1 (866) 928-1240

Because of the dynamic nature of the Internet, any web addresses or links contained in this book may have changed since publication and may no longer be valid. The views expressed in this work are solely those of the author and do not necessarily reflect the views of the publisher, and the publisher hereby disclaims any responsibility for them.

Any people depicted in stock imagery provided by Thinkstock are models, and such images are being used for illustrative purposes only. Certain stock imagery © Thinkstock.

ISBN: 978-1-5127-7410-8 (sc)
ISBN: 978-1-5127-7411-5 (hc)
ISBN: 978-1-5127-7409-2 (e)

Library of Congress Control Number: 2017901774

Print information available on the last page.

WestBow Press rev. date: 02/16/2017

TABLE OF CONTENTS

INTRODUCTION

The Daily Guide is composed of prayers and devotions designed to be used every day. These are my personal daily prayers I've chosen to share with you. I try to follow these prayers constantly and it is true that, at times, I've prayed quickly and had to stop and meditate on what I was saying. These prayers help keep my mind focused on the Lord all throughout the day and I like to pray to Him often. He is my unseen companion – I can communicate with Him as I can with no one else. I cannot see my Lord but He is real and He is always with me.

There are moments of prayer when I am in distress or when I feel lonely and isolated from the world. Sometimes I feel anxious about the safety or well being of loved ones and at such moments I've shed tears with a pained heart and the a feelings of despair. Sometimes I pray and a great sense of relief comes over me. At all these times, I may shed tears with feelings of gratefulness. I firmly believe that God hears my prayers all the time.

I do not pray out of a sense of obligation and I can talk to Him at anytime through my day.

The Hebrew word for "to pray" *l'hitpalel* (תְּפִלָּה / *těphillah*) does not mean "to ask" or "to petition" God. It is derived from a stem, *pll* (פָּלַל / *palal*). It means "to judge"; therefore, l'hitpalel, ("to pray"), could also be translated as "to judge oneself." Here lies a clue to the real purpose for engaging in prayer. Whether we petition God to give us what we need, thank Him for whatever good was granted, or extol Him for His awesome attributes, all prayer is intended to help make us into better human beings through a relationship with our Maker.

Spontaneous prayer may come easily to some when others may ask, "What do I say?" and "How do I say it?". I often see people ask for prayer from a respectable person as if their prayer might carry more weight. However, I believe that every person has the same right to approach God and to do so might well be more meaningful than to seek out intercessors. God wants a relationship with each and every individual.

I realize that some people lack the ability to express their innermost feelings and thoughts. Even though God knows our inner most thoughts, it helps us to focus on God through guided prayers; ridding us of distractions so that we can hear the voice of God from within.

Prayer does not belong exclusively to the followers of any one faith. All people who believe in God are moved at one time or another to utter a heartfelt prayer to Him.

To get the most out of any book, you must take the time to analyze the words you encounter and if you judge them worthy, you must take them within your way of thinking. Just as important, you then must act in accordance with what you have learned and embraced. This deliberate effort is going to make "The Daily Guide" a significant part of the price of success.

As you say these prayers and read the daily scripture readings consistently, you will begin to memorize them and take them to heart.

When the mind conceives and believes, that is when the mind of man can succeed.

Guidelines for using The Daily Guide

1. Decide when you want to do these prayers. There are morning prayers, afternoon prayers, evening prayers and a bedtime prayer (to be said before going to sleep). If things come up and you can't get to them, don't feel condemned or beat yourself up. Remember that what you are doing is out of your love and devotion to God – it is a way to clear the mind of distractions so that you can hear from Him. To be successful using this book, try to stay consistent as much as possible.

2. Always stay focused on what you are reading and saying in the prayers and scriptures. One way to stay focused is to repeatedly read each line and scripture a few times. I know that is can be time consuming but it is nevertheless very rewarding. Sometimes I will read each prayer 22 times, memorizing as I go. The daily morning prayers, for example, take about an hour.

3. Read each Psalms, Proverbs and devotional as recommended for each day. Memorize desirable affirmations or scriptures that stood out to you so to impress indelibly on your subconscious mind (spirit).

4. Check yourself daily to see if you are acquiring the desirable habit. Keep a daily record so that you can evaluate your progress.

You are guaranteed results using "The Daily Guide" if you use it and apply it to your everyday life. God has given you unlimited potential, all you have to do is learn how to tap into it, convert it and use it.

DAILY GUIDED PRAYERS

The LORD is near to all who call upon Him,
to all who call upon Him in truth. (Psalms 145:18)

Morning Prayers

I thank You, living and eternal King,
for returning my soul within me in compassion.

Great is Your faithfulness.

To be devoted with reverence and respect to the LORD
is the beginning of wisdom.
All who do His commandments have a good understanding.
His praise endures forever.
Blessed be His name forever and ever.

Let Your Words be sweet in our mouths.
The spirit that You placed within me is pure.
You created it; You fashioned it;
You breathed it into me.
You preserve it within me,
and will one day take it from me
and restore it to me in the hereafter.

Therefore, as long as my spirit is within me,
I will give thanks before You.
I give thanks before You LORD my God,
Master of all creation,
LORD of all spirits.
Blessed are You, oh LORD,
who restores the spirits of the departed.

Oh LORD our God,
I pray that we will become accustomed
to walking in the way of Your Words,
and cling to Your precepts
so we will not fall into sin, iniquity, temptation or disgrace
or let the impulse to evil rule over us.
LORD, keep us far from evil people and worthless companions,
and help us cling to Your will to do good and to
good deeds as written in Your Word.
May we continually stay in Your Word and bend our will to Yours.
Thank You that today and everyday,
You have given us grace
(unmerited love, favor and empowerment).
Thank You that today and everyday,
You have given us grace to do Your will.

In Your sight and in the sight of all people,
You have bestowed upon us Your loving-kindness.
Blessed are You LORD,
who bestows loving-kindness upon His people.

It is our privilege to give You thanks and praise and lift You up.
It is our privilege to bless, sanctify and render praise

and give thanksgiving to Your name.
We are fortunate: how excellent is Your name.

אֶחָד יְיָ אֱלֹהֵינוּ יְיָ יִשְׂרָאֵל שְׁמַע
וָעֶד לְעוֹלָם מָלְכוּתוֹ כְּבוֹד שֵׁם בָּרוּךְ
יי הוּא הַמָשִׁיחַ יֵשׁוּעַ

Hear oh Israel, the LORD our God, the LORD is one.
Blessed is the name of His glorious kingdom for ever and ever.
Jesus the Messiah He is LORD.

Bless the LORD, oh my soul and all that is within me,
bless His holy name.
Bless the LORD, oh my soul
and forget none of His benefits:
Who forgives all my iniquities,
Who heals all disease,
Who redeems my life from the pit of
corruption, destruction and decay,
Who beautifies and dignifies me.
Who surrounds me with loving-kindness and tender mercy
and Who satisfies my mouth with good
things so that my youth is renewed.
I am like an eagle: strong, overcoming and soaring!

Blessed are You, LORD our God, King of the universe,
Who by His Word brings about all things.

Something good is going to happen to me today!
I am successful because Jesus is with me.

I keep my mouth from speaking evil.
I love life and I see good days!

The LORD God is a sun and shield:
the LORD will give grace, favor, and a future.
The LORD will give glory (honor, brilliance,
and supreme happiness):
no good thing will He withhold from those who walk uprightly
(those that dwell in His presence).

Our Father, which is in heaven, hallowed be Your name.
Your kingdom come and Your will be
done on earth, as it is in heaven.
Thank You for giving us this day our daily bread.
You've forgiven our debts, as we forgive our debtors.
You lead us not into temptation.
You've delivered us from evil.
It is Your kingdom, the power and the glory, forever.
Amen.

This I pray that the God of our LORD Jesus Christ,
the Father of glory,
may give to my family, friends and myself the spirit of wisdom
and revelation in the knowledge of Him
that the eyes of our understanding may be enlightened;
that we may know what is the expectation of His calling
and the riches of the glory of His inheritance is in the saints,
and what is the exceeding greatness of His power to us
who believe, according to the working of His mighty power.

Blessed are You, LORD our God, King of the universe,
Who gave to us Jesus the Messiah and the promised Holy Spirit.
Blessed are You.

The Spirit helps our weaknesses
because we do not know what to pray for like we should.
The Spirit Himself makes intercession for us with
utterances that cannot be understood.
If we pray in an unknown language, our spirit prays,
but we do not understand.
Therefore, we will pray with the spirit, and we
will pray with the understanding also;
we will sing with the spirit, and we will sing
with the understanding also.

Blessed are You, LORD, giver of the Holy Spirit.

The very God of peace sanctifies us wholly,
and we pray to God that our whole spirit, soul and body
be preserved blameless all the way to the coming
of our LORD Jesus the Messiah.

Stop – personal prayer (fifteen minutes).

Praised is the LORD, the eternal source of all blessings.

Praised are You, oh LORD our God, King of the universe,
Who chose us from among all people by giving us His Word.

Praised are You, oh LORD, giver of the Word.

Blessed are You, LORD our God, King of the universe,
Who gave us Jesus the Messiah and the
commandments of the New Covenant.

Blessed are You, LORD, giver of the New Covenant.

***Stop and do a daily devotional and meditate
on each scripture reference given.***

Praised are You, oh LORD our God, King of the universe,
Who gave us the Word of truth,
endowing us with everlasting life.
Praised are You, oh LORD, giver of the Word.

Blessed are You, LORD our God, King of the universe,
Who gave to us the Word of truth
and planted everlasting life in our midst.

Blessed are You, LORD, giver of the New Covenant.

Afternoon Prayers

Blessed are You, LORD our God, King of the universe,
Who by His Word brings about all things.
Blessed are You, LORD our God, King of the universe.
You sustain the whole world with Your goodness,
loving favor and kindness.
You give food to all flesh
and Your loving-kindness endures forever.
In Your great goodness, our sustenance has never failed us.
It will never fail us for the sake of Your great name.
You are God who provides nourishing food for all
and are beneficent to all,
preparing food for all Your creatures.

Blessed are You, LORD, who provides food for all.
We thank You, LORD our God,
for the desirable, good and ample land
which You granted to our fathers as a heritage.
We thank You for the covenant and the Word.
We thank you for life and sustenance in plenty.
Blessed are You, LORD, for the land and for the food.
Thank You for Your compassion upon Your people.
Thank You for Your compassion upon Jerusalem, Your city.
Thank You for Your compassion upon the
royal house of Your anointed David.
Exalt the glory of Your temple,
and give us double comfort.
Blessed are You, LORD,
Who in Your loving-kindness rebuilds Jerusalem. Amen.

Blessed are You our God, our Father and our King,
Who is kind and deals kindly with all.
You have made us worthy in the Messiah,
You make us worthy in the life of the world to come.
He Who creates peace in His celestial heights
create peace for us all. Amen.

Thank You that You have blessed our bread and water
and have taken sickness away from us;
therefore, we will fulfill the number of our days in health and wealth.

אֶחָד יְיָ אֱלֹהֵינוּ יְיָ יִשְׂרָאֵל שְׁמַע
וָעֶד לְעוֹלָם מַלְכוּתוֹ כְּבוֹד שֵׁם בָּרוּךְ

Hear oh Israel, the LORD our God, the LORD is one.
Blessed is the name of His glorious kingdom for ever and ever.

You shall love the Lord your God with all your heart,
with all your soul and with all your might.

God said, "These words that I command you this
day are to be your love and affection.
You are to teach them diligently to your children.
You are to talk about them at home and abroad, night and day.

You are to bind them as a sign upon your hand;
they are to be frontlets between your eyes,
and you are to inscribe them on the doorposts
of your homes and on your gates."

Jesus said, "A new commandment I give unto you,
that you love one another; as I have loved you,
that you also love one another."

With a great love You love us, LORD our God,
and with exceedingly great mercy You sympathize with us.
Our Father, our King,
for the sake of our forefathers who trusted in You,
whom You taught the laws of life,
may You have mercy for us and teach us alike.
Our Father, the merciful Father, Who has mercy,
who has loving-kindness upon us
and gives us the insight to understand and to become wiser,
to listen, learn and teach,
observe, follow and maintain
all the words of the teaching of Your Word with love.
Enlighten our eyes with Your Word,
affix us to Your commandments,
unify us to love
and to deeply respect Your name

and we will not be ashamed forever and ever.
In Your great, awesome and holy name I have trusted,
and I will rejoice and delight in Your salvation
(safety, protection, health, healing and deliverance).
You brought peace
(health, safety, prosperity, nothing missing and nothing broken)
to me from the four corners of the earth,
and You lead us with pride to sovereignty in our country.
You are God Who brings salvation,
You have chosen us from among all nations and languages.
You have brought us closer to Your great name forever in truth,
to thank You and distinguish Your oneness with love.
Blessed are You, LORD, Who chooses His people with love. Amen.

Master of the universe who has reigned,
before anything was created,
at the time that everything was created at His will,
His name was proclaimed "King",
after all has ceased to exist,
He, the awesome one, will reign alone.
He was and He is, and He shall be in Glory.
He is one – and there is no second to compare to Him,
none to declare as His equal,
without beginning, without end,
He has the might and dominion.
He is my God and my living Redeemer,
and my Rock (my strength) in times of struggle
and my Rock at times of trouble.
He is my standard and a refuge for me,
He is the portion in my cup on the day I call.
In His hand I will deposit my spirit,
when I am asleep – I shall awaken,

and with my body shall my spirit remain.
The LORD is with me and I shall not fear.

All my children have turned to me and my influence.
All my children have come back to me from the land of the enemy.
God said, "Assuredly (I pledge it)
the wicked (malicious, spiteful with bitter,
ill will) shall not go unpunished,
but the seed of the righteous shall be delivered."
God rebukes him who fights against me and He saves my children.
God gives me wisdom that my enemies are not able to gain say.
My writings elevates my love, honor and
character above my enemies.
They are ashamed that taunted me saying, "Where is your God?".
I raise my eyes and I look around for all my
children are assembling and coming to me.
My children have returned to me seven times better.
I have sevenfold restoration of everything that
was stolen and kept back from me.
I am seven times happier than I was before.

Stop – personal prayer (fifteen minutes).
Read the Psalms and Proverb for today.

DAILY PSALMS AND PROVERBS

Read the Proverbs that corresponds with the current day. For example, if it is Sunday the 10th, you read Proverbs 10. If there are only 30 days in the month, read Proverbs 30 and 31 on the 30th.

Sunday - Psalm 24,
Monday- Psalm 48
Tuesday - Psalm 82
Wednesday - Psalm 94 / Psalm 95:1-3
Thursday - Psalm 81
Friday - Psalm 93

SABBATH PRAYER

Evening Prayers

Stop – personal prayer (fifteen minutes).

Blessed are You, LORD our God, Master of the universe,
whose Word brings on the evening.
May the living and eternal God rule over us always and forever.
Blessed are You, LORD, Who brings on the evening.

Praise the LORD, Who is to be praised forever and ever.

Blessed are You, LORD our God, Master of the universe,
Who forms light and creates darkness,
Who makes peace and creates all things.
Blessed are You, LORD, Who forms the lights.

Blessed are You LORD our God, King of the universe,
Who gave to us the way of salvation in Jesus the Messiah.
Blessed be He. Amen.

Bedtime Blessings

Blessed are You, oh LORD, our God, King of the universe,
who created day and night.
You roll away the light from before the darkness,
and the darkness from before the light.
Blessed are You LORD, who creates the evening twilight.

Hear oh Israel, the LORD our God the LORD is one.
Blessed be His name, whose glorious kingdom is forever and ever.

You shall love the LORD your God with all your heart,
with all your soul, and all your strength.

Blessed are You, LORD our God, King of the Universe,
who makes the bands of sleep fall upon my eyes
and slumber upon my eyelids.

Thank You, oh LORD my God, and the God of my fathers,
that You let me lie down in peace
and You let me rise up again in peace.

My spirit belongs to you: thou hast redeemed me,
oh LORD God of truth.

Saturday's Prayers

Taken from ISAIAH 58:13 – 14
If you hold back your foot on Sabbath
from pursuing your own interests on the LORD'S Holy Day;
if you call Sabbath a delight,
The LORD'S Holy Day, worth honoring;
Then honor it by not doing your usual things
Or pursuing your interests or speaking about them.
If you do, you will find delight in the LORD –
The LORD will make you ride on the heights of the land
And feed you with the heritage of your ancestor Jacob
For the mouth of Jacob has spoken.

Blessed are you LORD our GOD, King of the Universe,
who has sanctified us by Your Word
and calls us to hear the voice of the shofar (trumpet).

Blessed are You LORD our GOD, King of the universe,
Who has given us the way of salvation in Jesus the Messiah. Amen.

With joy I draw forth water from the springs of Salvation!

May your name be praised forever our King.
Unto You we offer blessings
and thanksgiving from this time forever.
Blessed are You LORD, GOD, King,
Who is exalted through praises,
You are GOD of thanksgiving,
Master of wonders,
Who chooses musical songs of praise,
You are King, LORD, giver of life.

How lovely are your tents, oh Jacob,
Your dwelling places, oh Israel.
LORD, through Your abundant grace I will enter Your presence,
In awe I will bow down to You.
LORD, I love Your presence where You dwell,
I love the place where Your Glory resides.
I will prostrate my self and bow,
I willingly bend the knee before the LORD my Maker.

As for me, may my prayers to You, oh LORD, be at the right time.
LORD, in Your abundant righteousness,
answer me with the truth of Your Salvation.

Bless the LORD, the blessed one.

Blessed is the LORD, the blessed one, for all eternity.

Remember the Sabbath day to keep it holy.

Six days shall you labor and do all your work;

But the seventh day is the Sabbath of the LORD your GOD,
in it you are to cease from your work and
abilities and trust in the LORD.

For in six days the LORD made the heaven and the earth,
the sea and all that is in them
and finished His work on the seventh day;
that is why the LORD blessed the Sabbath day and hallowed it.

Speak also unto the children of Israel saying:
"Above all, My Sabbaths you are to keep;

for it is a sign between Me and you throughout your generations,
that you may know that I am the LORD Who sanctifies you.

The Israelites are to observe the Sabbath,
Celebrating it for the generations to come
as an everlasting covenant.
It will be a sign between Me and the Israelites forever."
In six days the LORD made the heavens and the earth,
And on the seventh day He completed His work.

"It will come to pass that from one new moon to another
and from one Sabbath to another,
All flesh are to come to worship before Me."
says the LORD. (Isaiah 66:23)

אֶחָד יְיָ אֱלֹהֵינוּ יְיָ יִשְׂרָאֵל שְׁמַע
וָעֶד לְעוֹלָם מַלְכוּתוֹ כְּבוֹד שֵׁם בָּרוּךְ

Hear, oh Israel: The LORD our God, the LORD is one.
Praised be His sovereign glory forever and ever.

You are to love the LORD your God with
all your spirit, soul and body.

These words which I command you this day
are to be your love and affection.
You are to teach them diligently to your children.
You are to talk about them at home, abroad, night and day.

You are to bind them as a sign upon your hand;
they are to be frontlets between your eyes,

and you are to inscribe them on the doorposts
of your homes and on your gates.

You are to love your neighbor as God has loved you!

Who is like You LORD among the gods?
Who is like You glorified in holiness?
You are awesome in praise, working wonders
LORD, who is like You?

Give thanks to the LORD for He is good,
Give thanks to the LORD for His grace forever endures.

LORD, open my lips that my mouth may tell of Your glory.

Blessed are You LORD our God and God of our fathers,
God of Abraham, Isaac and Jacob,
the great, mighty and awesome God,
the most high God Almighty,
You bestows grace (love, favor and empowerment)
You create all,
You remember Your kindnesses,
You gave a Redeemer for Your name's sake with love.
oh King, Helper, Savior, and Shield,
blessed are You LORD, Shield of Abraham.

You are eternally mighty,
You are my Master,
You are the Resurrector of the dead;
You are great in salvation (safety, protection,
health, healing and deliverance).
You sustain the living with grace,

You resurrect the dead with great mercy,
You support the fallen,
You heal the sick,
You release the confined,
You keep Your Word to those who have already turned to dust.
Who is like You, oh master of mighty deeds,
Who is comparable to You,
oh King Who causes death and restores life
and makes salvation sprout?
You are faithful to resurrect the dead.
Blessed are You, LORD, Who resurrects the dead.

You are holy and Your name is holy,
and every day holy ones will praise You. Selah.
Blessed are You, LORD, the holy God.

You grant knowledge and teach insight to human beings.
Endow me graciously with Your knowledge, insight and wisdom.
Blessed are You, LORD, the giver of wisdom.

Bring us back, our Father, to Your Word,
and bring us closer, our King, to Your service
and make us return in complete repentance
(change of heart, mind and direction).
Blessed are You, LORD, Who desires repentance.

Forgive us, our Father, for we have erred,
pardon us, our King, for we have intentionally sinned,
for You pardon and forgive our sins (past, present and future).
Blessed are You, LORD, the merciful one Who pardons abundantly.

Behold our affliction, take up our grievance,
and save me soon for the sake of Your name,
for You are a powerful Redeemer.
Blessed are You, LORD, the Redeemer of Israel.

Heal us LORD - and we shall be healed,
save us - and we shall be saved,
for You are our praise,
Bring complete recovery for all our ailments.

You are LORD and King,
the faithful and compassionate Healer.
Blessed are You, LORD, Who heals the sick of His people.

Blessed are You, Jesus our Messiah
"Who His own self bore our sins in His own body on the tree,
that we, being dead to sins, should live unto righteousness:
by whose stripes we are healed." (1 Peter 2:24)

Bless for us, LORD, our GOD, this year and
all its kinds of crops for the best,
and give a blessing;
Give dew and rain for a blessing on the face of the earth,
and satisfy us from Your goodness,
and bless our year like the good years.
Blessed are You, LORD, Who blesses the years.

This is my best year so far
– it gets better and better!

God takes pleasure in my prosperity.
I am His servant;

therefore, I declare that my needs are met,
and I have plenty more to put in store.
I have all good and beneficial things.

Let them shout for joy, and be glad, that favor my righteous cause:
yea, let them say continually, "Let the LORD be magnified,
which has pleasure in the prosperity of his servant."

Wealth and riches shall be in his house:
and his righteousness endures for ever.

I have abundance and my storehouses (bank
accounts) are filled with plenty!

It is written, "But you are to remember the LORD your God:
for it is He that gives you power to get wealth,
that He may establish His covenant which He
swore to your fathers, as it is this day."

The blessings of the Lord makes me truly rich
and He adds no sorrow with them.

Sound the great shofar (horn) for our freedom,
and raise a standard to gather our exiles,
and gather us from the four corners of the earth.
Blessed are You, LORD, Who gathers the dispersed of His people.

LORD, restore our judges and leaders as in early times,
restore our advisers as it once was from the beginning,
remove from us agony and groaning,
and reign over us.

LORD, reign over us with grace and loving-kindness,
and justify us in judgment.
Blessed are You, LORD and King,
Who loves righteousness and judgment.

Lord, may Your compassion be stimulated
on the righteous and the devout,
may Your compassion be stimulated on the elders of Your people,
may Your compassion be stimulated on the house of Israel,
may Your compassion be stimulated on the remnant of their scribes,
may Your compassion be stimulated on the
righteous converts and on me,
may Your compassion be aroused, oh LORD, my God,
and give good reward to all who truly trust Your name,
may You put my share among them forever.
I will not be ashamed or disappointed because I trust in You.
Blessed are You, oh LORD, who supports
and safeguards the righteous.

To Jerusalem Your City
You will return with mercy and dwell in it,
as You have spoken,
may You rebuild it soon in my days for eternity,
may You establish the throne of David within it.
Blessed are You, oh LORD, the Builder of Jerusalem.

The offspring of David Your servant
may You swiftly make flourish
and exalt His honor with Your Salvation.
In Your Salvation (safety, protection, health, healing
and deliverance) I put my expectations.
Blessed are You, oh LORD, Who raises the ray of Salvation.

Hear my voice, oh LORD, my GOD,
have mercy and compassion for me,
and accept my prayers mercifully and willingly.
LORD, You listen to prayers and supplications.
After coming to You oh LORD, my King,
You do not turn me away empty-handed,
for You hear the prayers of Your people mercifully.
Blessed are You, oh LORD, Who hears prayers.

It is written "If we know that He hears us, whatsoever we ask,
we know that we have the petitions that we desired of Him."

This I pray that my children and I
may be accounted worthy to escape the
things that are to come to pass
and stand worthy before You.

Be favorable, oh LORD my God,
toward Your people and their prayers,
and restore the service to the Holy of Holies of Your Temple.
May the service of Your people always be favorable to You.
May my eyes behold Your return to Zion in compassion.
Blessed are You, oh LORD,
Who restores His Presence to Zion.

I thank You, for You are the LORD, my God
and the God of my forefathers forever and ever.
You are the Rock of my life,
and the shield of my Salvation (safety, protection,
health, healing and deliverance),
You are in every generation.
I will thank You and tell of Your glory

for my life which is in Your hands,
for my soul that is entrusted to You,
for Your miracles that are with me every day,
and for Your wonders and favors that happen all the time,
evening, morning and noon.
Your compassion is not fatigued,
Your merciful deeds have not ended,
and my expectations are on You.
For all these things, may Your name be blessed and exalted,
oh LORD our King, always, forever and ever be blessed and exalted;
and all the living will thank You
and praise Your name truly,
oh God, my Salvation and help.
Blessed are You, oh LORD,
to You it is proper to give thanks.

Establish peace, goodness and blessing upon me and all Your people.
Establish graciousness, grace and compassion
upon me and all Your people.
Bless me, my Father,
all of us as one with the light (understanding) of Your presence,
for with the light (understanding) of Your presence,
You gave us the Word of life
and a love of grace, righteousness, blessing, compassion, and peace.
Thank you that it is good in Your eyes to bless Your people,
in every season and in every hour with Your peace.

Blessed are You oh LORD,
Who blesses His people with peace
(health, safety, prosperity, nothing missing and nothing broken).

May the expressions of my mouth
and the thoughts of my love
and affection find favor before You, oh
LORD, my rock and my Redeemer.

My LORD, guard my mouth from speaking evil and deceitfully.
To those who curse me, make my soul silent,
and don't let them affect my mind, thoughts and emotions.
Let me be open to Your Word and what You have to say,
my soul will pursue You fervently.
Let my attention be only on You.
Speedily nullify the counsel and disrupt the plan
of those who plot evil things against me.
Act for the sake of Your name that I may represent You well.
Act for the sake of Your right hand,
Act for the sake of Your holiness and for the sake of Your Word.
Because You rescue Your beloved ones,
thank You that Your right hand has saved and responds to me.
May my words and my thoughts find favor before
You, oh LORD, my rock and my redeemer.

He Who makes peace in His heights,
thank You that You have made peace upon me.

Blessed be Jesus our Messiah Who has said,
"Behold, I give unto you power to tread on serpents and scorpions,
and over all the power of the enemy:
and nothing shall by any means hurt you."
"Do not let your hearts be troubled (distressed or agitated).
You believe in God; believe also in Me."

I have the power to tread over all the power of the enemy.
Therefore, I take authority over my thoughts and feelings.
Oh soul of mine, return to your peace.
I will not allow myself to be troubled (distressed or agitated).
I believe and trust in my LORD.

Blessed be He Who makes peace upon
me, and all His people. Amen.

Holy, Holy, Holy, is the LORD, God of Hosts,
Who was and is, and is to come.

Magnified and sanctified is His great name.
In the world which He has created according to His will,
May He establish His kingdom during my lifetime, swiftly and soon.
Let His great name be blessed forever and to all eternity. Amen.
Blessed, praised, and glorified is the name of the holy one.
Blessed and exalted, extolled and honored
is the name of the holy one.
Magnified and praised is the name of the holy one.
He is high above all the blessings, songs and
praise which are uttered in the world.
He is high above all comforts which are uttered in the world. Amen.

He who makes peace in His heights,
makes peace upon me and upon all His people. Amen.

Oh LORD, there is none like You among the gods,
and there is nothing like Your works.
Your kingdom is an everlasting kingdom,
and Your dominion is throughout all generations.
The LORD reigns,

the LORD has reigned,
the LORD will reign forever and ever.
The LORD will give strength unto His people;
the LORD will bless His people with peace.

Bless The LORD the blessed one.

Blessed is the LORD, the blessed one, for all eternity.

Blessed are You, LORD, our God, King of the Universe,
Who has chosen us from among all the people,
and given us Your Word.
Blessed are You, LORD, giver of the Word.
Amen.

Stop and read from the Old Testament.
Here are the recommended readings for every Sabbath:

Week 1: Genesis 1:1- 6:8
Week 2: Genesis 6:9-11:32
Week 3: Genesis 12:1-17:27
Week 4: Genesis 18:1-22:24
Week 5: Genesis 23:1-25:18
Week 6: Genesis 25:19-28:9
Week 7: Genesis 28:10-22:3
Week 8: Genesis 32:4-36:43
Week 9: Genesis 37:1-40:23
Week 10: Genesis 41:1-44:17
Week 11: Genesis 44:18-47:27
Week 12: Genesis 47:28 – 50:26
Week 13: Exodus 1:1-6:1
Week 14: Exodus 6:2-9:35
Week 15 : Exodus 10:1-13:16

Week: 16: Exodus 13:17 – 17:16

Week: 17: Exodus 18:1-20:26

Week: 18: Exodus 21:1-24:18

Week: 19: Exodus 25:1-27:19

Week: 20: Exodus 27:20 – 30:10

Week: 21: Exodus 30:11- 34:35

Week: 22: Exodus 35:1 -38:20

Week 23: Exodus 38:21 – 40:38

Week: 24: Leviticus 1:1-5:19

Week: 25: Leviticus 6:1 – 8:36

Week 26: Leviticus 9:1 – 11:47

Week: 27: Leviticus 12:1 – 13:59

Week: 28: Leviticus 14:1 – 15:33

Week: 29: Leviticus 16:1 – 18:30

Week: 30: Leviticus 19:1 - 20:27

Week: 31: Leviticus 21:1 -24:23

Week 32: Leviticus 25:1 – 26:2

Week: 33: Leviticus 26:3 – 27:34

Week: 34: Numbers 1:1-4:20

Week: 35:Numbers: 4:21-7:28

Week 36: Numbers 8:1-12:16

Week 37: Numbers 13:1-15:41

Week 38: Numbers 16:1-18:32

Week 39: Numbers 19:1 - 22:1

Week 40: Numbers 22:2-25:9

Week 41: Numbers 25:10-30:1

Week 42: Numbers 30:2-32:42

Week 43: Numbers 33:1-36:13

Week 44: Deuteronomy 1:1-3:22

Week 45: Deuteronomy 3:23-7:11

Week 46: Deuteronomy 7:12-11:25

Week 47: Deuteronomy 11:26-16:17

Week 48: Deuteronomy 16:18-21:9
Week 49: Deuteronomy 21:10-25:19
Week 50: Deuteronomy 26:1-29:9
Week 51: Deuteronomy 29:10-30:20
Week 52: Deuteronomy 31:1-30
Week 53: Deuteronomy 32:1-52
Week 54: Deuteronomy 33:1-34:12

After reading the Word of God

Blessed are You, LORD our God, King of the universe,
Who has given us the Word of Truth,
and has planted eternal life in our midst,
Blessed are You LORD, giver of the the Word. Amen.

He who blessed our fathers Abraham, Isaac and Jacob,
has blessed me who has come up to honor the LORD and His Word.
The holy one blesses me and my family
and sends blessing and prosperity on all the works of my hands.

Blessed are You LORD our God, King of the universe,
Who selected good prophets,
and was pleased with their words which were spoken truthfully.
Blessed are You LORD, Who chooses the prophets,
Your servant Moses,
Your people Israel,
and prophets of truth and righteousness.

Stop and read the historical and/or prophet readings
Here are the recommended historical/prophet readings:

Week 1: Isaiah 42:5-43:11

Week 2: Isaiah 54:1-55:5; 54:1-10

Week 3: Isaiah 40:27-41:16

Week 4: 2 Kings 4:1-37

Week 5: 1 Kings 1:1-31

Week 6.: Malachi 1:1-2:7

Week 7: Hosea 12:13-14:9

Week 8: Hosea 11:7-12:12, Obadiah 1:21

Week 9: Amos 2:6-3:8

Week 10: 1 Kings 3:15-4:1

Week 11: Ezekiel 37:15-28

Week 12: 1 Kings 2:1-12

Week 13: Isaiah 27:6-28:13; 29:22-23; Jeremiah 1:1-2:3

Week 14: Ezekiel 28:25-29:21

Week 15: Jeremiah 46:13-28

Week 16: Judges 4:4-5:31

Week 17 : Isaiah 6:1-7:1- 6, 9:6- 7

Week 18: Jeremiah 34:8-22, 33:25-26

Week 19: 1 Kings 5:12 – 6:13

Week 20: Ezekiel 43:10-27

Week 21: 1 Kings 18:1-39

Week 22: 1 Kings 7:13-26, 40-50

Week 23: 1 Kings 7:51 -8:21

Week 24: Isaiah 43:21-44:23

Week 25: Jeremiah 7:21-8:3, 9:22-24

Week 26: 2 Samuel 6:1-7:17

Week 27: 2 Kings 4:42 -5:19

Week 28: 2 Kings 7:3-20

Week 29: Ezekiel 22:1-19

Week 30: Amos 9:7-15

Week 31: Ezekiel 44:15-31

Week 32: Jeremiah 32:6-27

Week 33: Jeremiah 16:19-17:14

Week 34: Hosea 2:1-23

Week 35: Judges 13:2-25

Week 36: Zechariah 3:1-4:7

Week 37: Joshua 2:1-24

Week 38: 1 Samuel 11:14-12:22

Week 39: Judges 11:1-33

Week 40: Micah 5:6-6:8

Week 41:1 Kings 18:46- 19:1-21

Week 42: Jeremiah 1-2:28

Week 43:Jeremiah 2:4-28, 3:4

Week 44: Isaiah 1:1-27

Week 45: Isaiah 40:1-26

Week 46: Isaiah 49:14-51:3

Week 47: Isaiah 54:11-55:5

Week 48: Isaiah 51:12-52:12

Week 49:Isaiah 54:1-10

Week 50:Isaiah 60:1-22

Week 51:Isaiah 61:10-63:9

Week 52: Hosea 14:1-9, Micah 7:18-20, Joel 2:15-27

Week 53:2 Samuel 22:1-51

Week 54: Joshua 1:1-18

After reading the historical and/ or prophet readings

Blessed are You LORD our God, King of the universe,
Rock of all eternities,
Faithful in all generations,
the trustworthy God,
Who says and does,
Who speaks and makes it come to pass,
all of Whose Words are true and righteous.
Faithful are You LORD my God,
and faithful are Your Words,
for not one Word of Yours is turned back unfulfilled.
You are a faithful and compassionate LORD and King,
Blessed are You LORD, the God Who is faithful in all His Words.

He who blessed our fathers Abraham, Isaac and Jacob,
has blessed me who has come up to honor the
LORD and His Words of the prophets.
The holy one blesses me and my family
and sends blessing and prosperity on all the works of my hands.

Stop and read the Sabbath Psalms.
Here are the recommended Psalms readings:

Psalm 92, Psalm 93, Psalms 29, Psalms 95, Psalm 96, Psalm 97, Psalm 98, Psalm 99

After reading the Sabbath Psalms

He who blessed our fathers Abraham, Isaac and Jacob,
has blessed me who has come up to honor
the LORD and the Psalms.
The holy one blesses me and my family
and sends blessings and prosperity on all the works of my hands.

Blessed are You LORD, our God, King of the universe,
Who has given us Jesus the Messiah
and the commandments of the New Covenant,
blessed are You LORD, giver of the New Covenant.

Stop and read the New Covenant reading.
Here are the recommended New Covenant readings:

Week 1: John 1:1–14; Revelation 22:6–21
Week 2: Matthew 24:36–46; I Peter 3:18–22
Week 3: Romans 4:1–25
Week 4: II Peter 2:4–11
Week 5: I Corinthians 15:50–57
Week 6: Romans 9:6–13
Week 7: John 1:43–51
Week 8: Matthew 26:36–46
Week 9: Acts 7:9–16
Week 10: I Corinthians 2:1–5
Week 11: Luke 6:9–16
Week 12: I Peter 1:1–9
Week 13: Acts 7:17–29
Week 14: Romans 9:14–33
Week 15: Luke 22:7–30; I Corinthians 11:20–34
Week 16: John 6:15–71

Week 17: Matthew 5:8–20

Week 18: Matthew 5:38–42, 17:1–11

Week 19: Matthew 5:33–37

Week 20: Philippians 4:10–20

Week 21: I Corinthians 8:4–13

Week 22: II Corinthians 9:1–15

Week 23: Revelation 11:1–13, 15:5–8

Week 24: Romans 8:1–13

Week 25: Romans 8:1–13

Week 26: John 13:1–17:26

Week 27: John 18:1–19:42

Week 28: Acts 10:1–35

Week 29: Matthew 8:1–4, 11:2–6; Mark 1:40–45

Week 30: Matthew 9:20–26; Mark 5:24–34

Week 31: Romans 3:19–28, 9:30–10:13; Galatians 3:10–14

Week 32: Matthew 5:33–48, 15:1–11; I Peter 1:13–21

Week 33: I Peter 2:4–10

Week 34: Luke 4:16–21

Week 35: John 14:15–21, 15:10–12

Week 36: I Corinthians 12:12–20

Week 37: Acts 21:17–26

Week 38: I Corinthians 10:6–13

Week 39: Hebrews 3:7–19

Week 40: Romans 13:1–7

Week 41: John 3:10–21

Week 42: Romans 11:25–32; I Corinthians 1:20–31

Week 43: John 2:13–25

Week 44: Matthew 5:33–37

Week 45: Philippians 3:7–21; James 4:1–12

Week 46: Acts 9:1–21; I Timothy 3:1–7

Week 47: Matthew 23:31–39; Mark 12:28–34

Week 48: Romans 8:31–39

After reading the New Covenant

Blessed are You LORD our GOD, King of the universe,
Who has given us the Word of Truth
and has planted life everlasting in our midst.
Blessed are You LORD, giver of the New Covenant.

He who blessed our fathers Abraham, Isaac and Jacob,
has blessed me who has come up to honor
the LORD and the New Covenant.
The holy one blesses me and my family
and sends blessings and prosperity on all the works of my hands.

May the LORD make my sons, son-in-laws and
grandsons like Ephriam and Manassah.

I speak these blessings over my sons and my grandsons,
May the Lord bless them and keep them.
May He reveal Himself to them.
May He lift up His countenance and grant them peace.
May the Lord be with them forever.
May God bring them home to me
and unto the land prepared for them.
May God bless them and grant them long life.
May the Lord fulfill my Sabbath prayers for them.

May God make them good husbands and fathers.
May God prepare holy wives for them.
May the Lord protect and defend them.
May God's Spirit be within them
May God's Spirit fill them with grace
(unmerited love, favor and empowerment),
and may our family grow in happiness.
Thank you, LORD, for hearing my Sabbath prayers.
Amen.

May the LORD make my daughters, daughter-in-laws
and granddaughters
like Sarah, Rebecca, Rachel, Leah and Ruth.
I speak these blessings over them.
May the Lord bless them and keep them.
May the LORD reveal Himself to them.
May the LORD lift up His countenance and grant them peace.
May the LORD forever be with them.
May the LORD bring them to the land prepared for them.
May the LORD bless them and grant them long life.
May the LORD fulfill my Sabbath prayers for them.
May the LORD make them good mothers and wives.
May the LORD bring them a husband who will care for them.
May the Lord protect and defend them.
May His Spirit forever be within them
May His Spirit fill them with grace
(unmerited love, favor and empowerment),
and may our family grow in happiness.
Thank you, LORD, for hearing my Sabbath prayers.
Amen.

Stop – personal prayers

All my children have turned to me and my Godly influence and
have come back to me from the land of the enemy.
As it is written: "Assuredly (I pledge it) the wicked
(malicious, spiteful with bitter, ill will)
shall not go unpunished, but the seed of
the righteous shall be delivered."
God rebukes him who fights against me and He saves my children.
God gives me wisdom that my enemies are not able to gain say.
My writings elevate my love, honor and character above my enemies.
They are put to shame who taunted me,
asking, "Where is your God?".
With my own eyes I see their downfall and they
are trampled like mud in the streets.
I raise my eyes and I look for my children who
are all assembling and coming to me.
My children have returned to me seven times better.
I have sevenfold restoration of everything that
was stolen and kept back from me.
I am seven times happier than I was before.

This is the Word of GOD that Moses placed
before the children of Israel,
at the command of the LORD,
through Moses' hand.

It is a tree of life to those who take hold of it,
and those who support it are praiseworthy.
It's ways are ways of pleasantness
and all its paths are peace.
Bring us back to You, oh LORD
and we will come,
renew our days as of old.

There is none like our God,
there is none like our LORD,
there is none like our King,
there is none like our Deliverer.
Who is like our God?
Who is like our LORD?
Who is like our King?
Who is like our Deliverer?
We will give thanks to our God,
we will give thanks to our LORD,
we will give thanks to our King,
we will give thanks to our Deliverer.
Blessed be our God,
blessed be our LORD,
blessed be our King,
blessed be our Deliverer.
You are my God,
You are my LORD,
You are my King,
You are my Deliverer.
To You our fathers offered fragrant incense.

It is our privilege to praise the Master of all,
to acclaim the greatness of the one who forms all creation.
God did not make us like the nations of other lands,
and did not make us the same as other families of the Earth.
God did not place us in the same situations as others
and our destiny is not the same as anyone else.
I bend my knee, and bow down and give thanks,
before the Ruler, the Ruler of Rulers,
the holy one, blessed is God.
The one who spread out the heavens

and made the foundations of the Earth
and whose precious dwelling is in the heavens above
and whose powerful presence is in the highest heights.
The LORD is my God, there is none other.
My God is truth and nothing else compares.
It is written:
"You shall know today, and take to heart,
that the LORD is the only God,
in the heavens above and on Earth below.
There is no other."
It is written:
"The LORD will reign forever and ever."
It is written:
"The LORD will be Ruler over the whole Earth,
and on that day, God will be one,
and God's name will be one."

The LORD blesses me and keeps me,
The LORD makes His face shine upon me and is gracious to me,
The LORD lifts His countenance upon me
and gives me peace.

Master of the universe who has reigned,
before anything was created,
at the time that everything was created at His will,
"King" was His name proclaimed,
after all has ceased to exist,
He, the awesome one, will reign alone.
He was and He is, and He shall be in Glory.
He is one – and there is no second to compare to Him,
none to declare as His equal,
without beginning, without end,

He has the might and dominion.
He is my God, my living Redeemer,
and my Rock (my strength) in times of struggle.
He is my standard and a refuge for me,
He is the portion in my cup on the day I call.
In His hand I will deposit my spirit,
when I am asleep – I will awaken,
and with my body will my spirit remain.
The LORD is with me and I will not fear.

DAILY DEVOTIONALS

These devotionals can be used as a daily devotional. They are not numbered because they are not intended to be read in a specific order or time frame. Some may prefer to spend more time with some devotionals than others, and different people may want to read them in different orders.

As you study the Word, be open to hear from God. The rhema word you receive will cause your deliverance, results and manifestations. It is the revelation knowledge of God and His Word that gives you power and builds your confidence.

FAMILY RELATIONSHIPS

2 Peter 1:3-4 (KJV)
"According as his divine power hath given unto us all things that pertain unto life and godliness, through the knowledge of him that hath called us to glory and virtue: Whereby are given unto us exceeding great and precious promises: that by these ye might be partakers of the divine nature, having escaped the corruption that is in the world through lust."

God has given us all things that pertain to life and godliness, which includes the grace (love, favor and empowerment) to have strong and healthy relationships. Knowledge of the Word helps us to go from glory to glory in life – to be changed into the image of God.

We should learn to embrace the redemptive love of Jesus. His redemptive love changes us from the inside out; it makes us want to do the right thing.

> ### Ephesians 1:2-4 (KJV)
> *"Grace be to you, and peace, from God our Father, and from the Lord Jesus Christ. Blessed be the God and Father of our Lord Jesus Christ, who hath blessed us with all spiritual blessings in heavenly places in Christ: According as he hath chosen us in him before the foundation of the world, that we should be holy and without blame before him in love:*

> ### Ephesians 1:2-4 (Atarah)
> *"Grace (unmerited love, favor and empowerment) be to you, and peace (wholeness, nothing missing and nothing broken), from God our Father, and from the Lord Jesus Christ. Blessed be the God and Father of our Lord Jesus Christ, who has blessed us with all spiritual blessings in heavenly places in Christ: As He has chosen us (actually picked us out for Himself as His own) in Christ before the foundation of the world, that we should be holy (having the same mindset as Him), blameless, faultless and perfect in His sight, before Him in love."*

He chose us to be "*in Him*" before the foundation of the world.

God knew we would have family relationships. Our families are meant to be *"in Him."* Our children and marriages are chosen to be for Him, not for the world, so that *"we should be holy and without blame before him in love".*

When the Bible refers to blame in the above scripture, it also refers to the shame that comes along with blame. People experience shame when we hold their sins and weaknesses against them. However, God doesn't hold our sins and weaknesses against us; therefore, we shouldn't hold other people's against them. God doesn't remind us of our sinful past; instead, He tells us of our bright future. Likewise, we should strive to imitate Him in our relationships. Relationships that are full of shame and blame are not God's best.

God accepts us as we are. Our relationship with Him is not based on the Law. Under the Old Covenant, sacrifices to be in right-standing with God would be denied if they had even one flaw. However, today we are under the New Covenant, and God is not looking for reasons to reject or punish us. We are accepted in the Beloved—Jesus the Messiah.

Many people are complacent (self-satisfied) when it comes to their relationships, especially their family relationships. It is easy to make half-hearted attempts when resolving issues within the family. However, it is important that we take the time and effort it takes to pray and receive wisdom concerning our loved ones. Although we have God's Word for instruction, most of the incidences we face will require that we hear directly from the Spirit of God. It is vital to the success of our relationships that we receive instructions from the Spirit of God and obey those instructions.

ENEMIES OF HOLINESS

Holiness is a prerequisite to experiencing the manifestation of God's goodness. Holiness is the habit of being in one mind with God; the conduct of being aligned with God. Holiness is not based on religious tradition, but on the Word of God.

Developing in the love of God is an act of holiness.

There are multiple traps to be aware of.

> *"Thus saith the LORD, Stand ye in the ways, and see, and ask for the old paths, where is the good way, and walk therein, and ye shall find rest for your souls. But they said, We will not walk therein." Jeremiah 6:16 (KJV)*

You can avoid the traps of ungodliness by studying the paths that others have traveled before you; learn from their examples.

> *"This know also, that in the last days perilous times shall come. For men shall be lovers of their own selves, covetous, boasters, proud, blasphemers, disobedient to parents, unthankful, unholy, Without natural affection, trucebreakers, false accusers, incontinent, fierce, despisers of those that are good, Traitors, heady, highminded, lovers of pleasures more than lovers of God; Having a form of godliness, but denying the power thereof: from such turn away." 2 Timothy 3:1-5 (KJV)*

> *"Don't be naive. There are difficult times ahead. In the last days there will come great stress and trouble; things hard to deal with and hard to bear. As the end approaches, people will be lovers of self and self-centered,*

they will be lovers of money and aroused by a greedy desire for wealth, they will be proud, arrogant and insulting egotists. They will be abusive (blasphemous, scoffing), disrespectful and disobedient to parents. They will be ungrateful, unholy and profane. They will be without natural human affection (callous and inhuman). They will be unforgiving, slanderers (false accusers, troublemakers), cynical, loose in morals and conduct and they will despise and hate those that are good. They will be treacherous, ruthless, bloated windbags, rash, and inflated with self-conceit. They will be lovers of sensual pleasures more than and rather than lovers of God. They'll make a show of religion, having a form of godliness, but denying the power thereof: avoid such people." 2 Timothy 3:1 (Atarah)

In the last days, some people will experience the manifestation of God's goodness, while others will experience perilous times.

You have an enemy who wants to stop what you have been called to accomplish.

Trap #1: Immorality. Immorality eventually leads to failure and death; it will destroy you.

"Neither let us commit fornication, as some of them committed, and fell in one day three and twenty thousand." 1 Corinthians 10:8 (KJV)

"For she hath cast down many wounded: yea, many strong men have been slain by her." Proverbs 7:26 (KJV)

> *"Know ye not that ye are the temple of God, and that the Spirit of God dwelleth in you? If any man defile the temple of God, him shall God destroy; for the temple of God is holy, which temple ye are." 1 Corinthians 3:16-17 (KJV)*

There is a judgment associated with immorality.

> *"Can a man take fire in his bosom, and his clothes not be burned? Can one go upon hot coals, and his feet not be burned? So he that goeth in to his neighbour's wife; whosoever toucheth her shall not be innocent." Proverbs 6:27-29 (KJV)*

Approximately 23,000 people died in one day because of fornication.

> *"Neither let us commit fornication, as some of them committed, and fell in one day three and twenty thousand." 1 Corinthians 10:8 (KJV)*

Samson's life ended because of immorality (Judges 16).

Allow God to remove the "taste" of immorality from your life. Don't use your righteousness as an opportunity to sin. During the end times, there will be a great deal of seduction and demonically-influenced teaching of the Word (1 Timothy 4:1).

> *"Now the Spirit speaketh expressly, that in the latter times some shall depart from the faith, giving heed to seducing spirits, and doctrines of devils;" 1 Timothy 4:1 (KJV)*

Establish boundaries around your decision to live a life of holiness and stay focused on the Word of God – have the same mindset as Him.

Moses chose to suffer rather than enjoy the temporal pleasures of the world (Hebrews 11:25).

> *"Choosing rather to suffer affliction with the people of God, than to enjoy the pleasures of sin for a season;" Hebrews 11:25 (KJV)*

Trap #2: Financial Corruption. Financial corruption leads to death. Don't make money your idol (your "god made of gold"), or else your life will be destroyed. Gehazi, Elijah's servant, pursued money rather than God; as a result, he became sick with leprosy (2 Kings 5:20-27).

Holiness requires you making God your only source. Don't put your confidence in money.

When you covet, nothing that is yours appeals to you; you'll want what others have. Be content in what you have.

> *"Let your conversation be without covetousness; and be content with such things as ye have: for he hath said, I will never leave thee, nor forsake thee." Hebrews 13:5 (KJV)*

> *"Let your character and moral disposition be without covetousness; and be content with such things as you have: for He has said, I will never leave you, nor forsake you." Hebrews 13:5 (Atarah)*

In Joshua 7, Achan coveted money, and his family suffered as a result.

In Acts 5:1-11, Ananias and Sapphira died because of their wrong relationship with money.

God wants to manifest His goodness in your life, but it will require you to walk in true holiness, (dwelling in God's Word – thinking as He thinks and acting accordingly). The enemy understands the power of holiness and will attempt to hinder you from experiencing the goodness of God. Therefore, it's up to you to guard against the enemies of holiness.

THE ORIGIN OF PROSPERITY

"And thou say in thine heart, My power and the might of mine hand hath gotten me this wealth. But thou shalt remember the LORD thy God: for it is he that giveth thee power to get wealth, that he may establish his covenant which he sware unto thy fathers, as it is this day." Deuteronomy 8:17 (KJV)

"Beware lest you think and say in your heart, My own power and the might (abilities) of my hand have gotten me this wealth. You are to remember the Lord your God: for it is He that gives you power to get wealth, that He may establish His covenant which He swore to your ancestors, as it is this day." Deuteronomy 8:17 (Atarah)

Power is a necessary element to move you from one place in your life to another. God has given you power to get wealth. You must arise, or "change your posture and position," in order for prosperity to manifest itself in your life.

"Arise, shine; for thy light is come, and the glory of the LORD is risen upon thee." Isaiah 60:1 (KJV)

"Arise (get up) and shine (be radiant), for your light (understanding and guidance) has come, and the honor,

*dignity and the reputation of the Lord has risen upon
you!" Isaiah 60:1 (Atarah)*

Without light--the understanding of God's Word--you will stay the
same.

If you are a believer of Jesus as the promised Messiah, you are adopted
into His family and are now a seed of Abraham and have a right to the
promises of God.

Prosperity is born out of a covenant God made with His words—the
words found in the Bible. Therefore, the Bible is no ordinary book.

> *"This book of the law shall not depart out of thy mouth;
> but thou shalt meditate therein day and night, that thou
> mayest observe to do according to all that is written
> therein: for then thou shalt make thy way prosperous,
> and then thou shalt have good success." Joshua 1:8
> (KJV)*

God takes pleasure in your prosperity because He is magnified in it.
(Psalm 35:27).

> *"Let them shout for joy, and be glad, that favour my
> righteous cause: yea, let them say continually, Let the
> LORD be magnified, which hath pleasure in the prosperity
> of his servant." Psalm 35:27 (KJV)*

Society has reduced prosperity to money but God is interested in total
life prosperity, which includes, but is not limited to, money. Total life
prosperity is *"shalom"* meaning a continual well being and success.

Psalm 35:27 (KJV) says God, "hath pleasure in the prosperity of his
servant." Therefore, prosperity can't be bad if God takes pleasure in it.

Jesus restored all that the Devil stole.

Jesus came to preach the Gospel to the poor—those who were lacking something. It is good to give to the poor; however, you must remember to preach the Gospel to them as well.

> *"Jesus answered and said unto them, Go and shew John again those things which ye do hear and see: The blind receive their sight, and the lame walk, the lepers are cleansed, and the deaf hear, the dead are raised up, and the poor have the gospel preached to them." Matthew 11:4-5 (KJV)*

It is possible to be rich in material assets and poor in other areas of your life.

> *"Because thou sayest, I am rich, and increased with goods, and have need of nothing; and knowest not that thou art wretched, and miserable, and poor, and blind, and naked:" Revelation 3:17 (KJV)*

Although a person may be financially wealthy, he or she may be lacking meaningful relationships or be dying of cancer.

Total life prosperity begins in the soul.

> *"Beloved, I wish above all things that thou mayest prosper and be in health, even as thy soul prospereth." 3 John 1:2 (KJV)*

The prosperity of your soul must be your first priority because it determines your position in life. Soul prosperity comes from the revelation of God's Word. If you are "down on your luck," it is not because of luck, but because you are lacking the light of God's Word.

It is impossible for you not to prosper when the Word is operational in your heart.

The Word of God is your highway to the world of true wealth (Job 22:21-22).

> *"Acquaint now thyself with him, and be at peace: thereby good shall come unto thee. Receive, I pray thee, the law from his mouth, and lay up his words in thine heart." Job 22:21-22 (KJV)*

> *"Learn to be at peace with (God); in this way good will come to you. Please! Receive instruction from His mouth, and take His words to heart." Job 22:21-22 (Atarah)*

If you take the seed of God's Word and put it in your heart, then wealth and riches will be in your house.

> *"Praise ye the LORD. Blessed is the man that feareth the LORD, that delighteth greatly in his commandments. His seed shall be mighty upon earth: the generation of the upright shall be blessed. Wealth and riches shall be in his house: and his righteousness endureth for ever." Psalm 112:1-3 (KJV)*

Seek out people who believe right because the people you hang around influence the way you think. To break the poverty chain in your life; focus all your attention to what God says in His Word and do not be double minded.

The seed of God's Word controls the outcome of your endeavors in the kingdom of God. Prosperity is born out of truth.

> *"Gird thy sword upon thy thigh, O most mighty,
> with thy glory and thy majesty. And in thy majesty
> ride prosperously because of truth and meekness and
> righteousness; and thy right hand shall teach thee
> terrible things." Psalm 45:3-4 (KJV)*

Wisdom and light (understand) lead to mighty works.

> *"And when he was come into his own country, he
> taught them in their synagogue, insomuch that they
> were astonished, and said, Whence hath this man this
> wisdom, and these mighty works?" Matthew 13:54
> (KJV)*

Light (understanding) comes when revelation knowledge of the Word enters your heart (your spirit or subconscious mind).

The Word of God is seed.

> *"Now the parable is this: <u>The seed is the word of God</u>."
> Luke 8:11 (KJV)*

Every "Word seed" has a harvest time.

To prosper in any area, you have to have revelation knowledge of that particular area. God doesn't prosper you on the basis of your money seed, but on the basis of the light (understanding) you have inside of you. Once you have the light (understanding) of the Word of God, He will start to direct and guide you on what to do with your money. God's Word is your foundation for prosperity.

You cannot move toward prosperity without the seed of God's Word first entering your life. The Word provides the light (understanding) that is needed to break the chains of poverty. Your first concern must be the prosperity of your soul, which determines your position in life. When your soul is prospering, you will see it in your life. God's Word is your foundation for prosperity.

COVENANT FOR SECURITY AND UNSHAKEABLE BELIEF

"Beware that thou forget not the LORD thy God, in not keeping his commandments, and his judgments, and his statutes, which I command thee this day: Lest when thou hast eaten and art full, and hast built goodly houses, and dwelt therein; And when thy herds and thy flocks multiply, and thy silver and thy gold is multiplied, and all that thou hast is multiplied; Then thine heart be lifted up, and thou forget the LORD thy God, which brought thee forth out of the land of Egypt, from the house of bondage; Who led thee through that great and terrible wilderness, wherein were fiery serpents, and scorpions, and drought, where there was no water; who brought thee forth water out of the rock of flint; Who fed thee in the wilderness with manna, which thy fathers knew not, that he might humble thee, and that he might prove thee, to do thee good at thy latter end; And thou say in thine heart, My power and the might of mine hand hath gotten me this wealth. But thou shalt remember the LORD thy God: for it is he that giveth thee power to get wealth, that he may establish his covenant which he sware unto thy fathers, as it is this day." Deuteronomy 8:11- 18 (KJV)

When you obey God's commandments, you position yourself to live a prosperous life. After God has multiplied you, don't allow pride to cause you to forget God (verse 11-14).

God has given you the power (ability) to get wealth (verse 18). Power is the ability, or anointing, to get results.

There are several characteristics of the anointing that are available to believers.

> "And the spirit of the LORD shall rest upon him, the spirit of wisdom and understanding, the spirit of counsel and might, the spirit of knowledge and of the fear of the LORD;" Isaiah 11:2 (KJV)

When you keep your part of the covenant by obeying God, He will give you an anointing that will lead you to wealth. If you are a believer in Jesus the Messiah and have made Him your Lord, you have been adopted into the seed of Abraham and have a right to the promises of God.

God made a commitment to bless (make happy and empower to prosper) Abraham.

> "Now the LORD had said unto Abram, Get thee out of thy country, and from thy kindred, and from thy father's house, unto a land that I will shew thee: And I will make of thee a great nation, and I will bless thee, and make thy name great; and thou shalt be a blessing: And I will bless them that bless thee, and curse him that curseth thee: and in thee shall all families of the earth be blessed." Genesis 12:1-3 (KJV)

Abram went to Egypt during a time of famine; however, he left rich in cattle, silver and gold.

> *"And Abram went up out of Egypt, he, and his wife, and all that he had, and Lot with him, into the south. And Abram was very rich in cattle, in silver, and in gold."* Genesis 13:1-2 (KJV)

His riches can be attributed to the blessing (empowerment to prosper) that was on his life.

> *"The blessing of the LORD, it maketh rich, and he addeth no sorrow with it."* Proverbs 10:22 (KJV)

This blessing is also on Abraham's seed. Jesus' death on the cross made a way for the blessing of Abraham to come on the Gentiles (Galatians 3:13-14).

> *"Christ hath redeemed us from the curse of the law, being made a curse for us: for it is written, Cursed is every one that hangeth on a tree: That the blessing of Abraham might come on the Gentiles through Jesus Christ; that we might receive the promise of the Spirit through faith."* Galatians 3:13-14 (KJV)

As a believer in Jesus the Messiah and making Him your Lord, you belong to Him; therefore, you are Abraham's seed and heir to the promise.

> *"There is neither Jew nor Greek, there is neither bond nor free, there is neither male nor female: for ye are all one in Christ Jesus. And if ye be Christ's, then are ye*

Abraham's seed, and heirs according to the promise."
Galatians 3:28-29 (KJV)

Prosperity is part of the Covenant. God prospers you because of the covenant He has established with you.

The Blood Covenant

1 After these things, the word of the Lord came to Abram in a vision, saying, "Don't be afraid, Abram. I am your shield of defense and your reward will be exceedingly great." 2 Abram said, "Lord God, what can You give me, since I am childless and he who shall be the owner and heir of my house is this my steward Eliezer of Damascus?" 3 Abram continued, "Look, You have given me no child; and a servant born in my house is my heir." 4 Then the word of the Lord came to him, saying, "This man shall not be your heir, a son from your body will be your heir." 5 The Lord lead him outside his tent into the starlight and said, "Look now toward the heavens and count the stars, if you're able to number them, because so shall your descendants be." 6 Abram believed the Lord, and the Lord counted it to him as righteousness (right standing with God). 7 The Lord said to him again, "I am the same Lord, Who brought you out of Ur of the Chaldees to give you this land as an inheritance." 8 Abram said, "Lord God, how am I to know this, that it will all be mine?" 9 The Lord said to him, "Bring to Me a heifer three years old, a she-goat three years old, a ram three years old, a turtledove, and a young pigeon."10 Abram brought Him all these animals to Him and cut them down the middle into halves and laid each half opposite the other; but the birds he did not divide. 11 Vultures swooped down on the carcasses, but Abram drove them away.12 As the sun went down a deep sleep overcame Abram and a horror and great darkness came over him. 13 The Lord said to Abram, "Know positively that your descendants will be strangers dwelling as temporary residents in a land that is not theirs (Egypt), and they will be slaves there and will be afflicted and oppressed for 400 years. 14 But I will bring judgment on that nation whom they will serve and afterward they will come out with great possessions. 15 But you'll have a long and full life and be buried at a good old age.16 In the fourth generation your descendants shall come back here to Canaan again, for the iniquity of the Amorites is not yet full and complete." 17 When the sun had gone down and a thick darkness had come on and a smoking lamp and a flaming torch passed between those pieces. (See Genesis 15:1-17)

God used the covenant to convince man that His Word is solid. Blood covenants were the most powerful type of agreement known to man in Abraham's time. A covenant can only be broken by death. Loyalty is born out of covenant.

The covenant God made with Abraham was a process. God showed up and made a promise to Abraham. Abram questioned how he would know that God's promises would come to pass. God had a lengthy discussion with Abraham and established His covenant with him (v. 9-17).

God submitted His Word to that covenant, and He does the same today. God gives His promise first, and then He does what He promised to do. Everything begins with the Word.

The purpose of the covenant is to show man how loyal and faithful God is to His Word. Multiplication is part of the covenant.

1 When Abram was 99 years old the Lord appeared to Abram and said to him, "I am the Almighty God; walk in my presence, and be perfect.2 I will make my covenant between you and I, and I will multiply you exceedingly." 3 Abram fell on his face: and God continued speaking to him:4 "As for Me, this is my covenant with you: you will be a father of many nations.5 Your name will no

longer be Abram (exalted father), but your name will
be Abraham (father of many), because I have made you
a father of many.6 I will cause you to be very fruitful. I
will make nations of you; kings will descend from you.
7 I am establishing my covenant between you and I and
your seed after you, generation after generation, as an
everlasting covenant, to be a God to you, and to your
seed after you. 8 I will give you and your seed after you,
the land wherein you are now foreigners, all the land of
Canaan, for an everlasting possession; and I will be their
God." (See Genesis 17:1-8)

The Father of Creation changed Abram's name to Abraham, the "father of many nations."

Abraham was able to rest, or trust, in his covenant with God when he was told to sacrifice his son, Isaac (Genesis 22:1-17). Abraham had confidence in God's loyalty to His Word (verse 5). Abraham had an image of in his mind of sacrificing his son and God raising Isaac from the dead (Hebrews 11:17-19).

In a covenant relationship, whatever one party is willing to do, the other party must be willing to do the same and then some. Since Abraham had sacrificed his son already in his mind, God considered it done and sacrificed His only Son, Jesus. To raise Jesus from the dead, God used the same covenant image Abraham had of Isaac being raised from the dead. A covenant is the foundation for security and unshakeable belief.

If you are a stranger to your covenant, you are without hope and without God. (Ephesians 2:11-12).

"Wherefore remember, that ye being in time past Gentiles in the flesh, who are called Uncircumcision by that which is called the Circumcision in the flesh made by hands; That at that time ye were without Christ, being aliens from the commonwealth of Israel, and strangers from the covenants of promise, having no hope, and without God in the world:" Ephesians 2:11 (KJV)

When you keep the covenant before God (in remembrance), God's blessings will be seen in your life.

The subject of prosperity is greatly misunderstood due to erroneous teaching. Prosperity involves more than money and material assets; instead, it involves success in every area of life. Before we can experience this total life prosperity, we must understand and comply to the covenant we have with God.

COVENANT FOR SECURITY AND UNSHAKEABLE BELIEF PART 2

You must understand the details of your covenant with God before you can prosper.

You have been given the power to get wealth so that you may do your part to fulfill the covenant that God established with Abraham and his offspring.

"And thou say in thine heart, My power and the might of mine hand hath gotten me this wealth. But thou shalt remember the LORD thy God: for it is he that giveth thee power to get wealth, that he may establish his covenant which he sware unto thy fathers, as it is this day." Deuteronomy 8:17-18 (KJV)

Look at Joseph's life. As a result of his covenant with God, Joseph's life exemplified what it meant to be empowered to prosper.

Prosperity is in the covenant, but you won't prosper without a clear understanding of it.

God is a covenant-keeping God. The Bible is a book of covenants (agreements). For example: God made covenants with Abraham, Isaac, Jacob and others. God always makes a promise (establishes a covenant), and then carries out His end of the agreement. Being ignorant of your covenant with God leaves you without hope and without God.

> *"Wherefore remember, that ye being in time past Gentiles in the flesh, who are called Uncircumcision by that which is called the Circumcision in the flesh made by hands;* <u>*That at*</u> <u>*that time ye were without Christ, being aliens*</u> <u>*from the commonwealth of Israel, and strangers from the*</u> <u>*covenants of promise, having no hope, and without God*</u> <u>*in the world:"*</u> *Ephesians 2:11- 12 (KJV)*

God swore that He would never break or alter His promises because He bound Himself to His covenant.

> *"My covenant will I not break, nor alter the thing that is gone out of my lips." Psalm 89:34 (KJV)*

You will not worry about negative circumstances or beg God for things when you stand on your covenant rights.

God is, and has always been, serious about the terms of His covenant.

A covenant is "a pledge, promise or oath between two or more parties to carry out terms that are agreed on." A blood covenant is much more serious because the breaking of it is punishable by death. God established a blood covenant with man to assure mankind that He is committed to upholding His end of the covenant.

God is covenant-minded, because the covenant is imprinted on His mind (Psalm 111:5, AMP).

> *"He hath given meat unto them that fear him: <u>he will ever be mindful of his covenant</u>." Psalm 111:5 (KJV)*

> *"He has given food and provision to those who are devoted with reverence and respect to Him; He will remember His covenant forever." Psalm 111:5 (Atarah)*

Because you are in covenant with God, you are blessed and destined for increase; therefore, don't settle for decrease. (Deuteronomy 6:1-3)

> *"Now these are the commandments, the statutes, and the judgments, which the LORD your God commanded to teach you, that ye might do them in the land whither ye go to possess it: That thou mightest fear the LORD thy God, to keep all his statutes and his commandments, which I command thee, thou, and thy son, and thy son's son, all the days of thy life; and that thy days may be prolonged. Hear therefore, O Israel, and observe to do it; that it may be well with thee, and that ye may increase mightily, as the LORD God of thy fathers hath promised thee, in the land that floweth with milk and honey." Deuteronomy 6:1-3 (KJV)*

> *"Now this is the commandments, the laws and rulings which the LORD your God ordered me to teach you, that you are to obey in the land you are crossing over to*

possess, You are to be devoted with reverence and respect to the LORD your God and observe all his regulations and commandments that I am giving you - you, your child and your grandchild - as long as you live, and so that you will have long life. Therefore, listen, Israel, and take care to obey, so that things will go well with you, and so that you will increase greatly, as the LORD the God of your ancestors, promised you by giving you a land flowing with milk and honey."
Deuteronomy 6:1-3 (Atarah)

You can trust Him because He is mindful of you and your place in the covenant.

"O Israel, trust thou in the LORD: he is their help and their shield. O house of Aaron, trust in the LORD: he is their help and their shield. Ye that fear the LORD, trust in the LORD: he is their help and their shield. <u>The LORD hath been mindful of us: he will bless us</u>; he will bless the house of Israel; he will bless the house of Aaron. <u>He will bless them that fear the LORD</u>, <u>both small and great</u>." Psalm 115:9-13 (KJV)

"Oh Israel, trust in the Lord! He is your Help and your Shield. Oh house of Aaron (the priesthood), trust in the Lord! He is your Help and your Shield. You who are devoted with reverence and respect to the Lord, trust in the Lord! He is your Help and your Shield. <u>The Lord has been mindful of us: He will bless (make happy and empower to prosper) us</u>; He will bless the house of Israel; He will bless the house of Aaron. <u>He will bless those who are devoted with</u> <u>reverence and respect to Him, both small and great</u>." Psalm 115:9 (Atarah)

As long as you relate to God based on the covenant, He is not limited in what He can do in your life.

Remind God of what His covenant Word says.

Moses and Jehoshaphat understood the power of being in covenant with God.

> *The Lord said to Moses, "Go down! Hurry! Your people whom you brought up from the land of Egypt have become corrupt! So quickly they have turned aside from the way I ordered them to follow! They have cast a metal statue of a calf, worshiped it, sacrificed to it and said, 'Israel! Here is your god, who brought you up from the land of Egypt!'" The Lord continued speaking to Moses: "I have been watching these people and you can see how stiffnecked they are. Now leave Me alone, so that My anger can blaze against them and I can put an end to them! I will make a great nation out of you instead." Moses pleaded with the Lord God. He said, "Lord, why must Your anger blaze against Your own people, whom You brought out of the land of Egypt with great power and a strong hand? Why let the Egyptians say, 'It was with evil intentions that He led them out to slaughter them in the hills and wipe them off the face of the earth'? Turn from Your fierce anger! Relent! Don't bring such disaster on Your people! Remember Abraham, Isaac and Israel, Your servants to whom You swore by Your very self. You promised them, 'I will make your descendants as many as the stars in the sky and I will give all this land I have spoken about to your descendants and they will possess it forever.'" The Lord then changed His mind*

about the disaster He had planned for His people. (See Exodus 32:7-14)

Some time later, the people of Moab, and the people of Ammon with other Ammonites, came up to fight Jehoshaphat. Jehoshaphat was told, "A huge army from beyond the Sea, from Syria, is on it's way to fight you; right now they are in Hazazontamar, which is Engedi. Jehoshaphat was frightened, so he determined to seek the Lord. He proclaimed a fast throughout all Judah. Judah assembled to seek help from the Lord; they came from all the cities of Judah to seek the Lord. Standing in front of the new courtyard in the house of the Lord, among those assembled from Judah and Jerusalem, he said: "Oh Lord God of our fathers, are you not the God in heaven? Do You not rule all the kingdoms of the nations? In Your hand is there not power and might, so that none is able to withstand you? <u>Are You not our God, who drove out those living in the land ahead of Your people Israel and gave it to the seed of Abraham Your friend forever?</u> They who lived in it, built You a sanctuary for Your name and said, 'If calamity strikes us, such as war, judgment, disease or famine, we will stand before this house and in Your presence, (since Your name is in this house) and cry to You in our distress; and You will hear us and help us.' So now, see the people of Ammon, Moab and mount Seir, whom You would not let Israel invade when they came out of the land of Egypt, so that they turned away from them and did not destroy them, <u>Look and see how they are repaying us evil; they have come to throw us out of Your possession, which You gave us as an inheritance.</u> Oh our God! Won't You execute judgment against them? Because we haven't strength enough to defeat this huge

army coming against us, and we don't know what to do,
but our eyes are on You. All Judah stood before the Lord
with their little ones, their wives, and their children. (See
2 Chronicles 20:1)

You have a part to play in your covenant relationship with God. Don't be lazy in possessing your inheritance.

"And Joshua said unto the children of Israel, How long
are ye slack to go to possess the land, which the LORD
God of your fathers hath given you?" Joshua 18:3 (KJV)

Align your speaking with the covenant regardless of your circumstances. For example: Abraham refused to waver and speak contrary to God's promise.

"He (Abraham) staggered not at the promise of God
through unbelief; but was strong in faith, giving glory
to God; And being fully persuaded that, what he had
promised, he was able also to perform." Romans 4:20-
21 (KJV)

Obedience to God is a requirement; it is what guarantees that you will be a "peculiar treasure".

"And Moses went up unto God, and the LORD called
unto him out of the mountain, saying, Thus shalt thou
say to the house of Jacob, and tell the children of Israel;
Ye have seen what I did unto the Egyptians, and how I
bare you on eagles' wings, and brought you unto myself.
Now therefore, <u>if ye will obey my voice indeed, and keep</u>
<u>my covenant, then ye shall be a</u> peculiar treasure unto

*me above all people: for all the earth is mine:" Exodus
19:3-5 (KJV)*

Abraham showed that loyalty to God is a requirement of the covenant
(Genesis 26:1-5).

> *"And there was a famine in the land, beside the first
> famine that was in the days of Abraham. And Isaac
> went unto Abimelech king of the Philistines unto Gerar.
> And the LORD appeared unto him, and said, Go not
> down into Egypt; dwell in the land which I shall tell
> thee of: Sojourn in this land, and I will be with thee,
> and will bless thee; for unto thee, and unto thy seed,
> I will give all these countries, and I will perform the
> oath which I sware unto Abraham thy father; And I
> will make thy seed to multiply as the stars of heaven,
> and will give unto thy seed all these countries; and in thy
> seed shall all the nations of the earth be blessed; Because
> that Abraham obeyed my voice, and kept my charge, my
> commandments, my statutes, and my laws."*
> *Genesis 26:1-5 (KJV)*

God can't do anything in your life if you are not loyal to Him; therefore,
make loyalty your ultimate priority.

God requires that you respect Him, walk in His ways, love Him and
serve Him with all your heart and soul; this is for your good.

> *"And now, Israel, what doth the LORD thy God require
> of thee, but to fear the LORD thy God, to walk in all
> his ways, and to love him, and to serve the LORD thy
> God with all thy heart and with all thy soul, To keep the
> commandments of the LORD, and his statutes, which*

I command thee this day for thy good?" Deuteronomy
10:12-13 (KJV)

"So now, Israel, all that the LORD your God asks from
you is to be devoted with reverence and respect to the
LORD your God, follow all his ways, love him and serve
the LORD your God with all your heart and all your
being; to obey, for your own good, the commandments
and regulations of the LORD which I am giving you
today." Deuteronomy 10:12-13 (Atarah)

Don't continue living in sin, because your covenant with God is not
a license to sin. Obeying and showing reverence to God is a part of
worshiping Him on the basis of your covenant with Him.

"Give unto the LORD the glory due unto his name:
bring an offering, and come into his courts. O worship
the LORD in the beauty of holiness: fear before him, all
the earth." Psalm 96:8-9 (KJV)

"Give to the Lord the glory and honor due to His name:
bring an offering, and come into His presence. Oh
worship the Lord in the beauty of holiness. All the earth,
be devoted with reverence and respect to Him." Psalm
96:8-9 (Atarah)

Understand your covenant with God and then relating to Him based
on that covenant; doing that positions you to prosper in every area of
your life. You can live in peace by having the same mind-set as God.

COVENANT FOR SECURITY AND
UNSHAKEABLE BELIEF PART 3

Prosperity only responds to your understanding and practice of covenant details. What you don't know and understand will cost you.

> *"My people are destroyed for lack of knowledge: because thou hast rejected knowledge, I will also reject thee, that thou shalt be no priest to me: seeing thou hast forgotten the law of thy God, I will also forget thy children." Hosea 4:6 (KJV)*

If you are a stranger to your covenant, then you are without hope and without God in this world.

> *"Wherefore remember, that ye being in time past Gentiles in the flesh, who are called Uncircumcision by that which is called the Circumcision in the flesh made by hands; That at that time ye were without Christ, being aliens from the commonwealth of Israel, and strangers from the covenants of promise, having no hope, and without God in the world:" Ephesians 2:11- 12 (KJV)*

If you are without hope, then you have no reason to expect anything from God because you cannot hope for something that you do not know exists. If you believe in Jesus and have made Him your Lord, you can have hope because you are in covenant with God.

Understanding covenant details is the key to receiving your inheritance. Ignorance limits you.

The degree to which you receive God's Word will be the degree to which you receive the manifestation of His promises in your life.

Prosperity is in this covenant.

God always fulfills His part of the covenant as He promised to do it.

God has given you the power to get wealth so that He may establish His covenant on the earth.

> "And thou say in thine heart, My power and the might of mine hand hath gotten me this wealth. But thou shalt remember the LORD thy God: for it is he that giveth thee power to get wealth, that he may establish his covenant which he sware unto thy fathers, as it is this day." Deuteronomy 8:17-18 (KJV)

The "power" that it is talking about in this scripture is the "ability, enablement or anointing". Therefore, you can rightly say, "I am anointed by God to get wealth.".

The terms of the covenant are twofold. God has a part to play in the covenant, and so do you (Genesis 26:1-5). God has already done His part by establishing His promises through Abraham and Jesus. God's covenant allows you to partake of His resources. If you are in covenant with God, whatever belongs to Him belongs to you.

Your part of the covenant is to obey God's commands (Deuteronomy 10:12-13; Exodus 19:5). God wants you to obey His Word for your own good.

> "And now, Israel, what doth the LORD thy God require of thee, but to fear the LORD thy God, to walk in all his ways, and to love him, and to serve the LORD thy God with all thy heart and with all thy soul, To keep the commandments of the LORD, and his statutes, which

I command thee this day for thy good?" Deuteronomy 10:12-13 (KJV)

"So now, Israel, all that the LORD your God asks from you is to be devoted with reverence and respect to the LORD your God, follow all his ways, love him and serve the LORD your God with all your heart and all your being; to obey, for your own good, the commandments and regulations of the LORD which I am giving you today." Deuteronomy 10:12 (Atarah)

"Now therefore, if ye will obey my voice indeed, and keep my covenant, then ye shall be a peculiar treasure unto me above all people: for all the earth is mine:" Exodus 19:5 (KJV)

You can have confidence in the covenant because God swore an oath to Himself to bless and multiply you (Hebrews 6:13);

"For when God made promise to Abraham, because he could swear by no greater, he sware by himself," Hebrews 6:13 (KJV)

His promises and oaths are immutable and unchangeable. You must not doubt the covenant even when you don't see your prayers answered immediately. In His covenant, God has already given you everything you could ever want, need or desire. What you see or don't see should not stop you from believing and receiving the covenant God has established with you.

Covenant people know how to rest in the promises of God. Angels are available to assist you in receiving the manifestation of what God has promised, but you must rest (trust and have full confidence) in the covenant. (2 Chronicles 15:12-15).

Don't allow anything to disturb your rest (trust and full confidence). Abraham and Noah rested in the promises of God for years until they saw the manifestation of what He had promised them.

To obtain the promises of God, you must patiently endure. The enemy wants to take your focus off your covenant to change your attitude about what God has already said.

Patience does not mean "to put up with"; instead, it means "to be consistently, constantly the same". I like to call it "having tenacity". The covenant is designed to anchor your soul to God's promises.

By meditating on the promises of God daily, you will develop an inner image of the covenant. When you have developed an inner image, God sees it as a done deal. Change your vision by meditating on the covenant.

The only way to tap into the promises of God is to understand and practice covenant "details". God is a covenant-keeping God, He wants to perform the terms of His covenant; however, you must do your part, which is to believe, obey and rest in Him.

UNDERSTANDING YOUR COVENANT OF PROMISE

"And thou say in thine heart, My power and the might of mine hand hath gotten me this wealth. But thou shalt remember the LORD thy God: for it is he that giveth thee power to get wealth, that he may establish his covenant which he sware unto thy fathers, as it is this day." Deuteronomy 8:17-18 (KJV)

God promised to give you the power to get wealth. This power can take the form of ability, anointing, wisdom or enlightenment and is designed to lead to your wealthy place.

Angels are at your disposal. They do whatever it takes to carry out God's promise to bless Abraham's seed (those who believe in Jesus and have made Him their Lord). Although you may not see angels with your physical eyes, they exist in great multitudes. The Word of God is your guarantee that they exist. There are about 100 trillion angels available to the body of Christ to carry out God's will in the earth.

> "And I beheld, and I heard the voice of many angels round about the throne and the beasts and the elders: and the number of them was ten thousand times ten thousand, and thousands of thousands;" Revelation 5:11 (KJV)

When you get to heaven, you will see an innumerable company of angels, as well as the spirits of righteous people (Hebrews 12:22-23).

> "But ye are come unto mount Sion, and unto the city of the living God, the heavenly Jerusalem, and to an innumerable company of angels, To the general assembly and church of the firstborn, which are written in heaven, and to God the Judge of all, and to the spirits of just men made perfect," Hebrews 12:22-23 (KJV)

You won't fear the appearance of angels once you understand their purpose. Angels can speak and give direction.

> "And the angel of the Lord spake unto Philip, saying, Arise, and go toward the south unto the way that goeth

down from Jerusalem unto Gaza, which is desert." Acts
8:26 (KJV)

As long as you remain in the will of God, angels are charged with your protection and deliverance.

"For he shall give his angels charge over thee, to keep thee
in all thy ways." Psalm 91:11 (KJV)

"The angel of the LORD encampeth round about them
that fear him, and delivereth them." Psalm 34:7 (KJV)

"The Angel of the Lord encamps around those who are
devoted with reverence and respect to Him and each of
them He protects and delivers." Psalm 34:7 (Atarah)

"Then Nebuchadnezzar spake, and said, Blessed be the
God of Shadrach, Meshach, and Abednego, who hath
sent his angel, and delivered his servants that trusted
in him, and have changed the king's word, and yielded
their bodies, that they might not serve nor worship any
god, except their own God. Therefore I make a decree,
That every people, nation, and language, which speak
any thing amiss against the God of Shadrach, Meshach,
and Abednego, shall be cut in pieces, and their houses
shall be made a dunghill: because there is no other God
that can deliver after this sort." Daniel 3:28-29 (KJV)

"And, behold, the angel of the Lord came upon him, and
a light shined in the prison: and he smote Peter on the
side, and raised him up, saying, Arise up quickly. And
his chains fell off from his hands. And the angel said
unto him, Gird thyself, and bind on thy sandals. And so

he did. And he saith unto him, Cast thy garment about thee, and follow me. And he went out, and followed him; and wist not that it was true which was done by the angel; but thought he saw a vision." Acts 12:7-9 (KJV)

"And now I exhort you to be of good cheer: for there shall be no loss of any man's life among you, but of the ship. For there stood by me this night the angel of God, whose I am, and whom I serve," Acts 27:22-23 (KJV)

Angels have a main objective.

"Wherefore then serveth the law? It was added because of transgressions, till the seed should come to whom the promise was made; and it was ordained by angels in the hand of a mediator." Galatians 3:19 (KJV)

The terms of your covenant with God are administered, managed, supplied, executed, superintended, dispensed, distributed and furnished through the ministry of angels.

God's ranking system is: 1) God; 2) man; and 3) angels (Psalm 8:4-5).

"What is man, that thou art mindful of him? and the son of man, that thou visitest him? For thou hast made him a little lower than the angels (elohiym), and hast crowned him with glory and honour." Psalm 8:4-5 (KJV)

"I ask "What is man, that You are mindful of him and attend and care for him?" You have made him a little lower than Yourself, and have crowned him with glory (abundance, riches and dignity) and honor." Psalm 8:4-5 (Atarah)

"For thou hast made him a little lower than the angels..." (Psalm 8:5) was incorrectly translated. The word angels (elohiym) in this verse actually means "God."

Man was created a little lower than God, and angels were created lower than man. In Christ, you have a right to all that is God's and all that is at His disposal, including angels. Angels are ministering spirits assigned to minister to and for the heirs of salvation.

> "But to which of the angels said he at any time, Sit on my right hand, until I make thine enemies thy footstool? <u>Are they not all ministering spirits, sent forth to minister for them who shall be</u> <u>heirs of salvation</u>?" Hebrews 1:13-14 (KJV)

For God's promises to be established in your life, you must know it and decree them (Job 22:28).

> "Thou shalt also decree a thing, and it shall be established unto thee: and the light shall shine upon thy ways." Job 22:28 (KJV)

Angels only respond to the voice of God's Word that you decree.

> "Bless the LORD, ye his angels, that excel in strength, that do his commandments, hearkening unto the voice of his word. Bless ye the LORD, all ye his hosts; ye ministers of his, that do his pleasure." Psalm 103:20-21 (KJV)

After you know the promises of God and decree it, then Angels can carry out His pleasure in your life-your prosperity (Psalm 35:27).

> "Let them shout for joy, and be glad, that favour my righteous cause: yea, let them say continually, Let

the LORD be magnified, which hath pleasure in the prosperity of his servant." Psalm 35:27 (KJV)

Concentrating on circumstances rather than on God's promises causes many people to struggle. Your situation may seem impossible, but focus on your covenant instead. We order our conduct daily by the Word of God that we have come to believe and embrace and not by what we see with our physical eyes. (2 Corinthians 5:7)

"(For we walk by faith, not by sight:)" 2 Corinthians 5:7 (KJV)

"We order our conduct daily by the Word of God that we have come to believe and embrace and not by what we see with our physical eyes:" 2 Corinthians 5:7 (Atarah)

Angels are available even when things seem impossible. For example: the prophet Elisha and his servant were surrounded by the enemy's army but were delivered through the ministry of angels.

"Therefore, he sent horses, chariots and a large army there; they came by night and surrounded the city. The servant of the man of God rose early and went out, but to his surprise, he saw an army with horses and chariots around the city. Elisha's servant said to him, "Alas, my master! What shall we do? Elisha answered, "Fear not-don't worry about it; because we have more with us than they have with them." Then Elisha prayed, "Oh Lord, open his eyes so he can see". Then the Lord opened the young man's eyes, and he saw, and behold, the mountain was full of horses and chariots of fire round about Elisha. When they came down to him, Elisha prayed to the LORD, "Please strike these people blind"; and he

*struck them blind, as Elisha had asked." 2 Kings 6:14-
18 (Atarah)*

Don't fail to take advantage of angelic ministry: know your covenant rights, pray the Word of God, speak the Word of God and see the Word of God manifested in your life.

*"So shall my word be that goeth forth out of my mouth:
it shall not return unto me void, but it shall accomplish
that which I please, and it shall prosper in the thing
whereto I sent it." Isaiah 55:11*

*"Bless the Lord, you His angels, you mighty ones who
do His commandments, hearkening to the voice of His
word." Psalm 103:20 (Atarah)*

Rejoice, knowing that your covenant is established with God.

Multitudes of angels have been assigned by God to carry out the terms of His covenant with you. However, their work cannot be accomplished until you fulfill your part of the covenant.

REJECTION

It is not always easy to master emotions. One of the greatest fears that many of us have is the fear of rejection. *Rejection* is the feeling that you're unwanted, unloved or not accepted. Rejection is the feeling that you're never good enough. The fear of rejection is rooted in thoughts of inadequacy and insecurity. When someone is unsure of their worth as a person or falsely believes negative things about themselves, he or she will fear people's rejection based upon their own negative self–view.

Some people live their lives burying wounds and hurt that stem from being rejected. The problem is that burying the pain will not allow proper healing to take place. Some people cope with their feelings by constructing a false self–image and building walls around their hearts to protect themselves from being hurt or rejected again.

You may have heard the saying, "People spend the first part of their lives perfecting their disguise and the rest of it looking for the person that can see through it.". Many believers have perfected phoniness and their "disguise". When a person doesn't like himself on the inside, he has to wear a mask or project a false image of himself that he feels will cause him to be more accepted by others. This kind of person usually gains confidence from externalities like good looks, nice clothes, high position at job or a big salary. The problem is that this is not true, godly confidence. Real godly confidence comes from within and is not based upon external appearance or an abundance of *things*. If a person lives this way for too long, he or she will eventually become so comfortable with the mask they might find it difficult to ever regain contact with who they really are.

The solution to this soul sickness is knowing that God loves you. Only a person who is rooted in God's acceptance can accept themselves. When a person realizes that God loves them despite his or her imperfections, they are able to embrace the qualities that make them special and unique, in spite of what others think. This is so important, because many times, we focus on the rejection we may face from others without realizing that we have already internally rejected ourselves. Those who have rejected themselves usually suffer from a nagging sense of failing to measure up. A person's inferiorities are amplified when he or she faces rejection.

Jesus said,

> "All that the Father giveth me shall come to me; and
> him that cometh to me I will in no wise cast out." John
> 6:37 (KJV)

Everyone should focus on who they are according to the Word and who they are in Christ. As they do this, confidence begins to rise and it becomes easier to remove the masks that were once worn to protect the *real person*. Eventually, it becomes easier for them to be comfortable with his or her genuine self and there is no need for external "crutches". They will no longer feel that they have to protect themselves or their feelings. They are now free to express who they truly are without being ruled by the fear of rejection.

Being confident in who they really are will automatically attracts others. They say to themselves, *"God loves me and values me enough to give His most precious gift."*. True wholeness comes from an intimate love relationship with God. People must realize that there is no way to truly be happy with one's self outside of God. Anything else is just a cheap attempt to cover up wounds and pain with phoniness and external trappings that ultimately amount to nothing. Embraces the love of God and allow it to change you. Be secure and strong in Christ.

RIGHTEOUSNESS

In Christ you are righteous. God sent Jesus to Earth to redeem mankind from the curse of sin. Through Him, we are all able to come into relationship with God once again and remain in fellowship with Him forever. When Jesus sacrificed Himself on the cross, He did not just take on sin; He became sin so that a divine exchange could take place—our sin in exchange for His righteousness. Jesus not only died physically, He also died spiritually, experiencing separation from

God. When He defeated the enemy in Hell and was resurrected, the job was done. We now have the right to be called children of God, and righteousness is not something any of us can earn. There is no amount of good works that could ever qualify us to become righteous in God's eyes! Righteousness is a free gift we receive through Jesus.

I am the righteousness of God through Jesus.

> *"For he hath made him to be sin for us, who knew no sin; that we might be made the righteousness of God in him."*
> *2 Corinthians 5:21 (KJV)*

We are made righteous by Jesus Christ and not by any works of our own. We simply believe as Abraham did.

> *"What shall we say then that Abraham our father, as pertaining to the flesh, hath found? For if Abraham were justified by works, he hath whereof to glory; but not before God. For what saith the scripture? Abraham believed God, and it was counted unto him for righteousness. Now to him that worketh is the reward not reckoned of grace, but of debt. But to him that worketh not, but believeth on him that justifieth the ungodly, his faith is counted for righteousness. Even as David also describeth the blessedness of the man, unto whom God imputeth righteousness without works, Saying, Blessed are they whose iniquities are forgiven, and whose sins are covered. Blessed is the man to whom the Lord will not impute sin." Romans 4:1-8 (KJV)*

Focus more on who you are *in Christ* and your behavior will change. God has chosen us before the foundation of the world.
We are blameless and perfect in His sight.

"According as he hath chosen us in him before the foundation of the world, that we should be holy and without blame before him in love:" Ephesians 1:4 (KJV)

"As He has chosen us (actually picked us out for Himself as His own) in Christ before the foundation of the world, that we should be holy (having the same mindset as Him), blameless, faultless and perfect in His sight, before Him in love." Ephesians 1:4 (Atarah)

"In the body of his flesh through death, to present you holy and unblameable and unreproveable in his sight:" Colossians 1:22 (KJV)

"Now Christ has reconciled you to God in the body of His flesh through death, in order to present you holy, faultless (perfect) and guiltless in His presence." Colossians 1:22 (Atarah)

"Now we know that what things soever the law saith, it saith to them who are under the law: that every mouth may be stopped, and all the world may become guilty before God. Therefore by the deeds of the law there shall no flesh be justified in his sight: for by the law is the knowledge of sin. <u>But now the righteousness of God without the law is manifested</u>, being witnessed by the law and the prophets; <u>Even the righteousness of God which is by faith of Jesus</u> Christ unto all and upon all them that believe</u>: for there is no difference:" Romans 3:19-22 (KJV)

"Now we know that whatever the Law says, it speaks to those who are under the Law, so that every mouth may

be hushed and all the world may be held accountable to God. Therefore, by the deeds of the law there shall no flesh be justified and made righteous in His sight: for by the law is the knowledge of sin. *But now the righteousness of God has been revealed independently and altogether apart from the Law,* being witnessed by the Law and the Prophets, *We are made righteous by the Word of Jesus Christ that we've heard and come to believed* by analyzing and assimilating it into our way of thinking and then acting in accordance with what we have learned and have embraced and this is true for everyone who believes, no matter who we are." Romans 3:19-22 (Atarah)

"For Christ is the end of the law for righteousness to every one that believeth." Romans 10:4 (KJV)

"Christ is the end of the law, into righteousness (right-standing with God) to everyone that believes." Romans 10:4 (Atarah)

"For with the heart man believeth unto righteousness; and with the mouth confession is made unto salvation. For the scripture saith, Whosoever believeth on him shall not be ashamed. " Romans 10:10-11 (KJV)

"With the spirit (subconscious mind), mankind believes to righteousness (right standing with God); and with the mouth confession is made to salvation (safety, protection, health, healing and deliverance). The Scripture says that no man who believes in Him will ever be put to shame or be disappointed." Romans 10:10 (Atarah)

CONSECRATION: YOUR ACCESS TO PROSPERITY

Manifestation and accomplishment come from a strong foundation. A sturdy foundation is necessary to sustain any kingdom principle.

> *"If the foundations be destroyed, what can the righteous do?" Psalm 11:3 (KJV)*

Prosperity can't be established without the proper foundation.

Once we have a strong foundation, all people will flow to it.

> *"And it shall come to pass in the last days, that the mountain of the LORD'S house shall be established in the top of the mountains, and shall be exalted above the hills; and all nations shall flow unto it." Isaiah 2:2 (KJV)*

God will build us up to its highest point, then He will appear in His glory (Psalm 102:16).

> *"When the LORD shall build up Zion, he shall appear in his glory." Psalm 102:16 (KJV)*

Part of building a strong foundation is living a righteous life.

> *"Say ye to the righteous, that it shall be well with him: for they shall eat the fruit of their doings." Isaiah 3:10 (KJV)*

If the enemy can successfully destroy the foundation of God's Word in your life, he can see you fail over and over again.

Consecration is one element in the foundation of prosperity. God knows those who belong to Him; if you believe in Jesus and have made Him your Lord, you must depart from iniquity.

> *"While they promise them liberty, <u>they themselves are the servants of corruption: for of whom a man is overcome, of the same is he brought in bondage</u>."* 2 Peter 2:19 (KJV)

> *"They promise them freedom, <u>but they themselves are slaves of corruption; for a person is slave to whatever has defeated him</u>."* 2 Peter 2:19 (Atarah)

Departing from sin is a foundational key to prosperity. Until you depart from sin, the principles of the Word have nothing on which to stand. You can't expect prosperity and success when your life is filled with sin.

Jesus has set you free so that you can come out of the "jail" of sin. As a believer, you have been made the righteousness of God. Rely on the power of the Word to deliver you from sin.

> *"All scripture is given by inspiration of God, and is profitable for doctrine, for reproof, for correction, for instruction in righteousness:"* 2 Timothy 3:16 (KJV)

Return to God when you sin and miss the mark. Sin will cause you to "die", or to change your position in relation to God and brings the feelings of guilt and shame. Adam had the choice when he took in from the 'Knowledge of Good and Evil' (Genesis 2:15-17), but he chose to disobey God. He was clothed with the glory of God, but he changed when he took in from the 'Knowledge of Good and Evil'. As a result of his guilt and shame, he hid from God (Genesis 3:9-10).

Sin will escort you out of plenty and into poverty; sin is the mother of all poverty. Sin always has a consequence. The consequence of Adam's sin was having to leave the garden of plenty.

Before you can see the abundant blessings of God poured out on your life, you must have a relationship with God and His Word, and let it cleans you and purify you of sin as you yield to the promptings and guidance of the Lord. (Malachi 3:3-4).

Every time you say "no" to sin, you are saying "yes" to prosperity (wholeness) in your life. It is a day to day process.

> *"All things are lawful for me, but all things are not expedient: all things are lawful for me, but all things edify not." 1 Corinthians 10:23 (KJV)*

> *"All things are lawful (permissible and we are free to do anything we please), but not all things are beneficial, expedient, profitable and wholesome. All things are lawful, but not all things are constructive to character and edifying." 1 Corinthians 10:23 (Atarah)*

God has not called His children to remain in the dark. Once you believe in Jesus and made Him your Lord, it has been given to you to know the mysteries of the kingdom of God.

> *"And he said unto them, <u>Unto you it is given to know the mystery of the kingdom of God</u>: but unto them that are without, all these things are done in parables:" Mark 4:11 (KJV)*

God has knowledge that will bring results in your life. The common denominator for your escape from problematic situations is revelation from God.

The natural, carnal-minded man is on the outside of revelation knowledge. He is "without" God or the knowledge of God.

> "But the natural man receiveth not the things of the Spirit of God: for they are foolishness unto him: neither can he know them, because they are spiritually discerned."
> 1 Corinthians 2:14 (KJV)

God will show His secrets to those who are devoted with reverence and respect to Him (Psalm 25:14).

> "The secret of the LORD is with them that fear him; and he will shew them his covenant." Psalm 25:14 (KJV)
> "The secret (satisfying companionship) of the Lord is with them who are devoted with reverence and respect to Him; and He will reveal to them His covenant with all that it contains." Psalm 25:14 (Atarah)

Walking in the fear of God means the be devoted with reverence and respect to God. When you walk in devotion with reverence and respect to the Lord, you allow God to do wonderful things in your life.

What you do every day is what you develop; therefore, learn to develop in your relationship with God and His Word and accept responsibility for where you are. Don't be like a dog and "return to your vomit," or return to the way you did things when you were unsaved (2 Peter 2:20-22; Proverbs 26:11; Revelation 22:15).

"For if after they have escaped the pollutions of the world through the knowledge of the Lord and Saviour Jesus Christ, they are again entangled therein, and overcome, the latter end is worse with them than the beginning. For it had been better for them not to have known the way of righteousness, than, after they have known it, to turn from the holy commandment delivered unto them. But it is happened unto them according to the true proverb, The dog is turned to his own vomit again; and the sow that was washed to her wallowing in the mire."
2 Peter 2:20-22 (KJV)

"As a dog returneth to his vomit, so a fool returneth to his folly." Proverbs 26:11 (KJV)

"For without are dogs, and sorcerers, and whoremongers, and murderers, and idolaters, and whosoever loveth and maketh a lie." Revelation 22:15 (KJV)

A person who is living like a dog will not prosper. Jesus' advice to dogs is to depart from iniquity. God wants to have a relationship with you and help you to stop. You become a candidate for kingdom prosperity when you live a consecrated life.

You must be consecrated to God for kingdom principles to work effectively in your life. Consecration, or "setting yourself apart to and for God" is one element in the foundation of prosperity (wholeness of every area of your life). You must have a relationship with God and His Word and let it cleans and purify you of sin as you yield to the promptings and guidance of the Lord.

CONSECRATION: YOUR ACCESS
TO PROSPERITY, PART 2

True prosperity has a foundation. Prosperity (wholeness in every area of life) isn't based on emotions, but on an understanding of those things that are in the Word of God that we hear over and over and come to understand.

According to Psalm 11:3, if there is no foundation, you won't be able to accomplish anything. One element of the foundation for prosperity is consecration. Consecration, is "setting yourself apart to and for God, to be devoted or set apart for a definite purpose; separated from a common to a sacred use; separated or dedicated to the service and worship of God". Consecration can be translated to mean "perfected" or "newly made".

> *"For the law maketh men high priests which have infirmity; but the word of the oath, which was since the law, maketh the Son, who is consecrated for evermore."*
> *Hebrews 7:28 (KJV)*

> *"The Law sets up men in their weakness as high priests, but the Word of God's oath, which after the institution of the Law, makes the Son, Who has been made perfect forever."*
> *Hebrews 7:28 (Atarah)*

> *"By a new and living way, which he hath consecrated for us, through the veil, that is to say, his flesh;" Hebrews 10:20 (KJV)*

You are to have a relationship with God and His Word and yield to His guidance and promptings so that you separate yourself from iniquity.

By having this relationship with God and His Word and departing from iniquity, you lay down the foundation for prosperity.

> *"Nevertheless the foundation of God standeth sure, having this seal, The Lord knoweth them that are his. And, Let every one that nameth the name of Christ depart from iniquity"*
> *2 Timothy 2:19 (KJV)*

Job 22:23-24 says that God will build up those who return to Him and put away iniquity. There is compensation when you return to God, have that relationship with Him and say "no" to sin – it is written you will have gold, like dust. That sounds like prosperity.

> *"If thou return to the Almighty, thou shalt be built up, thou shalt put away iniquity far from thy tabernacles. Then shalt thou lay up gold as dust, and the gold of Ophir as the stones of the brooks." Job 22:23-24 (KJV)*

When you are devoted with reverence and respect to the Lord it involves hating iniquity. The Lord teaches those who are devoted with reverence and respect to Him the way they should go. Remember that the word 'fear' actually refers to being devoted with reverence and respect to the Lord. (Psalm 25:12, 14)

God reveals His covenant and its deep, inner meaning to them and gives revelation to those who have consecrated themselves.

> *"What man is he that feareth the LORD? him shall he teach in the way that he shall choose." Psalm 25:12 (KJV)*

> *"The secret of the LORD is with them that fear him; and he will shew them his covenant." Psalm 25:14 (KJV)*

<u>The fear of the Lord is dedicating yourself to Him, walking in respect of His Word and departing from iniquity by hating evil, sin and wrongdoing.</u>

Walking in the fear of the Lord is the beginning of revelation knowledge, but a fool despises wisdom and instruction.

> *"The fear of the LORD is the beginning of knowledge: but fools despise wisdom and instruction." Proverbs 1:7 (KJV)*

God blesses the person who departs from the counsel of the ungodly (Psalm 1:1).

> *"Blessed is the man that walketh not in the counsel of the ungodly, nor standeth in the way of sinners, nor sitteth in the seat of the scornful." Psalm 1:1 (KJV)*

Be cautious of those with whom you associate or from whom you take advice, because they may steer you the wrong way.

Delight in God's law. Meditate on in it day and night so that it will be in you.

"But his delight is in the law of the LORD; and in his law doth he meditate day and night." Psalm 1:2 (KJV)

If you depart from iniquity, you will be rewarded; you will be like a tree planted by rivers of water, and everything that you do will prosper.

> *"And he shall be like a tree planted by the rivers of water, that bringeth forth his fruit in his season; his leaf also*

shall not wither; and whatsoever he doeth shall prosper."
Psalm 1:3 (KJV)

We see this in the life of Joseph. Joseph prospered everywhere he went: Potiphar's house, in the field as a servant, in jail and as Prime Minister of Egypt.

It is time to return to the garden of plenty. Adam's sin moved them out of the garden (plenty). They were driven out of plenty and into lack (Genesis 3:24).

"Plenty" is still available to believers. It is time for believers to have that restored relationship with God and step out of sin and back into plenty, because this is the way the kingdom of God operates.

Adam's moving from life to death because of sin put everyone under a curse, but because of Jesus, you have moved from death to life. Now that you are alive with God, there is a garden waiting for you- a place of plenty.

As you consecrate yourself to God and His Word and turn from iniquity, plenty begins to shows up. The Almighty will be your defense; you will have plenty of silver.

> *"Yea, the Almighty shall be thy defence, and thou shalt*
> *have plenty of silver." Job 22:25 (KJV)*

Be obedient to the Word of God; it is your action that will return you to the garden of plenty. For your obedience, God will make your wilderness like Eden and your deserts like the Garden of the Lord.

> *"For the LORD shall comfort Zion: he will comfort all*
> *her waste places; and he will make her wilderness like*
> *Eden, and her desert like the garden of the LORD; joy*

and gladness shall be found therein, thanksgiving, and
the voice of melody." Isaiah 51:3 (KJV)

Uprightness and right-standing with God elevates a nation, while sin
brings a nation down.

"Righteousness exalteth a nation: but sin is a reproach
to any people." Proverbs 14:34 (KJV)

Your access to the wealthy place begins with being devoted with
reverence and respect to the Lord. Being devoted with reverence and
respect to the Lord is the beginning of wisdom, and wisdom is the
mother of all wealth.

Desire wisdom more than anything.

"Happy is the man that findeth wisdom, and the man
that getteth understanding." Proverbs 3:13 (KJV)

"Length of days is in her right hand; and in her left hand
riches and honour." Proverbs 3:16 (KJV)

"For wisdom is better than rubies; and all the things that
may be desired are not to be compared to it." Proverbs
8:11 (KJV)

God will rebuild your wastelands when you repent and allow yourself
to be cleansed of sin.

"Thus saith the Lord GOD; In the day that I shall have
cleansed you from all your iniquities I will also cause you
to dwell in the cities, and the wastes shall be builded."
Ezekiel 36:33 (KJV)

You must practice holiness to keep yourself spiritually fit. Holiness is having the same mindset as God because right believing will equal right living.

> *"But refuse profane and old wives' fables, and exercise thyself rather unto godliness. For bodily exercise profiteth little: but godliness is profitable unto all things, having promise of the life that now is, and of that which is to come." 1 Timothy 4:7-8 (KJV)*

> *"Refuse profane and old wives' fables, and exercise yourself rather to godliness. Though bodily exercise is profitable in the flesh, godliness is profitable to all things, since it holds promise both for the present life and for that life to come." 1 Timothy 4:7-8 (Atarah)*

> *"Meditate upon these things; give thyself wholly to them; that thy profiting may appear to all." 1 Timothy 4:15 (KJV)*

Holiness is "aligning your thoughts and actions with God's Word". Get into the habit of living a holy life. Employing godliness will profit you in this life and in the life to come.

Prosperity is not just about money. Christians need to know that there is total life prosperity, or wholeness and continuous well-being for every area of their lives. To experience total life prosperity, you must first understand how it works. Consecration is a key element of this kind of prosperity.

THE PROSPEROUS LIFE IS NOT FOR FOOLS

A firm foundation in the things of God is your key to prosperity (wholeness in ever area of life). If your foundations for success have been destroyed, you cannot accomplish anything for God.

> *"If the foundations be destroyed, what can the righteous do?" Psalm 11:3 (KJV)*

God desires for you to succeed in life and this requires consecration.

> *"Nevertheless the foundation of God standeth sure, having this seal, The Lord knoweth them that are his. And, Let every one that nameth the name of Christ depart from iniquity." 2 Timothy 2:19 (KJV)*

To consecrate means, "To set yourself apart to and for God, to be devoted to Him and set apart for a definite purpose; separated from a common to a sacred use; dedicated to the service and worship of God." Accepting Jesus as your Lord is an example of consecration; it's a decision to dedicate your life to obeying and living for God.

Fools do not prosper. Fools say in their hearts that there is no God.

> *"The fool hath said in his heart, There is no God. They are corrupt, they have done abominable works, there is none that doeth good. The LORD looked down from heaven upon the children of men, to see if there were any that did understand, and seek God. They are all gone aside, they are all together become filthy: there is none that doeth good, no, not one. Have all the workers of iniquity no knowledge? who eat up my people as they eat bread, and call not upon the LORD. There were they in great fear: for God is in the generation of the righteous.*

Ye have shamed the counsel of the poor, because the LORD is his refuge. Oh that the salvation of Israel were come out of Zion! when the LORD bringeth back the captivity of his people, Jacob shall rejoice, and Israel shall be glad." Psalm 14:1-7 (KJV)

The condition of your heart determines whether or not you are a fool. Everything you do for God is weighed in relation to the condition of your heart. The position of your heart determines the direction of your life.

You must seek God, require of and research Him to prosper (verse 2). Fools don't seek God; therefore, they don't prosper.

A fool is a "worker of iniquity" who lacks knowledge and understanding (verse 4).

Prosperity ruins a fool, because he won't handle it wisely.

> *"For the turning away of the simple shall slay them, and the prosperity of fools shall destroy them." Proverbs 1:32 (KJV)*

> *"The fools who turn their backs on my wise advice will be ruined. The prosperity of fools will destroy them." Proverbs 1:32 (Atarah)*

I heard it said and I find it to be true that "Money is an amplifier". It magnifies your present position and mindset. For example: money in the hands of a drug addict will perpetuate his addiction and a wealthy adulterer will be more extravagant in his adulterous affairs.

A fool mocks sin, finds pleasure in it, and thinks that sinning doesn't matter.

"Fools make a mock at sin: but among the righteous there is favour." Proverbs 14:9 (KJV)

Unbelievers are less likely to take God seriously when they witness believers living in sin.

God does not condemn you but He warns you of the danger of living in sin.

"For God sent not his Son into the world to condemn the world; but that the world through him might be saved." John 3:17 (KJV)

We have an enemy who attempts to condemn us, making us think that God doesn't love us.

Purity begets plenty, whereas impurity is an enemy to plenty. Many people make excuses for not prospering; they don't have that close relationship with God and do not realize that their sin is the problem.

When sin is destroyed, lack ceases to be a problem.

This may come as a shock, but your giving in tithes and offerings won't lead to prosperity until you establish a foundation of consecration "setting yourself apart to and for God and yielding to His promptings and guidance".

Turn your heart toward God and prosper. As you return to God and yield to Him and His promptings, what is rightfully yours by inheritance will return to you.

"Even from the days of your fathers ye are gone away from mine ordinances, and have not kept them. Return

unto me, and I will return unto you, saith the LORD of hosts." Malachi 3:7 (KJV)

Return to the Lord, have that relationship with Him, yield to Him and depart from iniquity, and you will have "gold as dust" (i.e. you will prosper as consistently as dust gathers).

> *"If thou return to the Almighty, thou shalt be built up, thou shalt put away iniquity far from thy tabernacles. Then shalt thou lay up gold as dust, and the gold of Ophir as the stones of the brooks. Yea, the Almighty shall be thy defence, and thou shalt have plenty of silver." Job 22:23-25 (KJV)*

Joseph's relationship with God and refusing to sin led to his promotion (Genesis 41:37-44).

> *"The plan seemed good in the eyes of Pharaoh and in the eyes of all his servants. Pharaoh said to his servants, "Isn't this the man we need? Are we going to find anyone else who has God's spirit in him like this?" So Pharaoh said to Joseph, "As your God has shown you all this, there is nobody as intelligent and discreet and understanding and wise as you are. You shall have charge over my house, and all my people shall be governed according to your word. Only in matters of the throne will I be greater than you are." Then Pharaoh said to Joseph, "I'm putting you in charge of the entire land of Egypt." Then Pharaoh removed his signet ring from his finger and slipped it on Joseph's hand. He clothed him in official robes of the best linen and put a gold chain around his neck. He made him ride in the second chariot which he had, and before he passed by officials shouted out,*

"Joseph is coming, bow and show respect!" Joseph was in charge of the entire land of Egypt. Pharaoh said to Joseph, "I am Pharaoh, but no one in Egypt will make a single move without your stamp of approval."" Genesis 41:37-44 (Atarah)

Great prosperity is available to you when you give God your focus and attention and yield to Him and His promptings. (Proverbs 23:26).

"My son, give me thine heart, and let thine eyes observe my ways." Proverbs 23:26 (KJV)

"Dear child, I want your full attention; please do what I show you." Proverbs 23:26 (Atarah)

Like King David, your heart must be perfect toward God for Him to show Himself strong in your life.

"For the eyes of the LORD run to and fro throughout the whole earth, to shew himself strong in the behalf of them whose heart is perfect toward him. Herein thou hast done foolishly: therefore from henceforth thou shalt have wars." 2 Chronicles 16:9 (KJV)

"And when he had removed him, he raised up unto them David to be their king; to whom also he gave testimony, and said, I have found David the son of Jesse, a man after mine own heart, which shall fulfil all my will." Acts 13:22 (KJV)

A perfect heart is "one that is pliable, sensitive and repentant toward God; willing to change and remain loyal to Him".

Your heart is where your treasure is.

"For where your treasure is, there will your heart be also." Matthew 6:21 (KJV)

As you prosper, refuse to make success your treasure; treasure God instead. You can live without material things, but not without God.

Do what is right because it is right and do it in a right manner. You are an upright and blessed believer who is called to depart from iniquity.

"Praise ye the LORD. Blessed is the man that feareth the LORD, that delighteth greatly in his commandments. His seed shall be mighty upon earth: the generation of the upright shall be blessed. Wealth and riches shall be in his house: and his righteousness endureth for ever." Psalm 112:1-3 (KJV)

Wealth and riches are in the houses of those who are consecrated to God.

Never seek things above seeking God.

You have a right to prosper and to be happy.

A firm foundation in the things of God, including the area of consecration toward Him, is essential to your prosperity. Likewise, not taking God seriously will hinder you. You must make a conscious decision to have a relationship with God and His Word and yield to Him and His promptings and depart from a life of sin so that He can show Himself strong in your life.

THE FOUNDATION OF COMMITMENT

Your heart is where your treasure is.

> *"For where your treasure is, there will your heart be also." Matthew 6:21 (KJV)*

> *"Where your treasure is, <u>is were your love and affections is</u>." Matthew 6:21 (Atarah)*

God is after your heart. When God has your heart, your sacrifices are acceptable to Him.

> *"For thou desirest not sacrifice; else would I give it: thou delightest not in burnt offering. The sacrifices of God are a broken spirit: a broken and a contrite heart, O God, thou wilt not despise. Do good in thy good pleasure unto Zion: build thou the walls of Jerusalem. Then shalt thou be pleased with the sacrifices of righteousness, with burnt offering and whole burnt offering: then shall they offer bullocks upon thine altar." Psalm 51:16-19 (KJV)*

When you make God your treasure and give Him your heart (love and affection), you can have whatever is in His hands. Your prosperity is determined by the motives of your heart. It is an act of perversion to seek after the creation and ignore the Creator.

The Macedonian Church prospered because they kept "first things" first (2 Corinthians 8:1-5).

> *"Moreover, brethren, we do you to wit of the grace of God bestowed on the churches of Macedonia; How that in a great trial of affliction the abundance of their joy and their deep poverty abounded unto the riches of*

their liberality. For to their power, I bear record, yea, and beyond their power they were willing of themselves; Praying us with much intreaty that we would receive the gift, and take upon us the fellowship of the ministering to the saints. And this they did, not as we hoped, <u>but first gave their own selves to the Lord, and unto us by the will of God</u>." 2 Corinthians 8:1-5 (KJV)

"Now, brothers, we must tell you about the grace (unmerited love, favor and empowerment) God has given to the churches of Macedonia; Despite severe trials, their joy and deep poverty has overflowed in a wealth of generosity. I tell you they have not merely given according to their means, but of their own free will they have given beyond their means. They begged and pleaded with us for the privilege of sharing in this service for God's people. They didn't do this in the way we had expected, <u>but first they gave themselves to the Lord and to us by the will of God</u>." 2 Corinthians 8:1-5 (Atarah)

The Macedonians first gave themselves to the Lord, and their prosperity became legendary. When you are committed to God, you are connected to Him and His pleasures. Plant yourself in the presences of God. The 'house of God' represents "His presence", To be planted means "to be committed".

"Those that be planted in the house of the LORD shall flourish in the courts of our God. They shall still bring forth fruit in old age; they shall be fat and flourishing;" Psalm 92:13-14 (KJV)

"Those that are planted in (committed to) the presence of the Lord will flourish in His presence. They will

bring forth fruit all the days of their life; they are full of excessive strength and vigor and rich in love, favor and contentment." Psalm 92:13-14 (Atarah)

When a tree is planted in the ground, it is committed to that spot; it doesn't uproot itself.

When you are committed, you flourish in the presence of God. If you are not flourishing, it's a matter of commitment. You must be planted (committed) to God and His Word long enough to establish roots deep enough so that you can grow and bear fruit.

Don't leave God when things don't work out the way you want them to.

A seed (God's Words) must be planted in your heart, you must become one with that Word and then you (being one with that Word) must die before the plant can grow; you must die to yourself; your own selfish desires, plans, career and decisions.

> *"Verily, verily, I say unto you, Except a corn of wheat fall into the ground and die, it abideth alone: but if it die, it bringeth forth much fruit. He that loveth his life shall lose it; and he that hateth his life in this world shall keep it unto life eternal. If any man serve me, let him follow me; and where I am, there shall also my servant be: if any man serve me, him will my Father honour." John 12:24-26 (KJV)*

Growth will not occur if every time trouble or pressure shows up, you become uprooted by filling your mind with thoughts that are contrary to those you have planted. Pressure comes to make you believe that the Word won't work in your life.

Once you prove your commitment, breakthrough is about to come into your life. It costs you something to be planted (committed). A tree is committed to its spot in the ground through storms, droughts and natural disasters alike. Likewise, we should be as strongly rooted in the Word of God.

A person who is committed to and strongly rooted in God and His Word is like a tree that brings forth fruit.

> *"Blessed is the man that walketh not in the counsel of the ungodly, nor standeth in the way of sinners, nor sitteth in the seat of the scornful. But his delight is in the law of the LORD; and in his law doth he meditate day and night. And he shall be like a tree planted by the rivers of water, that bringeth forth his fruit in his season; his leaf also shall not wither; and whatsoever he doeth shall prosper."*
> *Psalm 1:1-3 (KJV)*

When you are committed to the things of God, whatever your hands touch prospers. You become a tree of righteousness.

> *"To appoint unto them that mourn in Zion, to give unto them beauty for ashes, the oil of joy for mourning, the garment of praise for the spirit of heaviness; that they might be called trees of righteousness, the planting of the LORD, that he might be glorified." Isaiah 61:3 (KJV)*

The fruitfulness of a believer is apparent when he or she is thoroughly committed to God. Daniel's commitment to pray three times a day caused him to prosper past the lion's den. Joshua's commitment caused him to be promoted after Moses died.

Jesus gives a hint on how to live.

*"I am the vine, ye are the branches: He that abideth in
me, and I in him, the same bringeth forth much fruit: for
without me ye can do nothing." John 15:5 (KJV)*

When you remain attached to the vine, you will continuously draw
life from it. When the branch breaks away from the vine, it will dry up
and die. Your commitment to stay with and be strongly rooted in God
and in His Word determines the flow from God to you.

Commitment to and being strongly rooted in God and staying in
God's Word precedes transformation (Romans 12:1-2).

*"I beseech you therefore, brethren, by the mercies
of God, that ye present your bodies a living sacrifice,
holy, acceptable unto God, which is your reasonable
service. And be not conformed to this world: <u>but be ye</u>
<u>transformed by the renewing of your mind</u>, that ye may
prove what is that good, and acceptable, and perfect, will
of God." Romans 12:1-2 (KJV)*

Transformation has a price tag: deadly commitment. You must
commit yourself to the Word of God. There are sins of omission;
what you don't do might kill you. It was because of Jesus' commitment
to God that He willingly gave His life on the cross. He knew that He
had to die in order to be fruitful.

*"Therefore doth my Father love me, because I lay down
my life, that I might take it again. No man taketh it
from me, but I lay it down of myself. I have power to
lay it down, and I have power to take it again. This
commandment have I received of my Father." John
10:17-18 (KJV)*

In order for the principles of God's Word to produce results in your life, they must be supported by the necessary foundation (Psalm 11:3). Being committed to and strongly rooted in God and His Word is part of the foundation for living a prosperous life. When you are committed to the things of God, your life will be fruitful.

THE FOUNDATION OF LOVE AND AFFECTION

There are five key foundations to wholeness in every area of life. These foundations are: covenant, consecration, commitment, love and affection. The things of God cannot be accomplished on your behalf if the foundations have been destroyed in your life (Psalm 11:3).

> *"If the foundations be destroyed, what can the righteous do?" Psalm 11:3 (KJV)*

Today I want to talk to you about serving God with love and affection. Affection is "delightsome commitment; an expression of love". When you're affectionate toward God, you are excited about serving Him.

If you fail to serve God with gladness of heart, you will become vulnerable to your enemies and eventually serve them.

> *"Because thou servedst not the LORD thy God with joyfulness, and with gladness of heart, for the abundance of all things; Therefore shalt thou serve thine enemies which the LORD shall send against thee, in hunger, and in thirst, and in nakedness, and in want of all things: and he shall put a yoke of iron upon thy neck, until he have destroyed thee." Deuteronomy 28:47-48 (KJV)*

> *"Because you didn't serve the Lord your God with joy and gladness in your heart when you had such an*

> *abundance of everything; The Lord will allow your*
> *enemies to come against you; and you will serve him*
> *when you are hungry, thirsty, poorly clothed and lacking*
> *everything; you will have a yoke of iron on your neck*
> *until it destroys you." Deuteronomy 28:47-48 (Atarah)*

Rejoice over what God has done in your life, rather than complaining about your situation.

It should never be a burden for you to serve the Lord. God wants to be celebrated, not tolerated; He doesn't want to be a burden to you. Don't ever say that He's "given you a burden" for something, because you'll remove yourself from His presence.

> *"And the burden of the LORD shall ye mention no more:*
> *for every man's word shall be his burden; for ye have*
> *perverted the words of the living God, of the LORD*
> *of hosts our God. Thus shalt thou say to the prophet,*
> *What hath the LORD answered thee? and, What hath*
> *the LORD spoken? But since ye say, The burden of the*
> *LORD; therefore thus saith the LORD; Because ye say*
> *this word, The burden of the LORD, and I have sent*
> *unto you, saying, Ye shall not say, The burden of the*
> *LORD; Therefore, behold, I, even I, will utterly forget*
> *you, and I will forsake you, and the city that I gave you*
> *and your fathers, and cast you out of my presence: And*
> *I will bring an everlasting reproach upon you, and a*
> *perpetual shame, which shall not be forgotten." Jeremiah*
> *23:36-40 (KJV)*

Giving without cheerfulness is a waste of time; it is has no future.

Being loving and affectionate toward God is your greatest commandment; it's crucial (Matthew 22:37-40).

> *"Jesus said unto him, Thou shalt love the Lord thy God with all thy heart, and with all thy soul, and with all thy mind. This is the first and great commandment. And the second is like unto it, Thou shalt love thy neighbour as thyself. On these two commandments hang all the law and the prophets." Matthew 22:37-40 (KJV)*

King Solomon's love toward the Lord opened the door to be blessed with "supernatural plenty," or abundance.

> *"And Solomon loved the LORD, walking in the statutes of David his father: only he sacrificed and burnt incense in high places. And the king went to Gibeon to sacrifice there; for that was the great high place: a thousand burnt offerings did Solomon offer upon that altar. In Gibeon the LORD appeared to Solomon in a dream by night: and God said, Ask what I shall give thee." 1 Kings 3:3-5 (KJV)*

Love and affection require action.

> Jesus said, *"He that hath my commandments, and keepeth them, he it is that loveth me: and he that loveth me shall be loved of my Father, and I will love him, and will manifest myself to him." John 14:21 (KJV)*

If your motives are selfish, don't ask God for anything—He refuses to share places with another "god" in your life. God is the only true god!

"Ye ask, and receive not, because ye ask amiss, that ye may consume it upon your lusts. Ye adulterers and adulteresses, know ye not that the friendship of the world is enmity with God? whosoever therefore will be a friend of the world is the enemy of God." James 4:3-4 (KJV)

"Or you do ask God for them and fail to receive because you ask with wrong purpose and selfish motives. Your intention is to spend it in sensual and selfish pleasures. You are like unfaithful wives, having illicit love affairs with the world and breaking your marriage vow to God. Do you not know that being the world's friend is being God's enemy? So whoever chooses to be a friend of the world is an enemy of God and His ways." James 4:3-4 (Atarah)

When loving God is the motive behind all that you do, He response to that love.

Nothing good happens on your behalf if the Lord is not at the center of your life.

Your quality of love and affection for God will determine your effectiveness in the kingdom of God.

"And though I bestow all my goods to feed the poor, and though I give my body to be burned, and have not charity, it profiteth me nothing." 1 Corinthians 13:3 (KJV)

"If I give everything I own to the poor, if I give my body to suffer burnout and yet I don't love, I've gotten nowhere.

> *Therefore, no matter what I do, if I don't love it profits me nothing." 1 Corinthians 13:3 (Atarah)*

Love and affection toward God leads to prosperity. Prosperity is also "making satisfactory progress." If you have not progressed beyond where you've been for years, something is out of place in your life. Never be satisfied with circumstances in your life that are less than God's best. Your path through life should shine brighter every day.

> *"But the path of the just is as the shining light, that shineth more and more unto the perfect day." Proverbs 4:18 (KJV)*

Having love and affection towards God makes you a conqueror.

Delight in the Lord and His commandments and you'll prosper. (Psalm 1:2; Psalm 112:1).

> *"But his delight is in the law of the LORD; and in his law doth he meditate day and night." Psalm 1:2 (KJV)*

> *"Praise ye the LORD. Blessed is the man that feareth the LORD, that delighteth greatly in his commandments." Psalm 112:1 (KJV)*

When playing the Christian "game," you must know the rules to win.

Seek the Lord first and you won't lack any good thing.

> *"The young lions do lack, and suffer hunger: but they that seek the LORD shall not want any good thing." Psalm 34:10 (KJV)*

Don't be a "money hunter" or you'll suffer.

Lasting prosperity comes from carrying the divine presence of God. Set all of your might, love and affection toward the house of God (presence of God), just as King David did (1 Chronicles 29:1-3).

> David said,"... *I have set my affection to the house of my God, I have of mine own proper good,* of gold and silver, which I have given to the house of my God, over and above all that I have prepared for the holy house," 1 Chronicles 29:1-3 (KJV)

Follow this action plan for showing love and affection toward the things of God.

1. Pray.

> "But ye, beloved, building up yourselves on your most holy faith, praying in the Holy Ghost, Keep yourselves in the love of God, looking for the mercy of our Lord Jesus Christ unto eternal life." Jude 1:20-21 (KJV)

2. Examine your motives.
3. Be committed to God and His Word, reading and meditating His Words (the Bible).

Of all the things that you can do for the kingdom of God, developing love and affection toward the Lord is the greatest. Prospering in the things of God depends on your love and commitment to living for Him. Therefore, set your love and affection toward God so that you may position yourself to live in His divine presence and experience supernatural progress throughout life.

ACTIONS OF KINGDOM PROSPERITY

In the kingdom of God, prosperity (wholeness in every area of your live) is determined by how much you give (love, forgiveness, etc); in the world, it is determined by what you have.

God will prosper you in a way that is different from how the world prospers you.

Free yourself from the fear of giving. Do all things in God, not in or by yourself.

Giving is truly living. Give to live and live to give.

A lack of giving leads to "spiritual constipation". You can't just take and not give.

God's Word has four dimensions: principle, reproof, correction and instruction in righteousness.

> *"All scripture is given by inspiration of God, and is profitable for doctrine, for reproof, for correction, for instruction in righteousness: That the man of God may be perfect, throughly furnished unto all good works." 2 Timothy 3:16 (KJV)*

Many enjoy the principles, such as "If you do this, then you'll receive this". Most don't gravitate toward instruction; therefore, they miss out on much of what God desires to give and do for them.

Acquaint yourself with God, be at peace and good will come to you.

> *"<u>Acquaint now thyself with him</u>, and be at peace: thereby good shall come unto thee".*

Job 22:21 (KJV)

Agree with God; conform to and acquaint yourself with Him. Seek the Provider, not His provision. You were created to seek God.

Love is the first dimension of giving.

> *"And he (Jesus) answering said, <u>Thou shalt love the Lord thy God with all thy heart, and with all thy soul, and with all thy strength, and with all thy mind</u>; and thy neighbour as thyself." Luke 10:27 (KJV)*

Love is a commandment. God's commandments give you access to His kingdom.

> *"Christ hath redeemed us from the curse of the law, being made a curse for us: for it is written, Cursed is every one that hangeth on a tree:" Galatians 3:13 (KJV)*

When talking about prosperity many people preach from Malachi, saying that if we don't tithe that we are cursed. However, as we see in Galatians 3:13 Christ Jesus has redeemed us from the curse of the Law. According to Numbers 23:8 whom the Lord has blessed cannot be cursed.

We can't pick and choose what Laws we are going to obey. If you are going to beat someone over the head about tithing, then what about the other 316 Laws, such as not eating pork or meat and dairy together? Or gluttony? Or obeying the Sabbath (which by law is the seventh day)? (See a list of laws and curses in Duet 27)

> *"For as many as are of the works of the law are under the curse: for it is written, Cursed is every one that*

continueth not in all things which are written in the book of the law to do them." Galatians 3:10 (KJV)

"All who depend on the Law, who are seeking to be justified by obedience to the Law, are under a curse and doomed to disappointment and destruction. It is written in the Scriptures cursed be everyone who does not continue to abide (live and remain) by all the precepts and commands written in the Book of the Law and to practice them." Galatians 3:10 (Atarah)

I know that preachers like to keep this Law because they think that the tithes will go down and people will not give if they speak the truth–however, they should put their trust in the Lord.

People who love God will want to give. It's in their hearts to do. People who love God do it out of their love and affection for Him. People will give more out of love than they will ever give out of obligation.

God is not going to curse us for anything we do or don't do because Jesus redeemed us from the curse of the Mosaic Law; all of God's wrath was poured out on Jesus. We can chose to do as we desire, and although we are not going to be cursed by God there are still laws that affect us today. When we break one of these laws, there are still natural and physical consequences to our actions.

"All things are lawful unto me, but all things are not expedient: all things are lawful for me, but I will not be brought under the power of any." 1 Corinthians 6:12 (KJV)

"Everything is permissible (allowable and lawful) for me; but not everything is beneficial. Everything is lawful

for me (I have the right to do anything), but I will not become the slave of anything or be brought under its power." 1 Corinthians 6:12 (Atarah)

There are actions such as love that will open you up to receive kingdom prosperity. Many Christians debate over parts of the Mosaic Law, such as tithing. Some people try to put themselves under the Law and try to fulfill certain parts of the Law simply under obligation, while others keep the Law simply because they love God. God wants us to love and honor Him, and our actions will grow out of that love and not out of obligation.

WORK OPENS THE CHANNEL TO PROSPERITY

The diligent worker will become rich.

"He becometh poor that dealeth with a slack hand: but the hand of the diligent maketh rich." Proverbs 10:4 (KJV)

The enemy doesn't want you to work; he knows that without a job there is no channel through which blessings can flow into your life.

"A man's gift maketh room for him, and bringeth him before great men." Proverbs 18:16 (KJV)

"Seest thou a man diligent in his business? he shall stand before kings; he shall not stand before mean men." Proverbs 22:29 (KJV)

The decisions you make regarding work determine your position in life. God cannot bless the work of your hand if they are not working. The work of your hands is the channel through which you receive the blessing.

> *"The LORD shall open unto thee his good treasure,*
> *the heaven to give the rain unto thy land in his season,*
> <u>*and to bless all the work of thine hand: and thou shalt*</u>
> <u>*lend unto many nations, and thou shalt not borrow."*</u>
> *Deuteronomy 28:12 (KJV)*

There is no future for the idle man in God's covenant. You have a choice between hard work and a hard life. Just as the blessing can come on the labor of your hands, so can a drought come on it (Haggai 1:2-11).

There are people who work two jobs and still experience drought, because of lack of Wisdom. You must also have the relationship with God and His Word and get the wisdom from God on how to manage your money. Then you must be obedient to His guidance.

It is the Lord's will for you to work.

> *"But Jesus answered them, My Father worketh hitherto,*
> *and I work." John 5:17 (KJV)*

God never ceases from work, and He wants His children to work also. There is dignity in labor.

A man who doesn't work shouldn't eat.

> *"For even when we were with you, this we commanded*
> *you, that if any would not work, neither should he eat."*
> *2 Thessalonians 3:10 (KJV)*

Stop wishing for things and start working. In all labor there is profit.

> *"In all labour there is profit: but the talk of the lips*
> *tendeth only to penury." Proverbs 14:23 (KJV)*

Keep doing what you know is right.

> *"And let us not be weary in well doing: for in due season we shall reap, if we faint not." Galatians 6:9 (KJV)*

Tireless input is required. The results of your working will occur in phases.

> *"And he said, So is the kingdom of God, as if a man should cast seed into the ground; And should sleep, and rise night and day, and the seed should spring and grow up, he knoweth not how. For the earth bringeth forth fruit of herself; first the blade, then the ear, after that the full corn in the ear." Mark 4:26-28 (KJV)*

The end is always better than the beginning.

Your work provides the channel through which the blessing flows to you. You will not be a beneficiary of the blessing if you are unemployed.

WORKING WITH DILIGENCE

Lack is usually associated with idleness or "the folding of the hands".

> *"He becometh poor that dealeth with a slack hand: but the hand of the diligent maketh rich." Proverbs 10:4 (KJV)*

You are commanded to work.

> *"And that ye study to be quiet, and to do your own business, and to work with your own hands, as we commanded you; That ye may walk honestly toward*

them that are without, and that ye may have lack of
nothing." 1 Thessalonians 4:11-12 (KJV)

"Also, make it your ambition to live quietly, to mind your
own business and to earn your living by your own efforts,
just as we told you. We want you living in a way that
will command the respect of outsiders, not depending on
anyone but self sufficient and lacking nothing."
1 Thessalonians 4:11-12 (Atarah)

The blessings of God will never override idleness. Idleness and laziness prevent the blessings of God from reaching you. Work is the "catcher" of God's blessing in the natural realm. The diligent worker will experience increase and promotion; however, a slothful or deceitful person will be brought under the rule of another. (Proverbs 12:24).

"The soul of the sluggard desireth, and hath nothing:
but the soul of the diligent shall be made fat." Proverbs
13:4 (KJV)

"The hand of the diligent shall bear rule: but the slothful
shall be under tribute." Proverbs 12:24 (KJV)

There should not be any laziness or injustice among believers.

"Much food is in the tillage of the poor: but there is that is
destroyed for want of judgment." Proverbs 13:23 (KJV)

Believers of Jesus should be the best employees. Don't look for ways to deceive your employer by wasting time and money on the job. You can lose your job when you cost the owner money.

Get out of the "servant" mentality and into the "owner" mentality. If you work hard, you will bear fruit. The anointing of God will find you when you are working.

When you do your part God will bring the increase. (1 Corinthians 3:6).

> *"I have planted, Apollos watered; but God gave the increase." 1 Corinthians 3:6 (KJV)*

Jesus and the Father are constantly at work. They are your examples. (John 5:17).

> *"But Jesus answered them, My Father worketh hitherto, and I work." John 5:17 (KJV)*

Increase responds to your personal input as a covenant person. Whatsoever you do prospers.

> *"And he shall be like a tree planted by the rivers of water, that bringeth forth his fruit in his season; his leaf also shall not wither; and whatsoever he doeth shall prosper." Psalm 1:3 (KJV)*

Your prosperity is determined by what you do.

God responds to the diligent with blessings. Continue to be diligent about your work.

> *"The soul of the sluggard desireth, and hath nothing: but the soul of the diligent shall be made fat." Proverbs 13:4 (KJV)*

You must work to prosper. All of the blessed patriarchs in the Bible were hard workers. Abraham was a 75-year-old cattle rancher. As a farmer, Isaac sowed during a famine and received a harvest that same year.

> *"Then Isaac sowed in that land, and received in the same year an hundredfold: and the LORD blessed him."*
> *Genesis 26:12 (KJV)*

Jacob was a specialist farmer who worked for Laban for seven years, and the Lord's blessing reached him. According to the law of diligence, something has to open up for you.

If the patriarchs worked, you have no excuse to be idle. If you are lazy, insufficiency is inevitable. You will find yourself a beggar.

> *"The sluggard will not plow by reason of the cold; therefore shall he beg in harvest, and have nothing."*
> *Proverbs 20:4 (KJV)*

"Fast" money will dwindle away.

> *"Wealth gotten by vanity shall be diminished: but he that gathereth by labour shall increase." Proverbs 13:11 (KJV)*

It is only through diligent labor that you will acquire lasting riches.

Don't wait for the conditions to be "just right" before becoming a diligent sower. (Ecclesiastes 11:4).

> *"He that observeth the wind shall not sow; and he that regardeth the clouds shall not reap." Ecclesiastes 11:4 (KJV)*

God's blessing responds to the diligent worker. Work provides a channel through which God's empowerment to prosper can manifest in the natural realm. Idle people cannot partake of God's covenant of blessing. You must work diligently if you expect to see increase in your life.

THINKING FOR KINGDOM PROSPERITY

God wants you to enjoy kingdom prosperity (wholeness in every area of your life). There are actions required to experience kingdom prosperity: you must have a relationship with God and His Word and yield to His promptings and guidance. Mere giving an offering is not enough for you to experience kingdom prosperity.

Although it is necessary to work, it is not sufficient enough for you to experience kingdom prosperity; it only provides you with a channel through which the blessing can flow. Creative work guarantees productivity, which guarantees wealth.

Wealth is the offspring of wisdom.

> *"Happy is the man that findeth wisdom, and the man that getteth understanding. For the merchandise of it is better than the merchandise of silver, and the gain thereof than fine gold. She is more precious than rubies: and all the things thou canst desire are not to be compared unto her. Length of days is in her right hand; and in her left hand riches and honour."*
> *Proverbs 3:13-16 (KJV)*

> *"The man who finds wisdom and gains understanding will be happy. Wisdom is more profitable than all the money in the bank, and her wages are better than a*

*big salary. Wisdom is more precious than all wealth;
nothing you desire can compare with her. Wisdom offers
you long life on one side and riches and honor on the
other." Proverbs 3:13 - 16 (Atarah)*

You must never become so "overly spiritual" that you neglect the natural aspects of prospering in the things of God; that's where the action of thinking comes in. Thinking is "the ability to coordinate thoughts productively for increased output." You must be sound, or highly productive, in your thinking. Think to create something productive that will make living great.

*"That the God of our Lord Jesus Christ, the Father
of glory, may give unto you the spirit of wisdom and
revelation in the knowledge of him:The eyes of your
understanding being enlightened; that ye may know
what is the hope of his calling, and what the riches of the
glory of his inheritance in the saints," Ephesians 1:17-18
(KJV)*

Wise work begets wealth. For example, a man who is laboring without seeing results will grow weary of the work; eventually, he'll quit working. He knows what to do but doesn't know how to do it- he lacks direction.

*"The labour of the foolish wearieth every one of them,
because he knoweth not how to go to the city." Ecclesiastes
10:15 (KJV)*

Knowing what to do without knowing how to do something creates a problem. The wisdom of knowing how to do a thing is what guarantees results. Work smarter, not just harder.

Abundance is deposited within you and must be drawn out. All of the wealth in the universe came as a result of wisdom (Psalm 104:24).

> *"O LORD, how manifold are thy works! in wisdom hast thou made them all: the earth is full of thy riches." Psalm 104:24 (KJV)*

Wisdom gives mankind supernatural ability.

> *"He putteth forth his hand upon the rock; he overturneth the mountains by the roots. He cutteth out rivers among the rocks; and his eye seeth every precious thing. He bindeth the floods from overflowing; and the thing that is hid bringeth he forth to light. But where shall wisdom be found? and where is the place of understanding?" Job 28:9-12 (KJV)*

> *"The mineworkers spark, overturns mountains at their roots, and cuts out galleries in the rock, all the while watching for something of value. He dams up streams to keep them from flooding and brings what was hidden out into the light. But where can wisdom be found? Where is the source of understanding?" Job 28:9-12 (Atarah)*

Wisdom helps you to create things and reveals hidden treasure to you. You have the ability (wisdom) to make a difference in the world.

> *"That no flesh should glory in his presence. But of him are ye in Christ Jesus, who of God is made unto us wisdom, and righteousness, and sanctification, and redemption:" 1 Corinthians 1:29-30 (KJV)*

To prosper, you must "count the cost." Set aside time to generate, create and analyze ideas. Don't move too quickly or prematurely. Be willing to meet with others who are doing something similar to what you desire to do so that you can learn from them. God will enlighten you with creative thoughts of your own.

Quiet your mind and spirit so you can hear from God.

> "For the Egyptians shall help in vain, and to no purpose: therefore have I cried concerning this, Their strength is to sit still." Isaiah 30:7 (KJV)

> "For thus saith the Lord GOD, the Holy One of Israel; In returning and rest shall ye be saved; in quietness and in confidence shall be your strength: and ye would not." Isaiah 30:15 (KJV)

> "And thine ears shall hear a word behind thee, saying, This is the way, walk ye in it, when ye turn to the right hand, and when ye turn to the left." Isaiah 30:21 (KJV)

He wants to direct your way through life.

> "In all thy ways acknowledge him, and he shall direct thy paths." Proverbs 3:6 (KJV)

Don't ever say, "There's no way out." Avoid stressing yourself out; instead, convince yourself that the answer lies within you (2 Corinthians 1:9). For example, the answer to the widow's dilemmas in 2 Kings 4:1-37 was found in her house.

> "But we had the sentence of death in ourselves, that we should not trust in ourselves, but in God which raiseth the dead:" 2 Corinthians 1:9 (KJV)

Engage wisdom. Just as a car's gears must be engaged to drive it, you must engage God's Word for it to benefit your life.

Don't associate with pessimistic "buzzards;" instead, associate with dreamers. Creative thinking brought Joseph out of slavery; it will deliver you out of your bondage such as lack, debt, sickness and any other aspect of the curse.

Every throne is created by wisdom; the throne of your life must be created. Creative wisdom is the principal thing needed to create what does not yet exist.

> *"Wisdom is the principal thing; therefore get wisdom: and with all thy getting get understanding." Proverbs 4:7 (KJV)*

You have the mind of Christ and possess the thoughts of God's heart.

> *"Know ye not that ye are the temple of God, and that the Spirit of God dwelleth in you?" 1 Corinthians 3:16 (KJV)*

You possess the wisdom that God used to create all things, including the devil.

> *"All things were made by him; and without him was not any thing made that was made." John 1:3 (KJV)*

Declare: "I operate in wisdom today!" You can think, speak and act like God.

Wisdom is an anointing—the power of God that removes burdens and destroys yokes.

"But unto them which are called, both Jews and Greeks, Christ the power of God, and the wisdom of God." 1 Corinthians 1:24 (KJV)

New thoughts can produce new things; therefore, command the world's attention and respect through creative thinking.

Don't take the credit for the wisdom that God gives you.

Be courageous and live sin free so that you can step out on what God reveals to you.

While giving and working are essential to experiencing "kingdom prosperity", these actions alone don't guarantee success. You must tap into the wisdom of God for true, creative thinking. Your practical use of this wisdom will produce positive results that will command the world's attention and respect—a true testimony to the value of God's kingdom.

WISDOM FOR KINGDOM PROSPERITY

God's wisdom is the principle thing.

"Happy is the man that findeth wisdom, and the man that getteth understanding. For the merchandise of it is better than the merchandise of silver, and the gain thereof than fine gold. She is more precious than rubies: and all the things thou canst desire are not to be compared unto her. Length of days is in her right hand; and in her left hand riches and honour." Proverbs 3:13-16 (KJV)

"Because strife, jealousy and selfishness are not God's kind of wisdom. Such things are earthly, unspiritual

(animal like), even devilish (demoniacal)." James 3:15 (Atarah)

There are three kinds of wisdom: heavenly wisdom, earthly wisdom and demonic wisdom. True wisdom is the gift of God. Heavenly wisdom is made available to you.

> *"Howbeit we speak wisdom among them that are perfect: yet not the wisdom of this world, nor of the princes of this world, that come to nought: But we speak the wisdom of God in a mystery, even the hidden wisdom, which God ordained before the world unto our glory: Which none of the princes of this world knew: for had they known it, they would not have crucified the Lord of glory." 1 Corinthians 2:6-8 (KJV)*

> *"Yet when we are among the full-grown (spiritually mature believers who are ripe in understanding), we do impart a higher wisdom (the knowledge of the divine plan previously hidden); but it is indeed not a wisdom of this present age or of this world nor of the leaders and rulers of this age, who are being brought to nothing and are doomed to pass away. On the contrary, we are communicating a secret wisdom from God which has been hidden until now but which, before history began, God had decreed would bring us glory. Which none of the Jewish leaders and princes (devils) of this world knew: for had they known, they would not have crucified the Lord of glory." 1 Corinthians 2:6-8 (Atarah)*

The wisdom that is from above is superior to any other kind of wisdom.

The God of wisdom will shed unique light (understanding) and wisdom on your life.

Wealth is found where wisdom dwells. God is still giving His people knowledge and skill, just as He did to Daniel. He has provided a way for you to tap into riches and wealth.

> "As for these four children, God gave them knowledge and skill in all learning and wisdom: and Daniel had understanding in all visions and dreams." Daniel 1:17 (KJV)

All the treasures of wisdom and knowledge can be found in Christ. Wisdom dwells in Jesus and Jesus dwells in you; therefore, wealth is inside of you, waiting to come out. You are a treasure of wisdom and knowledge. You have productive wisdom inside of you.

Reasoning makes you rich.

> "Through wisdom is an house builded; and by understanding it is established: And by knowledge shall the chambers be filled with all precious and pleasant riches." Proverbs 24:3-4 (KJV)

The creative abilities within you will only come to light (understanding) when you adequately exercise your senses. The degree of mental action you engage in determines how far you excel in life. Wisdom will not operate without reasoning. You must be a thinker, because God is a thinker. It takes facts and the application of truth to those facts to bring forth positive results. Christians often try to deny the existence of the physical realm. There are natural things that must be dealt with through supernatural means.

There are three ways to exercise your senses:

1) Take time. Time is the greatest asset in the school of creativity. Daniel took time in order to get the necessary revelation to bring before the king. They prayed revelation-expectant prayers.

> *"Then Daniel went in and asked the king to give him time to tell the king the interpretation. Daniel went home and made the matter known to Hananiah, Mishael, and Azariah, his companions, so that they could ask the God of heaven for mercy concerning this secret and thus save Daniel and his companions from dying along with the wises of Babylon. Then the secret was revealed to Daniel in a vision at night and Daniel blessed the God of heaven in these words: "Blessed be the name of God from eternity past to eternity future! For wisdom and power are His alone;" Daniel 2:16-20 (Atarah)*

Revelation-expectant prayers are "prayers that communicate trust and belief in God with an expectation to receive directions from on High." When you ask God a question, expect to hear from Him. God will teach you how to profit and lead you in the way you should go.

> *"Thus saith the LORD, thy Redeemer, the Holy One of Israel; I am the LORD thy God which teacheth thee to profit, which leadeth thee by the way that thou shouldest go." Isaiah 48:17 (KJV)*

It is better to take your time and be slow and sure than to be fast and fail. Don't rush into things—sit down, think and count the cost. Be discreet in your affairs; use wisdom to avoid error and select the best course of action.

"A good man sheweth favour, and lendeth: <u>he will guide his affairs with discretion.</u>" Psalm 112:5 (KJV)

"This book of the law shall not depart out of thy mouth; but thou shalt meditate therein day and night, that thou mayest observe to do according to all that is written therein: for <u>then thou shalt make thy way prosperous, and then thou shalt have good success.</u>" Joshua 1:8 (KJV)

2) Seek information. Decisions based on quality information will always lead to distinction. Get the facts related to your situation. Locate resources and materials that will enhance your decisions, such as books and tapes. Daniel needed information in order to make quality decisions. (Daniel 9:2).

"In the first year of his reign I Daniel understood by books the number of the years, whereof the word of the LORD came to Jeremiah the prophet, that he would accomplish seventy years in the desolations of Jerusalem." Daniel 9:2 (KJV)

3) Mediate. Meditation is "processing acquired information to make quality decisions." Every success is tied to meditation. Man is first a thinker, then a worker (Psalm 1:2-3).

"But his delight is in the law of the LORD; and in his law doth he meditate day and night. And he shall be like a tree planted by the rivers of water, that bringeth forth his fruit in his season; his leaf also shall not wither; and whatsoever he doeth shall prosper." Psalm 1:2-3 (KJV)

Engage wisdom by maintaining a "there is a way out" attitude, praying "revelation-expectant" prayers and laying hold of the materials that will release light (understanding) in your situation.

Once God has given you the direction on what to do, it is just as important to act in a timely manner and do as He's directed you to. If God has revealed something to you and you do not do it, that is sin. Sin corrupts your mentality.

> *"Therefore to him that knoweth to do good, and doeth it not, to him it is sin." James 4:17 (KJV)*

> *"He that walketh with wise men shall be wise: but a companion of fools shall be destroyed." Proverbs 13:20 (KJV)*

> *"But there is a spirit in man: and the inspiration of the Almighty giveth them understanding." Job 32:8 (KJV)*

Don't practice something that will stop enlightenment from coming. Stay away from sin – do what you know it right.

True wisdom is the gift of God. You can't operate wisdom without reasoning, or engaging your senses. Where wisdom and reasoning exist, there also exists wealth. Engage the wisdom of God by maintaining a "there is a way out" attitude, praying "revelation-expectant" prayers and laying hold of the resources and materials that will lead to wisdom showing up to give you the answers you need.

TRUSTING GOD FOR KINGDOM PROSPERITY

Trusting God is a key to your prosperity (wholeness in every area of your life).

The man who puts his trust in God is blessed.

> "Blessed is the man that trusteth in the LORD, and whose hope the LORD is." Jeremiah 17:7 (KJV)

> "Blessed (happy and empower to prosper) is the man that trusts in the Lord, and whose confidence is in the Lord." Jeremiah 17:7 (Atarah)

Trusting God makes for a successful, whole and profitable life.

You must be totally dependent on God.

It takes trust to make your prosperity —healing, wholeness, deliverance, soundness and financial success—complete.

Trusting God does not dismiss the need for obeying natural laws. It takes the super, plus the natural, to equal abundant living (super + natural = abundance).

God must have a natural channel through which He can manifest every spiritual truth. For example: Your job is one channel God uses to bring blessings to you. Another example: God can also use your relationships to flow His blessings to you.

> "Give, and it shall be given unto you; good measure, pressed down, and shaken together, and running over, shall men give into your bosom. For with the same

measure that ye mete withal it shall be measured to you again." Luke 6:38 (KJV)

You can't ignore natural laws and then try to grab hold of spiritual laws; God originated both.

Doing things in the natural does not violate your trust in God—if your trust is in God and not in man. For example, taking medicine or going to the doctor does not necessarily violate your trust in God; however, are you trusting them, or are you trusting God to heal you by using them?

If you truly believe the Word of God then you will have corresponding action (in the natural realm) and this manifests spiritual truths. You can't believe God for favor to get a job if you've never left your house to apply for one.

You must know the difference between God using a man to bless you and your trusting in man.

> *"Thus saith the LORD; Cursed be the man that trusteth in man, and maketh flesh his arm, and whose heart departeth from the LORD." Jeremiah 17:5 (KJV)*

I cannot tell you how many people tell me they are trusting God but when I ask them the scriptures that they are stand on (believing on), they can't give me one. You always have to start with the Word.

If you have a relationship with God and follow His promptings, guidance and directions you should be enjoying God's blessings and continually experiencing sufficiency. If not, your trust may be in something else and not in God.

"Now therefore thus saith the LORD of hosts; Consider your ways. Ye have sown much, and bring in little; ye eat, but ye have not enough; ye drink, but ye are not filled with drink; ye clothe you, but there is none warm; and he that earneth wages earneth wages to put it into a bag with holes. Thus saith the LORD of hosts; Consider your ways." Haggai 1:5-7 (KJV)

Trusting God is the highway to a triumphant life (Psalm 34:8).

"O taste and see that the LORD is good: blessed is the man that trusteth in him." Psalm 34:8 (KJV)

Take no though for your life.

"Therefore I say unto you, Take no thought for your life, what ye shall eat, or what ye shall drink; nor yet for your body, what ye shall put on. Is not the life more than meat, and the body than raiment? Behold the fowls of the air: for they sow not, neither do they reap, nor gather into barns; yet your heavenly Father feedeth them. Are ye not much better than they? Which of you by taking thought can add one cubit unto his stature? And why take ye thought for raiment? Consider the lilies of the field, how they grow; they toil not, neither do they spin: And yet I say unto you, That even Solomon in all his glory was not arrayed like one of these. Wherefore, if God so clothe the grass of the field, which to day is, and to morrow is cast into the oven, shall he not much more clothe you, O ye of little faith? Therefore take no thought, saying, What shall we eat? or, What shall we drink? or, Wherewithal shall we be clothed? (For after all these things do the Gentiles seek:) for your heavenly Father

> knoweth that ye have need of all these t hings. But seek
> ye first the kingdom of God, and his righteousness; and
> all these things shall be added unto you." Matthew 6:25-
> 33 (KJV)

The only way you can successfully "take no thought for your life" is to trust God; then everything else will be added to you.

Every spiritual blessing that leads to abundant life requires both you doing your part and God doing His. No one who trusts in God will be desolate (bare or without).

> "The LORD redeemeth the soul of his servants: and
> none of them that trust in him shall be desolate." Psalm
> 34:22 (KJV)

Faith and trust are two different things. Faith is "taking the Word of God and analyzing and assimilating it into your way of thinking and then acting in accordance with what you have learned and have embraced – also a pleasant emotion caused by the belief in the Word of God that causes assurance, calmness and peace. " while trust is "commitment to God and His Word."

Faith breeds confidence, while trust breeds commitment. Faith can fail (Luke 22:32); trust, like Mount Zion, can't be removed and stands fast forever (Psalm 125:1).

> "They that trust in the LORD shall be as mount Zion,
> which cannot be removed, but abideth for ever." Psalm
> 125:1 (KJV)

Your faith, or confidence, can be cast away if the conflict is too heavy; trust causes you to outlast every conflict every time.

"Cast not away therefore your confidence, which hath
great recompence of reward." Hebrews 10:35 (KJV)

If the situation or circumstances get too hard, you stop reading the Word of God, analyzing and assimilating it into your way of thinking and think more on the situation and it dampens your confidence, causing you to cast away your confidence and belief in God and His Word.

Nothing can move you when your trust is in God – you are committed to Him and His Word. When you are committed to God and His Word, analyzing and assimilating His Word into your way of thinking that produces confidence and causes assurance, you are like a tree that is strongly rooted; no matter what comes your way you remain the same and stay on that Word that will bring forth much fruit.

<u>Faith believes that God can do what He promises; trust says, "Even if God doesn't do it, my position remains the same."</u> Three Hebrew children trusted God and knew God could save them, but they wouldn't worship the king's golden image even if God didn't save them.

"Shadrach, Meshach, and Abednego, answered and said
to the king, O Nebuchadnezzar, we are not careful to
answer thee in this matter. If it be so, our God whom we
serve is able to deliver us from the burning fiery furnace,
and he will deliver us out of thine hand, O king. But if
not, be it known unto thee, O king, that we will not serve
thy gods, nor worship the golden image which thou hast
set up." Daniel 3:16-18 (KJV)

Trust along with faith is like a tree that's been planted—it's not going anywhere whether it's raining, sunny or snowing. It's committed and it will bear fruit.

Once you learn to trust God, you must learn to rest in Him. God only fights once you take your rest. Your rest provokes divine intervention.

> *"The LORD shall fight for you, and ye shall hold your peace." Exodus 14:14 (KJV)*

God's part is to fight the battle; your part is to rest. You must labor to enter into the rest of God. Rest is not a call for inaction, but trust.

> *"Let us labour therefore to enter into that rest, lest any man fall after the same example of unbelief." Hebrews 4:11 (KJV)*

Even though you are resting in God, you must still do corresponding actions that complement that rest. You know you are at rest when no circumstance can cause you to waver from what you know God is doing. Stay away from people who have only negative things to say.

When you trust and have faith in God, you become unbeatable in life. Whatever you put in God's hands is secure. You must know that the power of God is working in you and for you!

Many people love and believe God, but few trust Him. There is a difference between faith and trust; while you may be operating in faith, you may not be operating in trust. The man who learns to trust God will be anointed, empowered and blessed.

TRUST GOD NOT THINGS

Trusting God empowers you to prosper (be successful in every area of life).

> *"Blessed is the man that trusteth in the LORD, and whose hope the LORD is." Jeremiah 17:7 (KJV)*

> *"Blessed (happy and empower to prosper) is the man that trusts in the Lord, and whose confidence is in the Lord." Jeremiah 17:7 (Atarah)*

Trust is eternal and everlasting. It demands the supernatural empowerment of God to operate in your life. When you trust God, you can rest in Him. Supernatural intervention only manifests for those who rest in God.

Having a relationship with God and His Word and yielding to His promptings and guidance demonstrates your trust in God.

Yield to and obey His promptings with joyfulness and without fear, because you know that God is your Source.

> *"The LORD hear thee in the day of trouble; the name of the God of Jacob defend thee; Send thee help from the sanctuary, and strengthen thee out of Zion; Remember all thy offerings, and accept thy burnt sacrifice; Selah. Grant thee according to thine own heart, and fulfil all thy counsel. We will rejoice in thy salvation, and in the name of our God we will set up our banners: the LORD fulfil all thy petitions. Now know I that the LORD saveth his anointed; he will hear him from his holy heaven with the saving strength of his right hand. Some trust in chariots, and some in horses: but we will remember the name of*

the LORD our God. They are brought down and fallen: but we are risen, and stand upright. Save, LORD: let the king hear us when we call." Psalm 20:1-9 (KJV)

It is difficult to enter into God's kingdom when your trust is in riches.

*"And when he was gone forth into the way, there came one running, and kneeled to him, and asked him, Good Master, what shall I do that I may inherit eternal life? And Jesus said unto him, Why callest thou me good? there is none good but one, that is, God. Thou knowest the commandments, Do not commit adultery, Do not kill, Do not steal, Do not bear false witness, Defraud not, Honour thy father and mother. And he answered and said unto him, Master, all these have I observed from my youth. Then Jesus beholding him loved him, and said unto him, **One thing thou lackest:** go thy way, sell whatsoever thou hast, and give to the poor, and thou shalt have treasure in heaven: and come, take up the cross, and follow me. And he was sad at that saying, and went away grieved: for he had great possessions. And Jesus looked round about, and saith unto his disciples, How hardly shall they that have riches enter into the **kingdom of God**! And the disciples were astonished at his words. But Jesus answereth again, and saith unto them, Children, how hard is it for them that **trust in riches** to enter into the kingdom of God!" Mark 10:17-24 (KJV)*

The kingdom of God means "God's system of operation," not "heaven." The issue is trust, not money; God wants to see where your heart is (Luke 16:11).

"If therefore ye have not been faithful in the unrighteous mammon, who will commit to your trust the true riches?"
Luke 16:11 (KJV)

"Therefore, if you have not been faithful in the unrighteous money (as this steward), who will entrust to you the true riches?" Luke 16:11 (Atarah)

The wrong relationship with money and material things will keep your heart from God. Your heart must be toward God, not your possessions. God wants your love and affection.

When your trust is in riches and material things, you will fall.

"He that trusteth in his riches shall fall: but the righteous shall flourish as a branch." Proverbs 11:28 (KJV)

"He who trusts in his riches will fall, but the righteous are a flourishing tree." Proverbs 11:28 (Atarah)

When your trust is in money and material things, you will find yourself in need and eventually get to the the point that you will have to depend on God. When you have many options to rely on, rely on God only because every other option is eventually going to fail.

God will not be the god of your life while you have money or material things on your throne. God will not share the throne.

Money and material things are uncertain.

"Charge them that are rich in this world, that they be not highminded, <u>nor trust in uncertain riches, but in the living God, who giveth us richly all things to enjoy</u>;"
1 Timothy 6:17 (KJV)

God and His Word are what make you rich. If you become prideful, you will think you no longer need God's way; then you'll have your own way and pride comes before a fall.

Don't be deceived by money. It can buy medicine, but it can't buy healing. It can buy a house, but it can't buy a peaceful home.

Trust in the Living God—He desires to do great things in your life. He wants to do more than just meet your needs; He wants you to enjoy life. God gives you things simply because He wants you to enjoy them.

Placing your trust in things rather than in God will cause you to betray Him.

Your heart must be firmly fixed, trusting in the Lord.

> *"He shall not be afraid of evil tidings: his heart is fixed, trusting in the LORD. His heart is established, he shall not be afraid, until he see his desire upon his enemies. He hath dispersed, he hath given to the poor; his righteousness endureth for ever; his horn shall be exalted with honour. The wicked shall see it, and be grieved; he shall gnash with his teeth, and melt away: the desire of the wicked shall perish." Psalm 112:7-10 (KJV)*

When your trust is in God, your heart is established and secure. God directs your path when your trust is in Him.

> *"Trust in the LORD with all thine heart; and lean not unto thine own understanding. In all thy ways acknowledge him, and he shall direct thy paths." Proverbs 3:5-6 (KJV)*

Trust is an expression of your commitment to God.

Trusting God requires your total dependence on Him alone. This depth of trust is the highway to continuous triumph. On the other hand, placing your trust in other things (such as money) more so than in God will lead to your destruction.

WAITING IS A PROCESS, NOT AN EVENT

There is a time for things to happen.

> "To every thing there is a season, and a time to every purpose under the heaven: A time to be born, and a time to die; a time to plant, and a time to pluck up that which is planted; A time to kill, and a time to heal; a time to break down, and a time to build up; A time to weep, and a time to laugh; a time to mourn, and a time to dance; A time to cast away stones, and a time to gather stones together; a time to embrace, and a time to refrain from embracing; A time to get, and a time to lose; a time to keep, and a time to cast away; A time to rend, and a time to sew; a time to keep silence, and a time to speak; A time to love, and a time to hate; a time of war, and a time of peace." Ecclesiastes 3:1-8 (KJV)

Don't make the mistake of doing things outside of God's timing. For example, people were praying for Peter's release from jail. After he was freed and came knocking at their door, they were too busy praying to receive him. The time for prayer was over—it was time to receive.

> "And when he had considered the thing, he came to the house of Mary the mother of John, whose surname was Mark; where many were gathered together praying. And as Peter knocked at the door of the gate, a damsel came to hearken, named Rhoda. And when she knew Peter's

voice, she opened not the gate for gladness, but ran in, and told how Peter stood before the gate. And they said unto her, Thou art mad. But she constantly affirmed that it was even so. Then said they, It is his angel. But Peter continued knocking: and when they had opened the door, and saw him, they were astonished." Acts 12:12-16 (KJV)

To avoid frustration and the temptation to quit, remember that there is a due season and an appointed time for every harvest.

"And he said, So is the kingdom of God, as if a man should cast seed into the ground; And should sleep, and rise night and day, and the seed should spring and grow up, he knoweth not how. For the earth bringeth forth fruit of herself; first the blade, then the ear, after that the full corn in the ear. But when the fruit is brought forth, immediately he putteth in the sickle, because the harvest is come." Mark 4:26-29 (KJV)

In Mark 4, Jesus compares God's kingdom to a man's sowing of seeds, thereby demonstrating the law of progression. The law of progression is "first the blade, then the ear and finally the full ear of corn." Once the progression has concluded, prepare your sickle for the harvest. For any harvest, someone must first cast his seed into the ground. He must continue to be attentive to his daily responsibilities as well as to his crop. The farmer understands the progression of his seed. Once it is sown, he knows his crop should grow. Like a farmer, you sow seed through your study of the Word of God, focusing and speaking that Word, which creates an image on the inside of you then you will find yourself acting in accordance with what you believe. As long as you don't dig it up, your seed will grow and produce a mighty harvest.

The three stages of the law of progression are blade time, stalk time and harvest time.

1) Blade time—you await the first evidence of growth. After the farmer sows the seed it looks like nothing is happening. During this barren season, patience is crucial. You can't succeed in blade time without patience. The farmer has an image of what is to come. You should develop a internal picture of your harvest. Patience is often defined as "putting up with." The Bible defines patience as "to hold steady; to be consistently, constantly the same." I like to call it tenacity, staying the same and being persistent. Patience (tenacity) will cause you to obtain the promise and bring forth fruit. (Hebrews 6:12, 15; Luke 8:15).

> *"That ye be not slothful, but followers of them who through faith and patience inherit the promises." Hebrews 6:12 (KJV)*

> *"That you be not lazy, but followers of them who take the Word of God, analyze and assimilate it into their way of thinking and then they acting in accordance with what they have learned and have embraced, they also have tenacity (perseverance). These people inherit the promises." Hebrews 6:12 (Atarah)*

> *"And so, after he had patiently endured, he obtained the promise." Hebrews 6:15 (KJV)*

> *"And so, after he (Abraham) had patiently endured, he obtained the promise." Hebrews 6:15 (Atarah)*

> *"But that on the good ground are they, which in an honest and good heart, having heard the word, keep it, and bring forth fruit with patience." Luke 8:15 (KJV)*

There will be a time with no physical evidence to motivate you, only God's Word. Blade time can be detrimental to a harvest, because believers are tempted to consume the sprout.

2) Stalk time—a tender sprout turns into a rough, rigid stalk.

> *"For the earth bringeth forth fruit of herself; first the blade, then the ear, after that the full corn in the ear." Mark 4:28 (KJV)*

This is the longest time for waiting. This stage separates the believers who know God's Word is true from those who hope His Word is true. Many believers quit during this time. Keep communing with God and His Word and being obedient to His guidance and promptings during this time.

3) Harvest time—the full ear of corn. God said that while the earth remains, the process of seedtime and harvest would remain.

> *"While the earth remaineth, seedtime and harvest, and cold and heat, and summer and winter, and day and night shall not cease." Genesis 8:22 (KJV)*

Combat the temptation to quit on God and His Word.

> *"Be not deceived; God is not mocked: for whatsoever a man soweth, that shall he also reap. For he that soweth to his flesh shall of the flesh reap corruption; but he that soweth to the Spirit shall of the Spirit reap life everlasting. And let us not be weary in well doing:*

for in due season we shall reap, if we faint not. As we
have therefore opportunity, let us do good unto all men,
especially unto them who are of the household of faith."
Galatians 6:7-10 (KJV)

Galatians 6 tells you not to be deceived. God said that you would reap a harvest from whatever you sow. Because you know He's not a liar, you can believe and know that His promises will come to pass.

Deception says that you have to see it for it to be true. Know that the seed grows down deep before it grows up to where it can be seen.

Your character is developed during this time. Don't be weary in well doing or lose heart and courage (verse 9).

The enemy will attack your mind with negative suggestions and thoughts.

"Fainting" takes place in your mind before it happens in your life (Hebrews 12:1-3).

"Wherefore seeing we also are compassed about with so
great a cloud of witnesses, let us lay aside every weight,
and the sin which doth so easily beset us, and let us run
with patience the race that is set before us, Looking unto
Jesus the author and finisher of our faith; who for the joy
that was set before him endured the cross, despising the
shame, and is set down at the right hand of the throne of
God. For consider him that endured such contradiction
of sinners against himself, lest ye be wearied and faint in
your minds." Hebrews 12:1-3 (KJV)

Don't fight thoughts with thoughts. You must fight thoughts with words that will stop the current thought to think about what you just said—open your mouth and speak God's Word aloud. You must know the Word before you can say it.

Defeat the temptation to quit by learning how to wait on the Lord. Though what you are praying for may tarry, wait for it because it will come. It's not a matter of the Word not working; it's a matter of timing.

> *"For the vision is yet for an appointed time, but at the end it shall speak, and not lie: though it tarry, wait for it; because it will surely come, it will not tarry." Habakkuk 2:3 (KJV)*

By waiting, you'll receive your promise in due season.

> *"The eyes of all wait upon thee; and thou givest them their meat in due season." Psalm 145:15 (KJV)*

> *"These wait all upon thee; that thou mayest give them their meat in due season." Psalm 104:27 (KJV)*

> *"If a man die, shall he live again? all the days of my appointed time will I wait, till my change come." Job 14:14 (KJV)*

The Bible says that if you wait on the Lord, you will inherit the earth.

> *"For evildoers shall be cut off: but those that wait upon the LORD, they shall inherit the earth." Psalm 37:9 (KJV)*

"Evildoers shall be cut off, but those who bind themselves together with the Lord (being of the same mind-set) shall inherit the earth." Psalm 37:9 (Atarah)

"Wait on the LORD, and keep his way, and he shall exalt thee to inherit the land: when the wicked are cut off, thou shalt see it." Psalm 37:34 (KJV)

"Bind yourself together with the Lord (be of the same mind-set as God, have a close intimate relationship with Him), and keep His way and He'll give you your inheritance in this land while you watch the wicked (those who are malicious, spiteful with bitter, ill will) lose it." Psalm 37:34 (Atarah)

How do you wait on the Lord? Waiting doesn't mean you remain idle. It's being like a waiter in a restaurant—giving God your complete attention and service.

Wait in the Hebrew means to collect or bind together, like a rope is twisted and intertwined together.

Waiting means "to serve God with worship and praise; to practice His presence and be so intimate with God and His Word that you have the same mindset as He does – thinking as He thinks, being one with Him."

Learn to be one with God and His Word and praise Him during blade time and stalk time.

They that wait on the Lord will have their strength renewed; they will be mounted on wings like eagles and run without weariness.

> "Hast thou not known? hast thou not heard, that the everlasting God, the LORD, the Creator of the ends of the earth, fainteth not, neither is weary? there is no searching of his understanding. He giveth power to the faint; and to them that have no might he increaseth strength. Even the youths shall faint and be weary, and the young men shall utterly fall: But they that wait upon the LORD shall renew their strength; they shall mount up with wings as eagles; they shall run, and not be weary; and they shall walk, and not faint." Isaiah 40:28-31 (KJV)

> "But they that wait and bind themselves together with the Lord will renew their strength; they will mount up with wings like eagles; they will run, and not be weary; and they will walk, and not faint." Isaiah 40:31 (Atarah)

The key to being successful during stalk time is to have a positive mental attitude and begin to nurture and cultivate your relationship with God and praise God; no matter what the situation looks like stay in the right mindset.

What do you do when you have seen a promise of God, prayed in agreement with it to God but haven't seen it manifest in your life? If you become skillful in waiting with patient endurance, there will never be a time when you won't see a harvest from the seeds you have sown in your heart. Just as a farmer must wait after sowing his field before harvesting his crop, so there is a process that demands a period of waiting before harvest time.

TALKING

Salvation, or wholeness in every area of your life, is available to you; however, you must speak.

What you speak confirms what you believe.

> *"For with the heart man believeth unto righteousness; and with the mouth confession is made unto salvation."* *Romans 10:10 (KJV)*

> *"We having the same spirit of faith, according as it is written, I believed, and therefore have I spoken; we also believe, and therefore speak;"* *2 Corinthians 4:13 (KJV)*

Your mouth is a key factor in tapping into God's prosperity (wholeness in every area of your life).

Don't stop speaking the Word (Joshua 1:8).

> *"This book of the law shall not depart out of thy mouth; but thou shalt meditate therein day and night, that thou mayest observe to do according to all that is written therein: for then thou shalt make thy way prosperous, and then thou shalt have good success."* *Joshua 1:8 (KJV)*

Your mouth gives expression to the things in the realm of the spirit. The spirit realm is controlled by the Word of God. The spirit realm is the parent realm; everything in the natural realm comes out of the spirit realm.

The spoken Word of God has creative power. Focus on what you have been speaking. God sees what you say as the conclusion of your expectation.

> "For verily I say unto you, That whosoever shall say unto this mountain, Be thou removed, and be thou cast into the sea; and shall not doubt in his heart, but shall believe that those things which he saith shall come to pass; he shall have whatsoever he saith." Mark 11:23 (KJV)

What have you been speaking? What God spoke are laws that will not be revoked.

> "Say unto them, As truly as I live, saith the LORD, as ye have spoken in mine ears, so will I do to you:" Numbers 14:28 (KJV)

Your mouth can destroy what you have built and stop your progress. Your tongue sets the course for your life; don't speak anything that will throw you off of God's course.

> "Even so the tongue is a little member, and boasteth great things. Behold, how great a matter a little fire kindleth! And the tongue is a fire, a world of iniquity: so is the tongue among our members, that it defileth the whole body, and setteth on fire the course of nature; and it is set on fire of hell." James 3:5-6 (KJV)

If you have spoken words that are contrary to God or His operation, quickly repent—make the necessary adjustments and get back on course. Speak the truth (what God says) despite the facts (circumstances). You determine your destination. Discover your destination based on what God's Word says.

Don't be afraid to speak what His Word says in private and in public. You are not speaking for anyone else's benefit but your own.

God is committed to the words of His servant, and they are confirmed.

> *"That <u>confirmeth the word of his servant,</u> and performeth the counsel of his messengers; that saith to Jerusalem, Thou shalt be inhabited; and to the cities of Judah, Ye shall be built, and I will raise up the decayed places thereof:" Isaiah 44:26 (KJV)*

Angels listen and preform the Word.

> *"Bless the LORD, ye his angels, that excel in strength, that do his commandments, hearkening unto the voice of his word." Psalm 103:20 (KJV)*

Talk and act in line with the Word of God. Until you talk of your salvation (wholeness in every area of your life), you can't have it. For example: don't look poor and expect riches; "fake it till you make it" by making the best of what you already have. Don't expect to remain where you are. Prosperity is produced by the Word of God that you have come to believe and embrace and it is expressed by what you say and do. Nurture your relationship with God and His Word and continually speak the Word of God.

> *"Let them shout for joy, and be glad, that favour my righteous cause: yea, let them say continually, Let the LORD be magnified, which hath pleasure in the prosperity of his servant. <u>And my tongue shall speak of thy righteousness and of thy praise all the day long.</u>" Psalm 35:27-28 (KJV)*

Your mouth is a master key;

"A man's belly shall be satisfied with the fruit of his mouth; and with the increase of his lips shall he be filled. Death and life are in the power of the tongue: and they that love it shall eat the fruit thereof." Proverbs 18:20-21 (KJV)

Speaking the Word of God is part of the process. However, don't speak God's Word in fear. Fear-based words won't bring the results you desire—they'll bring what you fear. Don't speak words that are not in line with God's Word.

"What man is he that desireth life, and loveth many days, that he may see good? Keep thy tongue from evil, and thy lips from speaking guile." Psalm 34:12-13 (KJV)

Until you speak, you really don't believe a thing.

"And blessed is she that believed: for there shall be a performance of those things which were told her from the Lord." Luke 1:45 (KJV)

Fill your heart with God's Word, and then speak it. Murmur, mutter, speak, talk and utter the Word of God that you have come to believe and have confidence in. Once you do that, you will find your actions lining up with what you have been focusing on. What you truly believe you will speak. Good things come from the fruit of your mouth.

"A man shall be satisfied with good by the fruit of his mouth: and the recompence of a man's hands shall be rendered unto him." Proverbs 12:14 (KJV)

"A man shall eat good by the fruit of his mouth: but the soul of the transgressors shall eat violence." Proverbs 13:2 (KJV)

There are certain things you should never say. What you say in private is responsible for your private circumstances. There is never not a reason why things happen the way they do—examine your words. Your word will tell you what you truly believe.

Your words determine the course of your life. God created you in His image and made you a creative being. You create your world by what you believe and speak. If you believe something, you will speak it. What you say confirms what you believe in your heart-- what you truly believe will come to pass in your life. Believe the Word of God and speak His Words; that's the good life!

THANKSGIVING

According to the Old Covenant Law, if you fail to give God the glory, your blessing will become a curse.

"And now, O ye priests, this commandment is for you. If ye will not hear, and if ye will not lay it to heart, to give glory unto my name, saith the LORD of hosts, I will even send a curse upon you, and I will curse your blessings: yea, I have cursed them already, because ye do not lay it to heart. Behold, I will corrupt your seed, and spread dung upon your faces, even the dung of your solemn feasts; and one shall take you away with it." Malachi 2:1-3 (KJV)

Now that we have received Jesus, we are no longer under the curse of the Laws.

*"Christ hath redeemed us from the curse of the law, being
made a curse for us: for it is written, Cursed is every one
that hangeth on a tree: That the blessing of Abraham
might come on the Gentiles through Jesus Christ; that
we might receive the promise of the Spirit through **faith.**"*
Galatians 3:13-14 (KJV)

Although we are not under the curses of the Law but under the
blessing, we walk by the Spirit of God that has been placed on the
inside of us. This spirit testifies and witnesses to us what is truth and
how we are to walk and not only that, He enables us to do what God
would have us to do. The Laws of God are good and to our benefit,
but we on our own ability cannot keep them. We must rely on God.
As you have this love relationship with God and His Word, you will
find yourself wanting to please Him more and more. Within this
relationship, you will find yourself fulfilling the demands of the Laws
(not under obligation but under love) with the ability to do all that you
could never have done before.

Out of your love for God and all that He has done for you don't take
credit for what God has done.

*"Hearken to me, ye that follow after righteousness, ye that
seek the LORD: look unto the rock whence ye are hewn,
and to the hole of the pit whence ye are digged. Look unto
Abraham your father, and unto Sarah that bare you: for
I called him alone, and blessed him, and increased him.
For the LORD shall comfort Zion: he will comfort all
her waste places; and he will make her wilderness like
Eden, and her desert like the garden of the LORD; joy
and gladness shall be found therein, thanksgiving, and
the voice of melody." Isaiah 51:1-3 (KJV)*

"Who against hope believed in hope, that he might become the father of many nations, according to that which was spoken, So shall thy seed be." Romans 4:18 (KJV)

Abraham was grateful to God. He even gave God glory before his miracle was made manifest. He didn't consider the impossibility of his situation; He refused to believe anything contrary to what God had promised.

To be thankful is to be fruitful; to be thankless is to be fruitless.

There is power in thanksgiving.

"Let the people praise thee, O God; let all the people praise thee. Then shall the earth yield her increase; and God, even our own God, shall bless us." Psalm 67:5-6 (KJV)

Praise provokes increase; murmuring blocks what God can do in your life. You have the grace to refrain from murmuring; don't walk with murmurers.

"A man shall be satisfied with good by the fruit of his mouth: and the recompence of a man's hands shall be rendered unto him." Proverbs 12:14 (KJV)

Thanksgiving must continue after the manifestation—then multiplication takes place. For example: Jesus gave thanks for the little, and the little became more than enough.

"And he commanded the people to sit down on the ground: and he took the seven loaves, and gave thanks, and brake, and gave to his disciples to set before them; and they did set them before the people. And they had a few small fishes: and he blessed, and commanded to set

them also before them. So they did eat, and were filled: and they took up of the broken meat that was left seven baskets." Mark 8:6-8 (KJV)

Water your seeds with thanksgiving. God is committed to bringing increase to whatever you plant and water.

"I have planted, Apollos watered; but God gave the increase." 1 Corinthians 3:6 (KJV)

Talking and giving thanks are forms of watering your seed; giving, working, thinking, trusting and waiting are forms of planting.

Take hold of God-given opportunities.

Preparation + opportunity = success.

Your relationship with God and His Word and being obedient to His promptings and guidance makes room for you; it establishes your throne. It is hard to accomplish things when you fail to take advantage of God-sent opportunities.

Opportunities can come from any man.

"As we have therefore opportunity, let us do good unto all men, especially unto them who are of the household of faith." Galatians 6:10 (KJV)

Every acceptable sacrifice determines your outcome and increases your worth.

"When the LORD turned again the captivity of Zion, we were like them that dream. Then was our mouth filled with laughter, and our tongue with singing: then

*said they among the heathen, The LORD hath done
great things for them. The LORD hath done great things
for us; whereof we are glad. Turn again our captivity,
O LORD, as the streams in the south. He that goeth
forth and weepeth, bearing precious seed, shall doubtless
come again with rejoicing, bringing his sheaves with
him."Psalm 126:1-6 (KJV)*

Every opportunity is God's design for the turning of your captivity.

You're not keeping the Laws to get God to move. God has already
provided all that you need and your response should be "Thank you".
Thanksgiving waters and helps to grow the Word seeds that you have
sown. Taking advantage of God given opportunity enables God to
turn your captivity. Out of your love and admiration for God give
thanks and be obedient to His guidance.

DEVELOPING IN THE LOVE OF GOD

The anointing comes in the form of spiritual gifts.

*"Now concerning spiritual gifts, brethren, I would
not have you ignorant. Ye know that ye were Gentiles,
carried away unto these dumb idols, even as ye were
led. Wherefore I give you to understand, that no man
speaking by the Spirit of God calleth Jesus accursed:
and that no man can say that Jesus is the Lord, but
by the Holy Ghost. Now there are diversities of gifts,
but the same Spirit. And there are differences of
administrations, but the same Lord. And there are
diversities of operations, but it is the same God which
worketh all in all. But the manifestation of the Spirit is
given to every man to profit withal. For to one is given*

by the Spirit the word of wisdom; to another the word of knowledge by the same Spirit; To another faith by the same Spirit; to another the gifts of healing by the same Spirit; To another the working of miracles; to another prophecy; to another discerning of spirits; to another divers kinds of tongues; to another the interpretation of tongues: But all these worketh that one and the selfsame Spirit, dividing to every man severally as he will. For as the body is one, and hath many members, and all the members of that one body, being many, are one body: so also is Christ. For by one Spirit are we all baptized into one body, whether we be Jews or Gentiles, whether we be bond or free; and have been all made to drink into one Spirit. For the body is not one member, but many."
1 Corinthians 12:1-14 (KJV)

"Now ye are the body of Christ, and members in particular. And God hath set some in the church, first apostles, secondarily prophets, thirdly teachers, after that miracles, then gifts of healings, helps, governments, diversities of tongues. Are all apostles? are all prophets? are all teachers? are all workers of miracles? Have all the gifts of healing? do all speak with tongues? do all interpret? But covet earnestly the best gifts: and yet shew I unto you a more excellent way." 1 Corinthians 12:27-31 (KJV)

The anointing removes burdens and destroys yokes. It is God's ability on your ability to do what you couldn't do.

"And it shall come to pass in that day, that his burden shall be taken away from off thy shoulder, and his yoke from off *thy neck, and the <u>yoke shall be destroyed because of the</u> <u>anointing</u>." Isaiah 10:27 (KJV)*

The anointing is the personality of the Holy Spirit. As we read in 1 Corinthians 12, all spiritual gifts come from the same Spirit. God does not want you to be ignorant concerning these things.

The manifestation of the Spirit is given to you for mankind's profit.

"But the manifestation of the Spirit is given to every man to profit withal." 1 Corinthians 12:7 (KJV)

Those who have believed and received Jesus have a special anointing inside of them. There is something wrong if things are not being made manifest in your life. God wants to use you to demonstrate to unbelievers that His Word will manifest in these last days. It's "show and tell" time in the body of Christ.

There are diversities of gifts, and everyone has a role to play (1 Corinthians 12:12, 14). The best gift to possess is the one that you need at the time.

Operating in spiritual gifts is commendable; however, there is a more excellent way (vv. 27-31). There is a way that is better, greater and more powerful than all anointings—walking in love (verse 31). Not everyone can prophesy or work miracles, but everyone can develop in love.

Without love, your spiritual gifts will fail.

"Though I speak with the tongues of men and of angels, and have not charity, I am become as sounding brass, or a tinkling cymbal. And though I have the gift of prophecy, and understand all mysteries, and all

knowledge; and though I have all faith, so that I could remove mountains, and have not charity, I am nothing. And though I bestow all my goods to feed the poor, and though I give my body to be burned, and have not charity, it profiteth me nothing. Charity suffereth long, and is kind; charity envieth not; charity vaunteth not itself, is not puffed up," 1 Corinthians 13:1-4 (KJV)

"Charity never faileth: but whether there be prophecies, they shall fail; whether there be tongues, they shall cease; whether there be knowledge, it shall vanish away." 1 Corinthians 13:8 (KJV)

Notice how 1 Corinthians 12 talks about the gifts and ends with earnestly desiring the best gifts and 1 Corinthians 13 immediately talks about how none of the gifts will work without love. You are wasting your time trying to get these gifts if you have not developed in love. Love never fails. The fruit of the Spirit is love.

Love has different components. Failure to develop in every component of love allows Satan to come in and disrupt/destroy your life. The character of Jesus is the love of God, which is the fruit of the Spirit.

Without love, you only see things in part.

"For we know in part, and we prophesy in part." 1 Corinthians 13:9 (KJV)

"For our knowledge is fragmentary (incomplete and imperfect), and our prophecy (our teaching) is fragmentary (incomplete and imperfect)." 1 Corinthians 13:9 (Atarah)

Many believers receive only part of their manifestations, instead of operating in wholeness. When you become developed in love, things will no longer be seen in part. If you allow your love to wax cold, your manifestations are placed "on ice".

Your power is in the love of God. To fail, you must step out of love. To have guaranteed victory means that you continue in your love walk.

God is love.

> *"Beloved, let us love one another: for love is of God; and every one that loveth is born of God, and knoweth God. He that loveth not knoweth not God; for God is love."* 1 John 4:7-8 (KJV)

Love never fails, because God never fails.

When Jesus returns, He will identify His family members by their love.

> *"Behold, what manner of love the Father hath bestowed upon us, that we should be called the sons of God: therefore the world knoweth us not, because it knew him not. Beloved, now are we the sons of God, and it doth not yet appear what we shall be: but we know that, when he shall appear, we shall be like him; for we shall see him as he is."* 1 John 3:1-2 (KJV)

Everything on this planet operates either by the law of life in Christ Jesus or by the law of sin and death.

> *"For the law of the Spirit of life in Christ Jesus hath made me free from the law of sin and death."* Romans 8:2 (KJV)

You operate either under the life cycle or the death cycle. God, Who is Love, operates under the life cycle; selfishness operates under the death cycle. From love, the Word of God that you have come to believe and embrace manifests to bring that which you believe to pass; from selfishness, fear manifests to bring the words of the devil to pass.

You cannot operate in love and selfishness at the same time. Love does not consider itself. It is "not about you".

God's divine order is the prerequisite to miracles. Ignoring the proper sequence of things will cause you to always ask why things are not working. You must know and operate in the proper sequence to see your heart's desires made manifest.

DEVELOPING IN THE LOVE OF GOD, PART 2

Selfishness is the root of everything that goes wrong in a believer's life. The devil is not your greatest enemy—you are! Satan wants to convince you that he's the problem so that you'll never accept responsibility for the things that have gone wrong in your life.

Godly character is unselfish and is the root to the power of God. Applying spiritual principles to your life without first having the character of God is fruitless.

Various spiritual gifts are available to every believer (1 Corinthian 12). Spiritual gifts, or anointings, are made available to you the moment you become born again; believers are impregnated with the anointing (the burden-removing, yoke-destroying power of God). Because the Holy Spirit dwells in your born-again spirit, you have wisdom, knowledge and supernatural ability.

God wants you to experience great manifestations of the Spirit so that you can profit in every area of your life (verse 7).

> *"But the manifestation of the Spirit is given to every man to profit withal."* 1 Corinthians 12:7 *(KJV)*

As a member of the body of Christ, you have specific assignments and have been empowered with access to spiritual gifts to accomplish them.

> *"For to one is given by the Spirit the word of wisdom; to another the word of knowledge by the same Spirit; To another faith by the same Spirit; to another the gifts of healing by the same Spirit; To another the working of miracles; to another prophecy; to another discerning of spirits; to another divers kinds of tongues; to another the interpretation of tongues: But all t hese worketh that one and the selfsame Spirit, dividing to every man severally as he will. For as the body is one, and hath many members, and all the members of that one body, being many, are one body: so also is Christ. For by one Spirit are we all baptized into one body, whether we be Jews or Gentiles, whether we be bond or free; and have been all made to drink into one Spirit. For the body is not one member, but many. If the foot shall say, Because I am not the hand, I am not of the body; is it therefore not of the body? And if the ear shall say, Because I am not the eye, I am not of the body; is it therefore not of the body? If the whole body were an eye, where were the hearing? If the whole were hearing, where were the smelling? But now hath God set the members every one of them in the body, as it hath pleased him. And if they were all one member, where were the body? But now are they many members, yet but one body.*

And the eye cannot say unto the hand, I have no need of thee: nor again the head to the feet, I have no need of you. Nay, much more those members of the body, which seem to be more feeble, are necessary: And those members of the body, which we think to be less honourable, upon these we bestow more abundant honour; and our uncomely parts have more abundant comeliness. For our comely parts have no need: but God hath tempered the body together, having given more abundant honour to that part which lacked: That there should be no schism in the body; but that the members should have the same care one for another. And whether one member suffer, all the members suffer with it; or one member be honoured, all the members rejoice with it. Now ye are the body of Christ, and members in particular. And God hath set some in the church, first apostles, secondarily prophets, thirdly teachers, after that miracles, then gifts of healings, helps, governments, diversities of tongues. Are all apostles? are all prophets? are all teachers? are all workers of miracles? Have all the gifts of healing? do all speak with tongues? do all interpret? 1 Corinthians 12:8-30 (KJV)

Although spiritual gifts are important, you must strive to purse the "excellent way"—a lifestyle of love.

"But covet earnestly the best gifts: and yet shew I unto you a more excellent way. Though I speak with the tongues of men and of angels, and have not charity, I am become as sounding brass, or a tinkling cymbal." 1 Corinthians 12:31; 13:1 (KJV)

The word "excellent" comes from the same root word as "love" and in the very next chapter, he talks about love (charity). Strive to excel in developing the character of God.

Love is the preeminent force; it should be the foundation of everything you do.

Spiritual gifts fail without love as their motivating force.

"Though I speak with the tongues of men and of angels, and have not charity, I am become as sounding brass, or a tinkling cymbal. And though I have the gift of prophecy, and understand all mysteries, and all knowledge; and though I have all faith, so that I could remove mountains, and have not charity, I am nothing. And though I bestow all my goods to feed the poor, and though I give my body to be burned, and have not charity, it profiteth me nothing. Charity suffereth long, and is kind; charity envieth not; charity vaunteth not itself, is not puffed up, Doth not behave itself unseemly, seeketh not her own, is not easily provoked, thinketh no evil; Rejoiceth not in iniquity, but rejoiceth in the truth; Beareth all things, believeth all things, hopeth all things, endureth all things. <u>Charity never faileth: but whether there be prophecies, they shall fail; whether there be tongues, they shall cease; whether there be knowledge, it shall vanish away.</u> For we know in part, and we prophesy in part. But when that which is perfect is come, then that which is in part shall be done away. When I was a child, I spake as a child, I understood as a child, I thought as a child: but when I became a man, I put away childish things." 1 Corinthians 13:1-11 (KJV)

Your character supports the love walk.

Love never fails, because God is love; there's no failure in Him.

> *"Charity never faileth: but whether there be prophecies,*
> *they shall fail; whether there be tongues, they shall cease;*
> *whether there be knowledge, it shall vanish away."*
> *1 Corinthians 13:8 (KJV)*

> *"Beloved, let us love one another: for love is of God; and*
> *every one that loveth is born of God, and knoweth God.*
> *He that loveth not knoweth not God; for God is love." 1*
> *John 4:7-8 (KJV)*

> *"And we have known and believed the love that God*
> *hath to us. God is love; and he that dwelleth in love*
> *dwelleth in God, and God in him." 1 John 4:16 (KJV)*

Like a tree, the different manifestations of the anointing—prophecy, healing, speaking in tongues and so on—are branches. God (Love) is the root and life of the tree.

Failure is a result of living without developing in the love of God. God (Love) is perfect; therefore, believers should strive to perfect His love within them.

> *"And hope maketh not ashamed; because the love of God*
> *is shed abroad in our hearts by the Holy Ghost which is*
> *given unto us." Romans 5:5 (KJV)*

Unfortunately, many believers are highly developed in selfishness.

Love and selfishness are "reciprocal" forces—they oppose one another. In mathematics, reciprocals are "alternates." For example: the reciprocal of 7/1 is 1/7. To be selfish is to "regard one's own interest;" selfishness is "a devotion to one's own interest."

Satan wants to take your focus from God; he wants you to focus on yourself. Adam and Eve were blinded by the idea that they could become like God, not realizing that they were already like Him (Genesis 3:1-5). When you're only concerned with yourself, you are no longer God-conscious; instead, you are self-conscious.

Your life is the sum total of operating under either the law of the Spirit of life or the law of sin and death.

> *"There is therefore now no condemnation to them which are in Christ Jesus, who walk not after the flesh, but after the Spirit. For the law of the Spirit of life in Christ Jesus hath made me free from the law of sin and death."* Romans 8:1-2 (KJV)

The law of the Spirit of life governs love, faith, the kingdom of God's system, the life cycle, health, prosperity, deliverance and eternal life. The law of sin and death governs selfishness, fear, the world's system, death, sickness, poverty and bondage.

To break free from selfishness, you must stop living by the law of sin and death and begin operating in love.

Perfected love casts out fear, selfishness and everything else that is governed by the law of sin and death.

> *"There is no fear in love; but perfect love casteth out fear: because fear hath torment. He that feareth is not made perfect in love."* 1 John 4:18 (KJV)

Cultivate the fruit of the Spirit, love, and examine your life for evidence of selfishness (Galatians 5:19-24). The fruit of love consists of the elements of joy, peace, longsuffering, gentleness, goodness, faithfulness, meekness and temperance (vv. 22-24). The fruits of the flesh (selfishness) are adultery, fornication, uncleanness, lasciviousness, idolatry, witchcraft, hatred, division, emulations, wrath, strife, seditions, heresies, envy, murder, drunkenness, reveling and the like (vv. 19-21).

Get rid of selfishness so that you can be free from bondage.

Let your actions of love be without selfishness (Romans 12:9, AMP).

> "Let love be without dissimulation. Abhor that which is evil; cleave to that which is good." Romans 12:9 (KJV)

> "Let your love be sincere (a real thing); hate what is evil, but hold fast to that which is good." Romans 12:9 (Atarah)

Selfishness hinders you from experiencing your God-given right to have positive results. Satan will try to deceive you into thinking that everyone and everything else, and not your own selfishness, are to blame for your life's troubles. The best thing that you can do is to cultivate the love of God within you. A heart that's motivated by love is connected to an unlimited supply of God's anointing.

Love

Love never gives up.
Love cares more for others than for self.
Love is not envious.
Love is not conceited, arrogant and inflated with pride.

Love doesn't force itself on others.

Love is not rude.

Love is not quickly angered.

Love does not insist on its own rights or its own way.

Love is not always "me first" (self seeking);

Love is not touchy or fretful or resentful.

Love doesn't keep score of the sins of others.

Love takes no account of the evil done to it.

Love pays no attention to a suffered wrong.

Love thinks no evil.

Love does not rejoice when others fall or make a mistake.

Love takes pleasure in the truth of God's Word.

Love puts up with anything.

Love always trusts God.

Love always looks for the best.

Love believes all things (trusts).

Love keeps going to the end.

Love never fails, it never fades out or becomes
obsolete or comes to an end,

1 Corinthians 13:4-8 (Atarah)

WHEN GOD IS FIRST

Setting priorities and putting first things first will either make you or break you.

> *"Prepare thy work without, and make it fit for thyself in the field; and afterwards build thine house."* Proverbs 24:27 (KJV)

Priority is "that which is of first importance; those things in which higher value is placed." Your schedule reflects your priorities. Make sure your schedule is indicative of your profession that God is first in your life.

During times of fasting and prayer, the ultimate aim is to replace the dictates of the flesh with the things of the Spirit.

Don't allow your flesh to control you; when you put your flesh under submission to your spirit, you put sin and selfishness under as well.

Make sure your fasting is sincere and not just for show.

If you are not praying and spending time in fellowship with God during a fast, you are simply on a "hunger strike" and will not receive anything from the Lord.

When fasting, cut out external, worldly distractions such as the news. Instead, replace them with increased prayer and Bible study time to aid your hearing clearly from God. Don't give in to the flesh by being moody; take the opportunity to develop in love.

Merely imitating the behavior of other Christians can get you off course and cause you to miss your destiny in God. You have to know what God is leading you to do. Everything is permissible for you, but not all things are profitable. For example: Spending beyond your means is lawful, but God wants you to be debt free.

> *"All things are lawful unto me, but all things are not expedient: all things are lawful for me, but I will not be brought under the power of any." 1 Corinthians 6:12 (KJV)*

> *"Everything is permissible (allowable and lawful) for me; but not everything is beneficial. Everything is lawful for me (I have the right to do anything), but I will not become the slave of anything or be brought under its power." 1 Corinthians 6:12 (Atarah)*

When following after your destiny in Christ, you must guard yourself against even noble distractions. When one of Jesus' disciples wanted to go bury his father, Jesus replied, "...let the dead bury their dead" (Matthew 8:18-22). Jesus was trying to get this man to see things from a heavenly viewpoint so that he wouldn't get off course.

If you don't get your priorities straight, then you'll allow circumstances and other people to set your priorities for you.

Your relationship with your spouse and children should not take precedent over your relationship with God.

> *"And this I speak for your own profit; not that I may cast a snare upon you, but for that which is comely, and that ye may attend upon the Lord without distraction." 1 Corinthians 7:35 (KJV)*

Rearrange your schedule so that you spend quality time with your family while maintaining your fellowship with God as top priority.

You will not be able to secure your undistracted devotion to the Lord without changing the way you think. Distractions are "intrusions of the mind to bring confusion." When distractions come, continue seeing things through the Word of God instead of what lies before you—or they will ultimately get you off course. Jesus told Jairus to not be afraid but only believe instead of allowing distractions to get him off course (Mark 5:35-36, 39).

When you walk in the Spirit, you see things from God's point of view; when you walk in the flesh, you see things from man's perspective, which provides several avenues for distraction. The fleshy person believes what he sees; a believer sees what he believes.

The person who sees things from a godly perspective will win in life. As long as you allow your flesh to control you, spiritual things can never take their rightful place as priority in your life. For example: Being tired should have nothing to do with whether or not you get up in the morning to pray. <u>You can't say God is first in your life when you continue to yield to your flesh</u>.

You must make walking in the Spirit and doing God's Word the highest priority in your life. The day you make the Word second place in your life will be the day you find yourself in the flesh, wondering why the Spirit isn't working for you.

God is before all things and holds everything in your life and this world together.

> *"For by him were all things created, that are in heaven,*
> *and that are in earth, visible and invisible, whether they*
> *be thrones, or dominions, or principalities, or powers: all*
> *things were created by him, and for him: And he is before*

*all things, and by him all things consist." Colossians 1:16
(KJV)*

It is an act of perversion for you to put a created thing before the Creator. Anything or anyone who occupies first place in your heart—including your career, family or marriage—is idolatry; guard yourself from letting that happen.

*"Little children, keep yourselves from idols. Amen." 1
John 5:21 (KJV)*

God can't do the things He wants to do for you when your job, sports or anything else is a higher priority than He is in your life. Don't allow a principle to take precedent over your relationship with God, or things still will not work.

You must be willing to disregard your personal interests to give to God. (2 Corinthians 8:5).

*"And this they did, not as we hoped, but first gave their
own selves to the Lord, and unto us by the will of God." 2
Corinthians 8:5 (KJV)*

*"They didn't do this in the way we had expected, but
first they gave themselves to the Lord and to us by the
will of God." 2 Corinthians 8:5 (Atarah)*

If you are a born again believer, you are naturally going to have the desire inside of you to serve God. God demands ultimate loyalty from you, so you can't keep making excuses for not serving Him.

*"And there went great multitudes with him: and he
turned, and said unto them, If any man come to me, and
hate not his father, and mother, and wife, and children,*

and brethren, and sisters, yea, and his own life also, he cannot be my disciple." Luke 14:25-26 (KJV)

"A huge number of people were walking along with Him, Jesus turned and told them:"Anyone who comes to me but refuses to let go of father, mother, spouse, children, brothers, sisters, even one's own self, they can't be my disciple. I must have ultimate loyalty above all." Luke 14:25-26 (Atarah)

When God is first in your life, you don't have to fear what man will do to you. Self-preservation is an indicator of fear and selfishness.

God must be in first place if He is to lead and guide you. You must put your confidence in God first.

"That we should be to the praise of his glory, who first trusted in Christ." Ephesians 1:12 (KJV)

"That we should live for the praise of His honor, who first trusted and had confidence in Christ." Ephesians 1:12 (Atarah)

When God sees that you trust Him and can't be moved off what you believe, things move and rearrange on your behalf.

Wrong priorities will cause things you desire to be dammed up.

"Having damnation, because they have cast off their first faith." 1 Timothy 5:12 (KJV)

If you want things to work right, you must rearrange your priorities and put God first.

You can't love the attachments of the world and expect to prosper.

> *"Love not the world, neither the things that are in the world.*
> *If any man love the world, the love of the Father is not in*
> *him. For all that is in the world, the lust of the flesh, and the*
> *lust of the eyes, and the pride of life, is not of the Father, but*
> *is of the world." 1 John 2:15-116 (KJV)*

When you allow other things to take first place over God, it is like breaking your marriage vow to Him. Your friendship with the world makes you God's enemy.

> *"Ye lust, and have not: ye kill, and desire to have, and*
> *cannot obtain: ye fight and war, yet ye have not, because*
> *ye ask not. Ye ask, and receive not, because ye ask amiss,*
> *that ye may consume it upon your lusts. Ye adulterers and*
> *adulteresses, know ye not that the friendship of the world*
> *is enmity with God? whosoever therefore will be a friend*
> *of the world is the enemy of God." James 4:2-4 (KJV)*

You can tell what your priorities are by how you spend your time, what you talk about and what you think about.

Most believers profess God as the top priority in their lives, but how they schedule their lives often contradicts their claims. In these last days, believers must take authority over their flesh and make God top priority in their lives in order to see their God given dreams made manifest.

WHO'S CONTROLLING YOUR LIFE?

Love is a new commandment that encompasses all the other commandments.

> *"A new commandment I give unto you, That ye love one*
> *another; as I have loved you, that ye also love one another.*
> *By this shall all men know that ye are my disciples, if ye*
> *have love one to another." John 13:34-35 (KJV)*

The way you treat your brothers and sisters in Christ is evidence of your love walk. Every time you mistreat someone, you are breaking this commandment. Before doing anything, ask, "How is this going to affect the other person?"

The process of being born-again is the process of passing from death to life.

> *"Marvel not, my brethren, if the world hate you. We*
> *know that we have passed from death unto life, because*
> *we love the brethren. He that loveth not his brother*
> *abideth in death." 1 John 3:13-14 (KJV)*

Jesus was the firstborn of many brethren.

> *"Who is the image of the invisible God, the firstborn of*
> *every creature:" Colossians 1:15 (KJV)*

> *"And he is the head of the body, the church: who is the*
> *beginning, the firstborn from the dead; that in all things*
> *he might have the preeminence." Colossians 1:18 (KJV)*

A man who doesn't love is spiritually dead.

The number one goal of every born-again believer must be to learn to walk in love.

As a born-again believer, you owe it to God to love him or her.

"Owe no man any thing, but to love one another: for he that loveth another hath fulfilled the law. For this, Thou shalt not commit adultery, Thou shalt not kill, Thou shalt not steal, Thou shalt not bear false witness, Thou shalt not covet; and if there be any other commandment, it is briefly comprehended in this saying, namely, Thou shalt love thy neighbour as thyself. Love worketh no ill to his neighbour: therefore love is the fulfilling of the law."
Romans 13:8-10 (KJV)

Jesus raised the bar from 'loving other as yourself' to 'love others as He (Jesus) loved us'.

"A new commandment I give unto you, <u>That ye love one another; as I have loved you</u>, that ye also love one another." John 13:34

Getting a revelation of the love of God will release the anointing of might in you.

"That he would grant you, according to the riches of his glory, to be strengthened with might by his Spirit in the inner man; That Christ may dwell in your hearts by faith; that ye, being rooted and grounded in love, May be able to comprehend with all saints what is the breadth, and length, and depth, and height; And to know the love of Christ, which passeth knowledge, that ye might be filled with all the fulness of God. Now unto him that is able to do exceeding abundantly above all that we ask or think, according to the power that worketh in us,"
Ephesians 3:16-20 (KJV)

Might is "an ability or anointing to do anything." Might comes from the Holy Spirit Who lives inside your spirit. The anointing of might dwells in you. Through the Spirit of might, you can do all things.

To tap into the Spirit of might, you must be rooted and grounded in love. If you want to fix your power shortage, you must fix your love shortage.

The love of God comes by way of revelation; it surpasses human knowledge or mental assent. Jesus was revealed to His disciples as the Anointed One (Matthew 16:13-18; John 1:40-42); their knowledge of Him needed to get past their mental assent. When the love of God is revealed to you, you will experience fullness—nothing needed or wanted. You refuse to walk in hate when you have a revelation of love.

If you are born again, you already possess the love of God. The day you received Jesus, the Holy Spirit entered your spirit and poured the love of God in you.

> *"And hope maketh not ashamed; because the love of God is shed abroad in our hearts by the Holy Ghost which is given unto us." Romans 5:5 (KJV)*

When love gets in you, Jesus and the Father get in you.

Love is power. What God can do through you, in you and for you is empowered by the love that is working in you. To love is to know God.

> *"He that loveth not knoweth not God; for God is love." 1 John 4:8 (KJV)*

Jesus was anointed with the Holy Spirit, love and power. (Acts 10:38).

"How God anointed Jesus of Nazareth with the Holy Ghost and with power: who went about doing good, and healing all that were oppressed of the devil; for God was with him." Acts 10:38 (KJV)

Jesus and the Father are one.

"And now I am no more in the world, but these are in the world, and I come to thee. Holy Father, keep through thine own name those whom thou hast given me, that they may be one, as we are." John 17:11 (KJV)

The same love that God loves Jesus with is in you.

"And I have declared unto them thy name, and will declare it: that the love wherewith thou hast loved me may be in them, and I in them." John 17:26 (KJV)

The Father, the Son and the Holy Spirit are one.

"For there are three that bear record in heaven, the Father, the Word, and the Holy Ghost: and these three are one". 1 John 5:7 (KJV)

Even though you function in different capacities, such as a child, spouse and businessperson, you are still one – you are still "you."

The Holy Spirit is love before He is power. Jesus was first anointed with the Holy Spirit, Who is love; power came about as a result. Jesus was anointed, or smeared, with love. You have the same love smeared on you that Jesus had on Him; therefore, you have access to the same power that controlled His life. There is no power apart from love.

Jesus was able to do great works because He allowed love, or compassion, to move Him.

> "But when he saw the multitudes, he was moved with compassion on them, because they fainted, and were scattered abroad, as sheep having no shepherd." Matthew 9:36 (KJV)

> "And Jesus went forth, and saw a great multitude, and was moved with compassion toward them, and he healed their sick." Matthew 14:14 (KJV)

When compassion moves you, it turns into power. Power that heals flows from compassion. The love of God can't dwell in a person who doesn't have compassion.

> "But whoso hath this world's good, and seeth his brother have need, and shutteth up his bowels of compassion from him, how dwelleth the love of God in him?" 1 John 3:17 (KJV)

You empower people by loving them. Compassion compels you to bear the burdens of others.

> "Brethren, if a man be overtaken in a fault, ye which are spiritual, restore such an one in the spirit of meekness; considering thyself, lest thou also be tempted. Bear ye one another's burdens, and so fulfil the law of Christ." Galatians 6:1 (KJV)

If there isn't a difference in how you love, you're just wearing a Christian T-shirt.

The "switch" of the law of Christ is turned on by your love walk.

Our loving one another is God's preeminent commandment; love fulfills every aspect of the law. Love is what connects you to power. How people know you are a true follower of Christ Jesus is by the love you display to others.

THE PERSONALITY OF THE HOLY SPIRIT

In the kingdom of God, 1+1+1 = 1.

> *"This is he that came by water and blood, even Jesus Christ; not by water only, but by water and blood. And it is the Spirit that beareth witness, because the Spirit is truth. For there are three that bear record in heaven, the Father, the Word, and the Holy Ghost: and these three are one."* 1 John 5:6 (KJV)

There is God the Father, God the Son and God the Holy Spirit: one God, but three different functions.

God is love.

> *"He that loveth not knoweth not God; for God is love."* 1 John 4:8 (KJV)

When you became born again, the Holy Spirit poured God's love into your heart.

> *"And hope maketh not ashamed; because the love of God is shed abroad in our hearts by the Holy Ghost which is given unto us."* Romans 5:5 (KJV)

Jesus asked the Father to give us His love.

> *"I in them, and thou in me, that they may be made*
> *perfect in one; and that the world may know that thou*
> *hast sent me, and hast loved them, as thou hast loved*
> *me." John 17:23 (KJV)*

God wants you to be strengthened with His might.

> *"That he would grant you, according to the riches of*
> *his glory, to be strengthened with might by his Spirit in*
> *the inner man; That Christ may dwell in your hearts*
> *by faith; that ye, being rooted and grounded in love,"*
> *Ephesians 3:16-17 (KJV)*

Might is "an ability or anointing to do anything". Christ, the Anointed One and His Anointing, dwells in your heart by faith. Love is the root to your faith, anointing and power.

You must have character before you can have power. Character is "doing what's right because it's right, and then doing it right." Walking in love is right.

The personality of the Holy Spirit (Hebrews: Ruach HaKodesh) is revealed in His name. Jesus called the Holy Spirit "the Comforter." His mission is to bring comfort to every area of your life—including anywhere you are experiencing discomfort.

Jesus had to leave so the Comforter could come. Jesus told the disciples it would be expedient for Him to go away.

> *"But now I go my way to him that sent me; and none of*
> *you asketh me, Whither goest thou? But because I have*
> *said these things unto you, sorrow hath filled your heart.*

Nevertheless I tell you the truth; <u>It is expedient for you</u>
<u>that I go away: for if I go not away, the Comforter will</u>
<u>not come unto you; but if I depart, I will send him unto</u>
<u>you.</u>" John 16:5-7 (KJV)

Expedient means "profitable; good; to their advantage".

The Comforter has come, and it is time for born-again believers to start walking in their advantage. When you operate in the love that the Holy Spirit has provided, it will ensure your comfort.

The Holy Spirit will reveal the true sons and daughters of God. Sonship with God is defined as "a man or woman who, by the power of God, brings deliverance and liberty to mankind.".

Believers should be doing greater works than what Jesus did while He was on the earth.

> *"Verily, verily, I say unto you, He that believeth on me,*
> *the works that I do shall he do also; and greater works*
> *than these shall he do; because I go unto my Father."*
> *John 14:12 (KJV)*

Religion considers it heresy to believe that you can act like God. The Holy Spirit is a Teacher Who will teach you how to be like God, a replica of God on earth. You are to resemble your heavenly Father.

Here are some attributes of the Holy Spirit:

1) The Holy Spirit is the oil of <u>joy</u>.

> *"To appoint unto them that mourn in Zion, to give unto*
> *them beauty for ashes, the oil of joy for mourning, the*
> *garment of praise for the spirit of heaviness; that they*

might be called trees of righteousness, the planting of the
LORD, that he might be glorified." Isaiah 61:3 (KJV)

You cannot be filled with the Holy Spirit and not have joy in your life.
You have been anointed with the oil of gladness.

> *"Thou lovest righteousness, and hatest wickedness:*
> *therefore God, thy God, hath anointed thee with the oil*
> *of gladness above thy fellows." Psalm 45:7 (KJV)*

Joy works like medicine.

> *"A merry heart doeth good like a medicine: but a broken*
> *spirit drieth the bones" Proverbs 17:22 (KJV)*

There's is a difference between joy and happiness: Happiness comes
from how you feel and may be subject to change but joy comes from
what you know from the Word of God. A joyful spirit will sustain you
through bodily pain or trouble.

> *"The spirit of a man will sustain his infirmity; but a*
> *wounded spirit who can bear?" Proverbs 18:14 (KJV)*

Bitterness brings trouble.

> *"Follow peace with all men, and holiness, without which*
> *no man shall see the Lord:" Hebrews 12:14 (KJV)*

2) The love of God that was poured into your heart determines your
access to revelation (enlightenment and direction). If you are not
developing in love, you will most likely not hear from God. Love
cannot communicate with strife. When you love others, it is proof
that you love God.

*"Jesus said unto him, Thou shalt love the Lord thy God
with all thy heart, and with all thy soul, and with all thy
mind. This is the first and great commandment. And the
second is like unto it, Thou shalt love thy neighbour as
thyself." Matthew 22:37-40 (KJV)*

Love is the platform by which the law and commandments function;
without the platform, you will just have a form of godliness with no
power.

It was Jesus' compassion that enabled Him to heal, deliver and set free.

3) When you are anointed with the Holy Spirit, your praise enters
   a higher dimension. High praise is a fundamental requirement
   for moving yourself to a place of rest so that God can take over
   your battles and you can become a spectator. You are sure to have
   sweatless victories when you operate on a high-praise frequency.

4) When the Holy Spirit shows up, so does <u>favor</u>. When you carry
   the anointing of the Holy Spirit, your name is sweet and creates
   an expectation; you'll "smell good" to God and enjoy love and
   favor from others.

   *"Because of the savour of thy good ointments thy name
   is as ointment poured forth, therefore do the virgins love
   thee." Song of Songs 1:3 (KJV)*

   *"The odor of your ointments is fragrant; your name is
   like perfume poured out. Therefore, everyone loves you."
   Song of Songs 1:3 (Atarah)*

People will want to do things for you because of the anointing that is
on your life. Success is the foundation of favor.

When the Holy Spirit, Who is love, came to live within you, He poured all that He is into you. As a result, you are equipped to love others beyond your natural, human ability to love. You are capable of walking in God's unconditional love.

CULTIVATING A LIFESTYLE OF THANKSGIVING

Give God a sacrifice of praise.

> *"By him therefore let us offer the sacrifice of praise to God continually, that is, the fruit of our lips giving thanks to his name." Hebrews 13:15 (KJV)*

A sacrifice is when there is pressure to do something—when you don't feel like doing it; when it's uncomfortable.

God wants you to praise Him continually with the fruit of your lips—open your mouth and say, "Thank You, Lord."

Giving thanks will cause you to become enlarged; it will "expand your capacity to receive more".

You must cultivate a lifestyle of thanksgiving. Cultivation is not automatic or only done when at church; it is purposely doing something every day.

Thanksgiving is a key to experiencing fullness—"nothing needed and nothing wanted".

Gratitude will keep you on course—maintain an attitude of gratitude.

The way to receive all that you've prayed for is to continually give thanks—it causes you to remain spiritually aligned with God.

Enter into God's presence with thanksgiving. For example: I look around at my children that I now have and I gave thanks, because God has given me more than I had before. I look around at all the many possessions that I now have and I give thanks because God has given back to me what was stolen from me. I am reminded of Psalm 34:1-3.

> *"I will bless the LORD at all times: his praise shall continually be in my mouth. My soul shall make her boast in the LORD: the humble shall hear thereof, and be glad." Psalm 34:1-2 (KJV)*

Give thanks for what you have instead of complaining about what you don't have.

Psalm 136:1-3 says to give thanks to God.

> *"O give thanks unto the LORD; for he is good: for his mercy endureth for ever. O give thanks unto the God of gods: for his mercy endureth for ever. O give thanks to the Lord of lords: for his mercy endureth for ever." Psalm 136:1-3 (KJV)*

It is good to give God thanks.

> *"It is a good thing to give thanks unto the LORD, and to sing praises unto thy name, O most High:" Psalm 92:1 (KJV)*

When you stay on the path of thanksgiving, you will be on the path of light and understanding. Complaining and grumbling will get you off the path of light and place you in darkness and confusion.

An ungrateful heart will push you into darkness and can cause what you do have to be taken away. Be thankful for what God has given you.

Those who compare themselves to others and what they have demonstrate an attitude of ingratitude and work in pride. Comparison is an insult to God.

There is nothing inferior or lowly about what God gives you. Be thankful for the little, and more will come to you. For example: Jesus took a boy's "two-piece fish dinner", blessed it and gave thanks—and it was multiplied to feed over 5,000 people (Matthew 14:15-21).

Don't be ungrateful for what you have been given. Thanksgiving involves remembering what God has done for you and valuing it.

Thanksgiving causes you to have grace.

> *"But he giveth more grace. Wherefore he saith, God resisteth the proud, but giveth grace unto the humble."*
> *James 4:6 (KJV)*

More grace (unmerited love, favor and empowerment) is required to see more of anything in your life.

A thankful person is a humble person—gratitude and humility go hand in hand.

Pride shows ingratitude. Pride always wants more and isn't satisfied with what it has. Pride says, "You owe me something"—you expect something from people. When it comes to people, expect nothing and appreciate everything; when it comes to God, expect everything and appreciate everything.

God resists the proud and ungrateful. For example: Lucifer wasn't grateful for all that God did for him; pride and ingratitude took root in him. Another example: Adam and Eve weren't grateful for what they had. Favor resists the proud.

Pride leads you to destruction and hell. For example: Korah gathered a group of Israelites against Moses and Aaron because he felt like they were taking on too much and not giving others a chance to "shine" (Numbers 16:2-3). He was guilty of that of which he was accusing others (Romans 2:1). Moses told him that he was ungrateful for all that the Lord had done for him (Numbers 16:8-10). God was so grieved that He caused the ground to open up and swallow him and his followers (verse 33).

Don't look at what others have; instead, give thanks for what God has done for you. You can't compare what you see of others to your own life- you're trying to compare their "highlight reel" to your "behind-the-scenes footage".

Guard your mouth and your attitude. Murmuring and complaining will undo all that you have striven to achieve. Murmuring displeases God. When you go from thanksgiving to murmuring, you go from light to darkness. Those who murmured in the wilderness were destroyed; it turned God against them. (Numbers 11)

People who murmur are natural failures; nothing works for them, which causes them to live a life of perpetual struggle.

A grateful heart is your fastest escape out of the trap of murmuring. Gratitude will cause God's presence to engulf you.

Thanksgiving pleases God; according to the Law, ingratitude leads you to a curse. Jesus did all things to please God – so should we. Thanksgiving and praise please God more than any other sacrifice.

> "I will praise the name of God with a song, and will magnify him with thanksgiving. *This also shall please*

the LORD better than an ox or bullock that hath horns and hoofs." Psalm 69:30-31 (KJV)

If you know God and don't give thanks to Him, your heart and imagination will be darkened. According to the Law, an attitude of ingratitude will open you up to a curse and cause you to want.

> *"These curses will serve as signposts, warnings to your children ever after. Because you didn't serve the Lord your God with joy and gladness in your heart when you had such an abundance of everything;The Lord will allow your enemies to come against you; and you will serve him when you are hungry, thirsty, poorly clothed and lacking everything; you will have a yoke of iron on your neck until it destroys you." Deuteronomy 28:46 (Atarah)*

God wanted us to be grateful so much that He made it an established law with a curse if not kept. Under the New Covenant, Christ Jesus has redeemed us from the curse of the Laws (Galatians 3:13). Now God wants us to be grateful, not out of obligation, but out of our love for Him. Under this New Covenant, we should find ourselves doing it more and better than those who did it out of obligation. Knowing God's love, we love God so much that we just have to give Him praise and thanksgiving and out of this, we get all of the blessings of Abraham.

> *"Christ hath redeemed us from the curse of the law, being made a curse for us: for it is written, Cursed is every one that hangeth on a tree: That the blessing of Abraham might come on the Gentiles through Jesus Christ; that we might receive the promise of the Spirit through faith." Galatians 3:13-14 (KJV)*

By giving thanks, you are made whole. For example: When Jesus healed the 10 lepers, only one turned back around and gave thanks. The others were healed, but Jesus told the one that turned back to give thanks that he was made whole, meaning there was no longer anything missing or broken in his life (Luke 17:14-19). While the other just got healed, the thankful one was healed and made whole; nothing missing and nothing broken.

Give thanks continually for what you have and for what is to come.

Your circumstances should not determine whether or not you give thanks.

Abraham didn't consider what things looked like—his old age and Sarah's barren womb—when he stood on the Word that God had given him.

> *"Who against hope believed in hope, that he might become the father of many nations, according to that which was spoken, So shall thy seed be. And being not weak in faith, he considered not his own body now dead, when he was about an hundred years old, neither yet the deadness of Sara's womb: He staggered not at the promise of God through unbelief; but was strong in faith, giving glory to God;" Romans 4:18-20 (KJV)*

In the middle of everything that is going on around you, give thanks no matter what the circumstances.

> *"In every thing give thanks: for this is the will of God in Christ Jesus concerning you." 1 Thessalonians 5:18 (KJV)*

Giving thanks is God's will for you. You won't be able to find His ultimate will for your life until you have cultivated a life of thanksgiving.

If you give thanks, you will experience multiplication.

> *"And out of them shall proceed thanksgiving and the voice of them that make merry: and I will multiply them, and they shall not be few; I will also glorify them, and they shall not be small." Jeremiah 30:19 (KJV)*

> *"From them will come thanksgiving and the sound of people celebrating. I will increase them; they will not be decreased; I will honor them; they will not be despised." Jeremiah 30:19 (Atarah)*

Thanksgiving is vital to expanding your capacity to receive from God. It should not be consigned to just Thanksgiving Day. God is a purposeful Being with a reason for desiring you to give thanks to Him—He desires to create a life of success, victory and fulfillment for you. Position yourself to receive more and more!

WHAT IT MEANS TO WALK IN THE SPIRIT

The "flesh" is the unrenewed, carnal mindset. Although the flesh includes the physical body, it is also a "central control system;" it is a way of thinking that tells your body what to do. The unseen flesh tells the physical flesh what to do.

Don't use the righteousness of God as an excuse to take advantage of fleshly or selfish opportunities.

> *"For, brethren, ye have been called unto liberty; only use not liberty for an occasion to the flesh, but by love serve*

*one another. For all the law is fulfilled in one word, even
in this; Thou shalt love thy neighbour as thyself. But
if ye bite and devour one another, take heed that ye be
not consumed one of another. This I say then, <u>Walk in
the Spirit, and ye shall not fulfil the lust of the flesh</u>."*
Galatians 5:13-16 (KJV)

The blessings of God are located in spiritual places; therefore, we must walk in the Spirit to tap into them.

*"Blessed be the God and Father of our Lord Jesus
Christ, <u>who hath blessed us with all spiritual blessings
in heavenly places in Christ</u>:" Ephesians 1:3 (KJV)*

The blessing is "God's supernatural ability on your natural ability;" it is the root to the fruit. Jesus has already blessed you. Meditating on, understanding, speaking and getting a revelation that you are blessed defeats that carnal mindset.

The "heavenly places" where the blessings are located are spiritual places. All of your blessings are located in the Spirit. You must walk in the Spirit to see supernatural results.

Jesus' words are spirit and life.

*"It is the spirit that quickeneth; the flesh profiteth
nothing: the words that I speak unto you, they are spirit,
and they are life." John 6:63 (KJV)*

The spirit of God quickens, or gives life to, the things you desire from God. <u>Jesus' words are the only things identified as spiritual</u>. If you are not in His Word, you are not in the Spirit. You will not be able to walk in the Spirit if you don't spend time reading, studying and acting on the Word of God.

You can't be spiritual without the Word of God; anything called "spiritual" that is not based on the Word of God is just being "spooky."

Walking in the Spirit = power, blessings and life; walking in the flesh = no profit, a curse and death.

Walking in the Spirit means that you first see within you what you believe, rather than believing what you see with your physical eyes.

God operating in your life comes from your walking in the Spirit.

Walking in the flesh opens you up to a curse, which is an empowerment to fail.

> *"Thus saith the LORD; Cursed be the man that trusteth in man, and maketh flesh his arm, and whose heart departeth from the LORD." Jeremiah 17:5 (KJV)*

The curse and the flesh go hand in hand; the flesh opens the door for Satan.

According to the Law, ingratitude also opens you up to the curse.

> *"I call heaven and earth to record this day against you, that I have set before you life and death, blessing and cursing: therefore choose life, that both thou and thy seed may live: That thou mayest love the LORD thy God, and that thou mayest obey his voice, and that thou mayest cleave unto him: for he is thy life, and the length of thy days: that thou mayest dwell in the land which the LORD sware unto thy fathers, to Abraham, to Isaac,*

*and to Jacob, to give them." Deuteronomy 30:19-20
(KJV)*

There is no honor in comparing yourself to others; there is no promotion in murmuring and complaining.

You are what you think you are; you can have what you think you can have.

> *"For as he thinketh in his heart, so is he: Eat and drink, saith he to thee; but his heart is not with thee." Proverbs 23:7 (KJV)*

> *"What he constantly thinks about is what goes to his subconscious mind (spirit) and this is what makes him the person he is. "Eat and drink!" he says to you, but his motives (what he has been constantly thinking about and that are now in his spirit) are not for your good. He will say something nice but won't mean a word of it." Proverbs 23:7 (Atarah)*

You are in a battle of words that are competing for residence in your mind. Everything starts in your thoughts. Don't accept the devil's suggestions; they are his most powerful weapons.

You'll never conquer anything until you conquer your thinking. You are spiritual or fleshy depending on your thought life. Walking in the flesh is a way of thinking; it is seeing yourself from man's point of view rather than from God's point of view. Fleshly thinking is a mindset that goes against the righteousness of God and the Word of God.

Strongholds exist in the mind; a stronghold is "a house made of thoughts." Don't try to use the flesh to pull down strongholds; you can't fight thoughts with thoughts.

> *"Now I Paul myself beseech you by the meekness and gentleness of Christ, who in presence am base among you, but being absent am bold toward you: But I beseech you, that I may not be bold when I am present with that confidence, wherewith I think to be bold against some, which think of us as if we walked according to the flesh. <u>For though we walk in the flesh, we do not war after the flesh: (For the weapons of our warfare are not carnal, but mighty through God to the pulling down of strong holds;) Casting down imaginations, and every high thing that exalteth itself against the knowledge of God, and bringing into captivity every thought to the obedience of Christ;</u> And having in a readiness to revenge all disobedience, when your obedience is fulfilled."* 2 Corinthians 10:1-6 (KJV)

Fight fleshy thoughts by speaking the Word of God (thoughts aren't spiritual, but the Word of God is).

The "flesh" is a mindset that is contrary to the Word of God. It will keep you from obtaining His blessings. If you are not in the Word, you are not in the Spirit. The way to keep from walking in the flesh, or an unrenewed mindset, is to walk in the Spirit.

WALKING IN THE SPIRIT VS.
WALKING IN THE FLESH

The blessings of God are located in the Spirit.

> "Blessed be the God and Father of our Lord Jesus Christ, <u>who hath blessed us with all spiritual</u> <u>blessings in heavenly places in Christ</u>:" Ephesians 1:3 (KJV)

Here we read in the Scriptures that God has <u>already</u> blessed you with all spiritual blessings.

The blessing is an ability that comes from God; it is His ability on your ability—His "super" on your "natural"—that enables you to do what you couldn't do before. There is a spiritual root to all physical manifestations. When you became born again, you received the root to everything that pertains to life and godliness in this physical world. Meditating on, understanding it, and getting a revelation of that along with speaking that you are blessed defeats the carnal mindset.

Jesus' words are spirit and life.

> "It is the spirit that quickeneth; the flesh profiteth nothing: the words that I speak unto you, they are spirit, and they are life." John 6:63 (KJV)

The Spirit of God quickens, or gives life to, the things you desire from God.

Walking in the Spirit is walking in agreement with the Word, which makes you spiritual. When you walk in the Spirit, you are on the path of life and experience supernatural results. When you walk in the Spirit, Satan has no access to you.

The only way to conquer the flesh is by walking in the Spirit.

> *"This I say then, Walk in the Spirit, and ye shall not fulfil the lust of the flesh." Galatians 5:16 (KJV)*

> *"Now the works of the flesh are manifest, which are these; Adultery, fornication, uncleanness, lasciviousness, Idolatry, witchcraft, hatred, variance, emulations, wrath, strife, seditions, heresies, Envyings, murders, drunkenness, revellings, and such like: of the which I tell you before, as I have also told you in time past, that they which do such things shall not inherit the kingdom of God." Galatians 5:19-21 (KJV)*

Fasting alone will not conquer the works of the flesh (of wrong thinking). Walking in the flesh is a mindset that is contrary to God and His Word. The flesh leads you away from manifestation, because it only understands what it sees and feels. The flesh equals no profit but a curse and death.

> *"Thus saith the LORD; Cursed be the man that trusteth in man, and maketh flesh his arm, and whose heart departeth from the LORD."*

You can choose life or you can choose death.

> *"I call heaven and earth to record this day against you, that I have set before you life and death, blessing and cursing: therefore choose life, that both thou and thy seed may live:" Deuteronomy 30:19 (KJV)*

When you have a carnal mindset, you go against your righteousness.

Right actions come from right thinking.

"For as he thinketh in his heart, so is he: Eat and drink, saith he to thee; but his heart is not with thee." Proverbs 23:7 (KJV)

"What he constantly thinks about is what goes to his subconscious mind (spirit) and this is what makes him the person he is. "Eat and drink!" he says to you, but his motives (what he has been constantly thinking about and that are now in his spirit) are not for your good. He will say something nice but won't mean a word of it." Proverbs 23:7 (Atarah)

Condemnation involves the flesh.

*"There is therefore now no condemnation to them which are in Christ Jesus, who walk not after the flesh, but after the Spirit. For the law of the Spirit of life in Christ Jesus hath made me free from the law of sin and death. For what the law could not do, in that it was weak through the flesh, God sending his own Son in the likeness of sinful flesh, and for sin, condemned sin in the flesh: That the righteousness of the law might be fulfilled in us, who walk not after the flesh, but after the Spirit. For they that are after the flesh **do mind** the things of the flesh; but they that are after the Spirit the things of the Spirit. <u>For to be carnally minded is death; but to be spiritually minded is life and peace</u>. Because the carnal mind is enmity against God: for it is not subject to the law of God, neither indeed can be. So then they that are in the flesh cannot please God. But ye are not in the flesh, but in the Spirit, if so be that the Spirit of God dwell in you.*

> *Now if any man have not the Spirit of Christ, he is none of his. And if Christ be in you, the body is dead because of sin; but the Spirit is life because of righteousness. But if the Spirit of him that raised up Jesus from the dead dwell in you, he that raised up Christ from the dead shall also quicken your mortal bodies by his Spirit that dwelleth in you. Therefore, brethren, we are debtors, not to the flesh, to live after the flesh. For if ye live after the flesh, ye shall die: but if ye through the Spirit do mortify the deeds of the body, ye shall live. For as many as are led by the Spirit of God, they are the sons of God." Romans 8:1-14 (KJV)*

The flesh does not submit to the laws of God. The Word of God will not work for a carnal minded believer. Sadly, most religions think like the world and yet try to live by the Word and still can't live by what they preach. Carnal minded people cannot please God.

Every believer is responsible for setting and changing his or her own mindset.

> *"If ye then be risen with Christ, seek those things which are above, where Christ sitteth on the right hand of God. Set your affection on things above, not on things on the earth." Colossians 3:1 (KJV)*

Your thoughts must be set on things that are higher than the things of the world.

Right actions won't change wrong thinking. However, right thinking will change your actions.

To receive more from God, you must do your part, which involves walking in the Spirit. Failure to change your mindset by aligning your thoughts with His Word will cause you to miss out on all that God wants to do in your life.

WINNING THE BATTLE BY RENEWING THE MIND

People are products of their thoughts. You are what you continually think.

> *"For as he thinketh in his heart, so is he: Eat and drink, saith he to thee; but his heart is not with thee." Proverbs 23:7 (KJV)*

You change your life by changing your mindset. Right thinking precedes right actions.

There are two sources of thoughts—God and Satan. Satan's greatest weapon is suggestion.

The devil wants you to worry and to think outside of God's Word so that he can gain access to your life. Do not allow him to gain a foothold.

> *"Neither give place to the devil." Ephesians 4:27 (KJV)*

An empty mind or one that hasn't been renewed with the Word, will give place to the devil.

Your thoughts determine your destiny.

Take hold of your thought life so that your life can be changed.

It is the premeditated thoughts that come from inside a person that defile them —those things on which their mind dwells; what they constantly think about.

> *"For from within, out of the heart of men, proceed evil thoughts, adulteries, fornications, murders, Thefts, covetousness, wickedness, deceit, lasciviousness, an evil eye, blasphemy, pride, foolishness: All these evil things come from within, and defile the man." Mark 7:21-23 (KJV)*

Notice the Bible says "...out of the heart", which means its not just a passing thought. Its something that you've let grow and take root inside of you, which only comes through meditation.

If you continue dwelling on the past, it will hinder your future. Feed your heart and mind with the right things so that your thoughts will line up properly with the Word of God.

What you meditate on is the source of your actions. For example: A person doesn't just wake up one morning and ask for a divorce. Divorce was a thought that had been nourished, nurtured and meditated on for a long time.

You need to develop the spirit from within. God wants you to hear Him-- the more time that you spend in the Word of God, the better you will be able to hear His voice.

God wants you to think from the source: His Word. When you take your mind off of God, you will fall. Adam and Eve fell when they took their minds off of God (Genesis 3).

Everything in life begins as a thought; it's a seed.

You can win the battle over your mind each and every time. Put off your old ways of thinking, and then set your mind and affection on higher things.

> *"That ye put off concerning the former conversation the old man, which is corrupt according to the deceitful lusts; And be renewed in the spirit of your mind; And that ye put on the new man, which after God is created in righteousness and true holiness." Ephesians 4:22-24 (KJV)*

> *"Set your affection on things above, not on things on the earth." Colossians 3:2 (KJV)*

> *"For which things' sake the wrath of God cometh on the children of disobedience: In the which ye also walked some time, when ye lived in them. But now ye also put off all these; anger, wrath, malice, blasphemy, filthy communication out of your mouth. Lie not one to another, seeing that ye have put off the old man with his deeds; And have put on the new man, which is renewed in knowledge after the image of him that created him: Colossians 3:6-10 (KJV)*

Rid yourself of fear, as it gives Satan access to your mind.

> *"For God hath not given us the spirit of fear; but of power, and of love, and of a sound mind." 2 Timothy 1:7 (KJV)*

Fear is an enemy of God; it is designed to get your thoughts off God. Be perfected in God's love, because perfected love casts out fear.

> *"There is no fear in love; but perfect love casteth out fear: because fear hath torment. He that feareth is not made perfect in love." 1 John 4:18 (KJV)*

Develop a sound, or disciplined, mind. An undisciplined mind is one whose thoughts wander; it is unstable. Concentrate on what you are doing. A disciplined mind is not easily confused.

A mind that is focused on the Word of God leads to perfect peace (Philippians 4:5-8).

> *"Thou wilt keep him in perfect peace, whose mind is stayed on thee: because he trusteth in thee. Trust ye in the LORD for ever: for in the LORD JEHOVAH is everlasting strength:" Isaiah 26:3-4 (KJV)*

> *"Let your moderation be known unto all men. The Lord is at hand. Be careful for nothing; but in every thing by prayer and supplication with thanksgiving let your requests be made known unto God. And the peace of God, which passeth all understanding, shall keep your hearts and minds through Christ Jesus. Finally, brethren, whatsoever things are true, whatsoever things are honest, whatsoever things are just, whatsoever things are pure, whatsoever things are lovely, whatsoever things are of good report; if there be any virtue, and if there be any praise, think on these things." Philippians 4:5-8 (KJV)*

Be aggressive in casting down evil thoughts with the Word. Study, listen to and speak the Word daily.

The mind is the control center of your life; it determines your destiny. By taking every thought captive and aligning your thoughts with God's way of thinking (which is His Word), you will walk in continuous victory.

CONQUERING AND OVERCOMING THE FLESH

In Matthew 26:36-41, Jesus identifies the flesh as a problem because it is weak. Many believers blame the devil for all the trouble in their lives, when in fact it is their worldly, sinful mindsets that are responsible. The fruit of anything, including sin, begins with a thought seed. The devil is happy to let you blame him because as long as you think he is responsible for all your problems, he can keep you defeated.

It is not God's design for you to conquer Satan—He has already defeated him.

> "And you, being dead in your sins and the uncircumcision of your flesh, hath he quickened together with him, having forgiven you all trespasses; Blotting out the handwriting of ordinances that was against us, which was contrary to us, and took it out of the way, nailing it to his cross; *And having spoiled principalities and powers, he made a shew of them openly, triumphing over them in it.*" *Colossians 2:13-15 (KJV)*

It is God's design for you to conquer your flesh.

To blame the devil for your problems instead of your carnal mindset is contrary to the Word—doing so makes you guilty of walking in the flesh.

All power and authority to rule in heaven and on earth has been given to Jesus. Satan has no access to your life when your thinking lines up with the Word of God.

You can't manifest the fruit of the Spirit without having the mindset of the Spirit; you can't experience the works of the flesh without a mindset of the flesh.

> *"For they that are after the flesh do mind the things of the flesh; but they that are after the Spirit the things of the Spirit." Romans 8:5 (KJV)*

You cannot walk in the Spirit without the Word of God, because the Word is Spirit and life.

> *"It is the spirit that quickeneth; the flesh profiteth nothing: the words that I speak unto you, they are spirit, and they are life." John 6:63 (KJV)*

Walking in the Word is what makes you spiritual. When you try to be spiritual without the Word, you are just being "spooky".

Walking in the Spirit is a way of thinking that lines up with God and His Word, while the flesh is a way of thinking that lines up with the devil and the world's way of thinking.

The flesh always opposes the Word of God. The flesh opposes your righteousness by saying you're just "a sinner saved by grace."

If you don't become diligent and get in the Word, you will be a carnal minded believer.

You have a choice of walking in the Word—which produces profit, blessings and life—or walking in flesh—which leads to no profit, the curse and death.

Right actions can't change wrong thinking, but right thinking changes wrong actions.

The blueprint for your life is comprised of how you think; your thoughts are your plans.

> "For as he thinketh in his heart, so is he: Eat and drink, saith he to thee; but his heart is not with thee." Proverbs 23:7 (KJV)

God has thoughts and plans for your welfare, success and peace in life.

> "For I know the thoughts that I think toward you, saith the LORD, thoughts of peace, and not of evil, to give you an expected end." Jeremiah 29:11 (KJV)

You must rid yourself of those things and people that challenge your decision to live by the Word—how can two walk together unless they agree?

> "Can two walk together, except they be agreed?" Amos 3:3 (KJV)

Surround yourself with people who think in line with the Word and who agree with your success.

The results of your blueprint may not come right away; but eventually, if you follow those plans with precise attention to detail, they will manifest.

When you set your mind to a way of thinking, that mindset then commands the chemicals in your body to line up with it—thus directing your body toward healing or sickness.

The key to achieving a mindset is leaving it set where you chose to set it.

Walking in the Spirit is what conquers walking in the flesh.

> "This I say then, Walk in the Spirit, and ye shall not fulfil the lust of the flesh." Galatians 5:16 (KJV)

Religion has said that you must stop negative actions before you can act on the Word; that you must act right for God to bless and accept you. The Word of God says that if you think in line with the Word it will stop negative actions. If you deal with the root to the action, the action dies. Jesus cursed the fig tree from the root and the tree died; when you deal with the root, the fruit dies.

> "And when he saw a fig tree in the way, he came to it, and found nothing thereon, but leaves only, and said unto it, Let no fruit grow on thee henceforward for ever. And presently the fig tree withered away." Matthew 21:19 (KJV)

A person can only change by renewing his mind.

> "I beseech you therefore, brethren, by the mercies of God, that ye present your bodies a living sacrifice, holy, acceptable unto God, which is your reasonable service. And be not conformed to this world: but be ye transformed **by the renewing of your mind**, that

ye may prove what is that good, and acceptable, and perfect, will of God." Romans 12:1-2 (KJV)

You must renew your mindset according to God's Word to prove the will of God for your life.

For you to think of yourself as superior or inferior is to walk in the flesh, because the Word says to be sober in your thinking. You must see yourself as God sees you.

> *"For I say, through the grace given unto me, to every man that is among you, not to think of himself more highly than he ought to think; but to think soberly, according as God hath dealt to every man the measure of faith." Romans 12:3 (KJV)*

> *"I say, through the grace (unmerited love, favor and empowerment) given to me, to every man that is among you, do not think of yourself more highly than you ought to think; but **think** <u>soberly</u> (not intoxicated with a wrong way of thinking), think according to the Word of God – as <u>God has dealt to every man the same amount of the Word of God to analyze and assimilate into your way of thinking</u>." Romans 12:3 (Atarah)*

To think soberly is to think in line with the Word of God.

A man changes his ways by changing his thoughts.

> *"Ho, <u>every one that thirsteth,</u> come ye to the waters, and he that hath no money; come ye, buy, and eat; yea, come, **buy** wine and milk without money and without price. Wherefore do ye spend money for that which is*

not bread? and your labour for that which satisfieth not? hearken diligently unto me, and eat ye that which is good, and let your soul delight itself in fatness. Incline your ear, and come unto me: hear, and your soul shall live; and I will make an everlasting covenant with you, even the sure mercies of David. Behold, I have given him for a witness to the people, a leader and commander to the people. Behold, thou shalt call a nation that thou knowest not, and nations that knew not thee shall run unto thee because of the LORD thy God, and for the Holy One of Israel; for he hath glorified thee. Seek ye the LORD while he may be found, call ye upon him while he is near: Let the wicked forsake his way, and the unrighteous man his thoughts: and let him return unto the LORD, and he will have mercy upon him; and to our God, for he will abundantly pardon. For my thoughts are not your thoughts, neither are your ways my ways, saith the LORD. For as the heavens are higher than the earth, so are my ways higher than your ways, and my thoughts than your thoughts. For as the rain cometh down, and the snow from heaven, and returneth not thither, but watereth the earth, and maketh it bring forth and bud, that it may give seed to the sower, and bread to the eater: So shall my word be that goeth forth out of my mouth: it shall not return unto me void, but it shall accomplish that which I please, and it shall prosper in the thing whereto I sent it. Isaiah 55:1-11 (KJV)

Change and success will only take place for those who are thirsty and crave them (verse 1). These things can take place in your life without money when your soul, or mind, thinks prosperity (verse 2). Your thinking determines whether your soul is dead or alive (verse 3). The wicked man forsakes his ways by changing his wicked thoughts and obtaining God's thoughts (verse 7).

The Bible is seed for thought. When you get His Word, you get His thoughts; when you get His thoughts, you get His ways that produce results and lead to the "high" way. No Word equals no high thoughts and no "highway."

Satan's words produce thoughts that produce his ways, and God's Word produces thoughts that produce His ways. You make your way prosperous, deal wisely and have good success by getting in the Word and meditating on it until it becomes your constant thought. This produces God's higher ways of success.

> *"Moses my servant is dead; now therefore arise, go over this Jordan, thou, and all this people, unto the land which I do give to them, even to the children of Israel."*
> *Joshua 1:2 (KJV)*

> *"This book of the law shall not depart out of thy mouth; but thou shalt meditate therein day and night, that thou mayest observe to do according to all that is written therein: for then thou shalt make thy way prosperous, and then thou shalt have good success." Joshua 1:8 (KJV)*

Don't look for the world to agree with your higher way of thinking; it cannot understand God's ways.

God will do exceedingly above what you ask or think according to the power that is at work within you.

> *"Now unto him that is able to do exceeding abundantly*
> *above all that we ask or think, according to the power*
> *that worketh in us," Ephesians 3:20 (KJV)*

The power of God that is at work in you is the love of God that was poured in you by the Holy Spirit.

> *"And hope maketh not ashamed; because the love of God*
> *is shed abroad in our hearts by the Holy Ghost which is*
> *given unto us." Romans 5:5 (KJV)*

Love thinks no evil; God can't produce an evil thought.

> *"Doth not behave itself unseemly, seeketh not her own,*
> *is not easily provoked, thinketh no evil;" 1 Corinthians*
> *13:5 (KJV)*

Paul said that he spoke and understood as a carnal, selfish, fleshy child because he thought as a child—but when He matured in love and put away selfish, childish thinking, He became a man and his world changed.

> *"When I was a child, I spake as a child, I understood as*
> *a child, I thought as a child: but when I became a man,*
> *I put away childish things." 1 Corinthians 13:11 (KJV)*

When your thoughts get in line with the power of love at work within you, then God will do what you think because you now carry His plan (Ephesians 3:20).

God is committed to His thoughts and plans for your life. When you begin to think His thoughts and take hold of His plans for peace, prosperity and deliverance, then you have His covenant guarantee that He will bring His plans to full fruition in your life.

> *"The LORD of hosts hath sworn, saying, Surely as I*
> *have thought, so shall it come to pass; and as I have*
> *purposed, so shall it stand:" Isaiah 14:24 (KJV)*

If you find His thoughts and plans for your life in the Word, then think on and develop them in your mind. You have His covenant guarantee that He will do exceedingly above all that you dare ask, think, desire, hope or dream.

God dares you to think in line with His Word and to agree with Him, because He wants to change your world and make a mark that can never be erased!

Most people try to change their lives by changing their actions. While this may work for a short period of time, lasting change comes only when one changes his way of thinking (his mindset). Only the person who forsakes his old mindset and takes on the thoughts of God will walk in the will of God for his life and have good success.

STEPS TO WALKING IN THE SPIRIT

You have been called to liberty, but you should not use your freedom as an incentive to sin.

> *"For, brethren, ye have been called unto liberty; only use*
> *not liberty for an occasion to the flesh, but by love serve*
> *one another." Galatians 5:13 (KJV)*

When you intentionally sin and rely on God's forgiveness, you defeat yourself; <u>what you practice doing determines what you become</u>. Don't fornicate or curse someone out just because you know you're the righteousness of God and are eligible to receive forgiveness.

Instead of giving place to the flesh, you should serve others (Galatians 5:13). You fulfill the entirety of the law when you love your neighbor as you love yourself.

> *"For all the law is fulfilled in one word, even in this; Thou shalt love thy neighbour as thyself."*
> *Galatians 5:14 (KJV)*

Your born-again spirit is in competition with your flesh for control of your life.

> *"But if ye bite and devour one another, take heed that ye be not consumed one of another. This I say then, Walk in the Spirit, and ye shall not fulfil the lust of the flesh. For the flesh lusteth against the Spirit, and the Spirit against the flesh: and these are contrary the one to the other: so that ye cannot do the things that ye would. But if ye be led of the Spirit, ye are not under the law. Now the works of the flesh are manifest, which are these; Adultery, fornication, uncleanness, lasciviousness, Idolatry, witchcraft, hatred, variance, emulations, wrath, strife, seditions, heresies, Envyings, murders, drunkenness, revellings, and such like: of the which I tell you before, as I have also told you in time past, that they which do such things shall not inherit the kingdom of God. But the fruit of the Spirit is love, joy, peace, longsuffering, gentleness, goodness, faith, Meekness, temperance: against such there is no law. And they that are Christ's have crucified the flesh with the affections and lusts."*
> *Galatians 5:15-24 (KJV)*

Every work of the flesh, as well as every fruit of the Spirit, begins with a thought. Your mind is the control center, or central processing center, of your human body. Your life is the sum total of how you think. Walking in the flesh is a mindset aligned with the world; walking in the Spirit is a mindset aligned with God's Word. You can't manifest the fruit of the Spirit without having the mindset of the Spirit; you can't experience the works of the flesh without a mindset of the flesh.

You think about fornication before actually committing the act. You think about loving others before you actually love them.

When you walk in the Spirit, you won't fulfill the lust of the flesh (verse 16).

You can't be spiritual without the Word of God.

You can't walk in the Spirit without the Word, because the Word is Spirit and life.

> *"It is the spirit that quickeneth; the flesh profiteth nothing: the words that I speak unto you, they are spirit, and they are life." John 6:63 (KJV)*

Living according to the Word is what makes you spiritual. When you try to be spiritual without the Word, you are just being "spooky."

Any way of thinking that doesn't align with the Word is walking in the flesh. This includes traditional religious doctrines. Daily study of the Bible is vital—your potential for walking in the Spirit is directly linked to your understanding of the Word.

> *"Study to shew thyself approved unto God, a workman that needeth not to be ashamed, rightly dividing the word of truth." 2 Timothy 2:15 (KJV)*

If you never read your Bible, then the only potential you have is to walk in the flesh.

You will only prosper and be in health to the degree that your soul prospers in these areas.

> "Beloved, I wish above all things that thou mayest prosper and be in health, even as thy soul prospereth."
> 3 John 1:2 (KJV)

You are made up of three parts: spirit, soul and body. You are a spirit, you possess a soul and you live in a body.

Your life is a production of your thoughts. If you don't have thoughts of health, prosperity and increase on your mind, you will never have those things in your life. Your thoughts are the plans (or blueprints) for your life. If you want to change your life, you must change the way you think. Generational curses, such as poverty and sickness in your family, will only be broken when you change the way you think about them.

God's ways are the highest ways. To walk in His ways, you must discover His thoughts from the Bible.

> "Let the wicked forsake his way, and the unrighteous man his thoughts: and let him return unto the LORD, and he will have mercy upon him; and to our God, for he will abundantly pardon. For my thoughts are not your thoughts, neither are your ways my ways, saith the LORD." Isaiah 55:7-8 (KJV)

God has a thousand ways to straighten out your marriage, help you raise your children and get you out of debt; however, as long as you continue to think according to the world, you place yourself outside of His ways.

God knows that you can't get His ways without first exchanging your thoughts with those that align with His Word. Many believers allow their thinking to be influenced by unsaved friends, talk shows, TV and movies that don't line up with the Word.

Satan's words produce thoughts that produce his ways; God's Word produces thoughts that produce His ways. God sent His Word so that you can think like He does and live His way.

Within your mind, God's Word and the devil's words battle for influence and control.

The devil tests you with sinful suggestions to see if he can control you; he knows that your thoughts govern your life.

He uses words in songs and images in the media to influence you, gain access to your thinking and use your body to express himself through you. He wants to see if you will accept and nourish his thoughts or cast them down.

Although a born-again believer can't be demon-possessed, they can be demon oppressed if they allow their thinking to be influenced by the devil.

Words from the devil were what produced devilish thoughts that delivered sin into the world. Sin could never have entered in if Adam and Eve had not received his words that produced his thoughts.

God established that only those with a physical body would have authority on earth; He then gave that authority to Adam. When Adam sinned, he forfeited his power; Satan took control of everything up to the throne of God.

God made a way to bring Jesus into the earth legally so that He could restore man's authority. The Old Testament is a covenant of words intended to produce thoughts that would one day become the flesh-- Who has all authority—Jesus Christ.

God sent an angel to Mary to deliver His Word. When she aligned her thinking to it by saying, "Be it unto me according to thy Word" (Luke 1:38), a way opened up and God stepped through her womb into a "legal earth suit."

God's Word will produce the path for you to reach success in every area of your life, receive your healing or become delivered from drugs; but you must first align your thinking with it.

There are practical steps for walking in the Spirit versus walking in the flesh. You must be aware of the conflict that you are in. <u>Your born-again spirit and your flesh are battling for control of your life</u>. You can use God's Word to cast down Satan's words, because God's Word is mighty!

> "*Casting down imaginations, and every high thing that exalteth itself against the knowledge of God, and bringing into captivity every thought to the obedience of Christ;*" 2 Corinthians 10:5 (KJV)

When you sin, don't punish your body—it's not the problem. Your fleshy way of thinking is what needs to be disciplined with the Word.

You must put first things first. If you want to conquer the lust of the flesh, walk in the Spirit by setting your mind on the Word first.

"For the flesh lusteth against the Spirit, and the Spirit against the flesh: and these are contrary the one to the other: so that ye cannot do the things that ye would."
Galatians 5:17 (KJV)

The religious world says you must be perfect before you come to God or attend church, but that is not what the Word of God says. <u>If you could stop sinning by yourself, you would have no need for God</u>. God knew you needed help to overcome sin—that's why He says, "Come to Me first."

Religion says to stop sinning first, and then the Holy Spirit will come in to empower you to overcome; but the Word of God says to align your thinking with the Word first for change to come.

The light of God's Word, not religious foolishness, always overcomes darkness.

"The entrance of thy words giveth light; it giveth understanding unto the simple." Psalm 119:130 (KJV)

Your flesh (carnal mindset) is in constant conflict with your born-again spirit for control of your life, and your mind is the battleground. When you recognize that you're in a war for your thought life and purpose to align your thinking with God's Word, you begin your march toward victory.

WHO IS THE HOLY SPIRIT?

Who is the Holy Spirit? The Holy Spirit is not an emotion or other outward manifestation such as "falling out." His presence will affect your emotions, because humans are emotional beings.

He is the Third Person of the Trinity, the personality in the order of the Godhead. He is in charge of the affairs of the kingdom of God and is the Chief Executor of divine programs on the earth. He is the Motivator, Energizer and Operator of every revealed plan or vision from God. He is the Revealer of the hidden treasures of the kingdom of God. He holds the key to the inheritance of the saints of God. He is the most valuable asset to a believer. He is the central figure in any breakthrough in life and is the only One worth leaning on.

The Holy Spirit's job is to reveal the sonship of God's people. He is the Spirit of Truth and has been sent to reveal the mind of God to those who are born again.

> *"I have yet many things to say unto you, but ye cannot bear them now. Howbeit when he, the Spirit of truth, is come, he will guide you into all truth: for he shall not speak of himself; but whatsoever he shall hear, that shall he speak: and he will shew you things to come." John 16:12-13 (KJV)*

If you are not born again, all He will point out to you is that you need to be. He has come to reveal wisdom, knowledge, abilities, enablements and mysteries to you to show you your significance, value and power. He wants to reveal your God-nature to you and cause you to live on a higher level than you are living now.

The Holy Spirit is a real Person with Whom you must develop a real relationship. He's your invisible Partner, giving you inside information. He'll cause things to work for you that won't work for others.

He can tell you about your future and straighten out your past; the key to these benefits is your realizing that He is a real Person. Just because He is invisible, it doesn't mean He's not real. For example:

You can't see the wind, but you can feel and see its effects. You should be going to Him for the plan for your life instead of coming up with a plan yourself and expect Him to sign off on it.

You must develop such an awareness of His presence that you can't wake up in the morning without saying "Good morning, Holy Spirit," or go for too long without talking with Him intimately. You must practice the presence of the Holy Spirit.

People may think you are crazy for talking to Someone they can't see, but you must move past that. The world can't receive Him, because they don't know Him and can't see Him.

> *"Even the Spirit of truth; whom the world cannot receive, because it seeth him not, neither knoweth him: but ye know him; for he dwelleth with you, and shall be in you."*
> *John 14:17 (KJV)*

He has a way of confirming His presence; you'll know He's there. The Holy Spirit can make the difference in your life. He's sent to comfort you.

The Holy Spirit has four main attributes. The Holy Spirit is the oil of joy.

> *"To appoint unto them that mourn in Zion, to give unto them beauty for ashes, the oil of joy for mourning, the garment of praise for the spirit of heaviness; that they might be called trees of righteousness, the planting of the LORD, that he might be glorified." Isaiah 61:3 (KJV)*

You cannot be filled with the Holy Spirit and not have joy in your life, because He literally injects the believer with joy and gladness.

This joy and gladness are supernatural and build your immunity to sickness and disease; however, you must learn to "let things go." Cast your cares on God. Joy comes from what you know from the Word of God. The more you comprehend God's Word, the more the Holy Spirit can instruct, minister and reveal to you; He compares spiritual things with spiritual things.

The love of God that was poured into your heart determines your access to revelation (enlightenment and direction); your access is based on your love walk.

> "And hope maketh not ashamed; because the love of God is shed abroad in our hearts by the Holy Ghost which is given unto us." Romans 5:5 (KJV)

If you continue to walk in selfishness, you hinder the Holy Spirit from speaking to you and you remain "stuck" in "average," having no results from the Word. If you have a grievance between you and someone else, you need to set it straight. The Spirit of God is grieved when there is envy, bitterness, strife and unforgiveness. They prevent Him from giving you the answers you need for your life. You must get your feelings under subjection to the Word. Love is the platform on which the laws and commandments function.

When you are anointed with the Holy Spirit, you enter into a higher dimension of praise. When you thank and praise God, giving Him the glory, the Holy Spirit comes in and elevates your praise.

> "He shall glorify me: for he shall receive of mine, and shall shew it unto you." John 16:14 (KJV)

High praise is always followed by supernatural intervention.

*"And at midnight Paul and Silas prayed, and sang praises
unto God: and the prisoners heard them. And suddenly
there was a great earthquake, so that the foundations of
the prison were shaken: and immediately all the doors
were opened, and every one's bands were loosed."*
Acts 16:25-26 (KJV)

When you enter into high praise, God comes in and sets an ambush against your enemies and conquers them.

*"Let the high praises of God be in their mouth, and a
twoedged sword in their hand;" Psalm 149:6 (KJV)*

*"And when they began to sing and to praise, the LORD
set ambushments against the children of Ammon, Moab,
and mount Seir, which were come against Judah; and
they were smitten." 2 Chronicles 20:22 (KJV)*

When you praise God in the "high praise dimension," the heavens will intervene and render the right judgment on your enemies, not even allowing them to speak negatively against you. (2 Samuel 6:14-23)

High praise is a fundamental requirement for God to take over so that you can become a reporter of your own battle.

When the Holy Spirit shows up, so does favor. When you carry the anointing of the Holy Spirit, your name is sweet and creates an expectation; you'll "smell good" to God and enjoy love and favor from others.

*"Because of the savour of thy good ointments thy name
is as ointment poured forth, therefore do the virgins love
thee." Song of Songs 1:3 (KJV)*

"The odor of your ointments is fragrant; your name is like perfume poured out. Therefore, everyone loves you."
Song of Songs 1:3 (Atarah)

You walk in the favor of God and in the comfort of the Holy Spirit.

"Let not mercy and truth forsake thee: bind them about thy neck; write them upon the table of thine heart: So shalt thou find favour and good understanding in the sight of God and man." Proverbs 3:3-4 (KJV)

Favor means, "to treat with high regard and approval; something granted out of good will rather than for payment or justice; a gift bestowed and not necessarily earned or bought; a token of love or friendship; preferential treatment provided with advantages and special privileges." When you acknowledge God's favor, it motivates Him to favor you even more. Favor from the Lord guarantees success. Therefore, believe that you receive success, comfort and ease from now on.

There are 10 benefits that the favor of God produces in your life through the Holy Spirit.

1. Supernatural increase and promotion.
2. Supernatural restoration of everything the Enemy has stolen.
3. Honor in the midst of your adversaries.
4. Increased assets, especially in the area of real estate (Deuteronomy 33:23; Deuteronomy 6:11-12).
5. Great victories in the midst of great impossibilities.
6. Recognition when you're least likely to receive it.
7. Prominence and preferential treatment.
8. Petitions granted by ungodly civil authorities.

9. Policies, rules and regulations changed/reversed to your advantage.
10. Battles won that you didn't even have to fight.

The Holy Spirit has come to guide you into the truths that you are a child of the Most High God and that you should settle for nothing less than God's best. As you develop your relationship with Him and allow Him to anoint your praise, you will experience favor with God and with man.

THE HOLY SPIRIT AND HIS ABILITY TO GET RESULTS

The Holy Spirit is the believer's key to power. Power is the "ability to get results". The day you became born again, the Holy Spirit was poured into your heart, planting a "power seed" within you.

> *"And hope maketh not ashamed; because the love of God is shed abroad in our hearts by the Holy Ghost which is given unto us." Romans 5:5 (KJV)*

When the Holy Spirit comes on you, you have power, ability, efficiency and might. With this power, you become the evidence of the Word and can demonstrate God's power to others.

> *"But ye shall receive power, after that the Holy Ghost is come upon you: and ye shall be witnesses unto me both in Jerusalem, and in all Judaea, and in Samaria, and unto the uttermost part of the earth." Acts 1:8 (KJV)*

You have an endowment that makes you a partaker of God's power. Don't be deceived into thinking that your ability can outdo the Holy Spirit's.

When Jesus was baptized, the Holy Spirit descended on Him. Only then was He able to get results in His ministry.

> *"Now when all the people were baptized, it came to pass, that Jesus also being baptized, and praying, the heaven was opened, And the Holy Ghost descended in a bodily shape like a dove upon him, and a voice came from heaven, which said, Thou art my beloved Son; in thee I am well pleased." Luke 3:21-22 (KJV)*

> *"And Jesus returned in the power of the Spirit into Galilee: and there went out a fame of him through all the region round about. And he taught in their synagogues, being glorified of all." Luke 4:14-15 (KJV)*

The Holy Spirit helps you to operate in God's capacity. He has come to make you a living testimony of God's glory and power.

The Holy Spirit empowers believers to live the Word. Peter denied Jesus three times, but after the Holy Spirit came on him, he boldly preached about Jesus—even when he was told not to.

> *"Be it known unto you all, and to all the people of Israel, that by the name of Jesus Christ of Nazareth, whom ye crucified, whom God raised from the dead, even by him doth this man stand here before you whole." Acts 4:10 (KJV)*

> *"But Peter and John answered and said unto them, Whether it be right in the sight of God to hearken unto you more than unto God, judge ye. For we cannot but speak the things which we have seen and heard." Acts 4:19-20 (KJV)*

The Holy Spirit is not optional to living a fruitful life. The Holy Spirit works in a believer's life in three stages.

> *"The hand of the LORD was upon me, and carried me out in the spirit of the LORD, and set me down in the midst of the valley which was full of bones, And caused me to pass by them round about: and, behold, there were very many in the open valley; and, lo, they were very dry. And he said unto me, Son of man, can these bones live? And I answered, O Lord GOD, thou knowest. Again he said unto me, Prophesy upon these bones, and say unto them, O ye dry bones, hear the word of the LORD. Thus saith the Lord GOD unto these bones; Behold, I will cause breath to enter into you, and ye shall live: And I will lay sinews upon you, and will bring up flesh upon you, and cover you with skin, and put breath in you, and ye shall live; and ye shall know that I am the LORD. So I prophesied as I was commanded: and as I prophesied, there was a noise, and behold a shaking, and the bones came together, bone to his bone. And when I beheld, lo, the sinews and the flesh came up upon them, and the skin covered them above: but there was no breath in them. Then said he unto me, Prophesy unto the wind, prophesy, son of man, and say to the wind, Thus saith the Lord GOD; Come from the four winds, O breath, and breathe upon these slain, that they may live. So I prophesied as he commanded me, and the breath came into them, and they lived, and stood up upon their feet, an exceeding great army." Ezekiel 37:1-10 (KJV)*

1) Bone returning to bone is the first stage. Ezekiel witnessed dry bones coming together. The Holy Spirit draws men to repentance, gathering them to God.

2) The second stage involves flesh and sinews coming together and rejoining the bone. When Ezekiel spoke to the bones, they were again covered with flesh and sinews. You reconnect to God. Form is given to what was previously scattered.

3) The third stage is the breath of life and power. The form still needs the breath of the Holy Spirit to have power or ability. Many Believers have the form of God, but no power.

There are hindrances to the Holy Spirit's operation.

1) Grieving, or quenching, the Holy Spirit will stop Him from moving in your life. Don't quench, or put out, the Holy Spirit.

> *"Quench not the Spirit." 1 Thessalonians 5:19 (KJV)*

You can grieve or suppress the Holy Spirit by holding on to bitterness, unforgiveness, wrath, anger and evil speaking; in other words, by refusing to walk in the love of God.

> *"And grieve not the holy Spirit of God, whereby ye are sealed unto the day of redemption. Let all bitterness, and wrath, and anger, and clamour, and evil speaking, be put away from you, with all malice: And be ye kind one to another, tenderhearted, forgiving one another, even as God for Christ's sake hath forgiven you." Ephesians 4:30-32 (KJV)*

2) Refusing to walk in love will block the Holy Spirit. Be kind to others, even when they aren't kind to you. God has forgiven you of so much more, so how can you not forgive?

3) Sin and wrong associations will hinder the work of the Holy Spirit in your life. Witness and minister to the unsaved, but don't become

their companions by "hanging out" with them. A companion of fools will be a fool.

> "He that walketh with wise men shall be wise: but a companion of fools shall be destroyed." Proverbs 13:20 (KJV)

Those who are friends with the world are enemies of God; you can't be a companion of the world and expect to commune with the Holy Spirit.

> "Ye adulterers and adulteresses, know ye not that the friendship of the world is enmity with God? whosoever therefore will be a friend of the world is the enemy of God." James 4:4 (KJV)

The Holy Spirit is not an emotion. He is the third Person of the Godhead. He infuses each believer with the power necessary to live a successful and fruitful life. Power, which is the ability to get results, is available to every believer by way of the Holy Spirit, Who helps believers to operate in God's capacity on the earth.

THE MINISTRY OF THE HOLY SPIRIT

The Spirit that raised Jesus from the grave dwells in you.

> "But if the Spirit of him that raised up Jesus from the dead dwell in you, he that raised up Christ from the dead shall also quicken your mortal bodies by his Spirit that dwelleth in you." Romans 8:11 (KJV)

The Holy Spirit causes your mortal body to become supernaturally alive to God. The Spirit of God lives inside of you. Evidence of your acknowledgment of His presence can be determined by your behavior. Fellowship with your unseen Partner causes His power to flow in your life. You cannot live a Spirit-filled life without the ministry of the Holy Spirit. He is grieved when you ignore Him.

Jesus baptizes with the Holy Spirit and with fire.

> *"I indeed baptize you with water unto repentance: but he that cometh after me is mightier than I, whose shoes I am not worthy to bear: he shall baptize you with the Holy Ghost, and with fire:" Matthew 3:11 (KJV)*

When you became born again, you received both the Holy Spirit and fire. Fire has a purifying, cleansing and sweeping affect. Anything that doesn't glorify God will be burned with unquenchable fire. The conviction you feel when ungodly things are present in your life is the Holy Spirit letting you know that He is present, fanning the fire in your life. Your refusal to pay attention quenches the Spirit. When He is quenched, His power and fire depart from you.

The Holy Spirit guides you into all truth.

> *"I have yet many things to say unto you, but ye cannot bear them now. Howbeit when he, the Spirit of truth, is come, he will guide you into all truth: for he shall not speak of himself; but whatsoever he shall hear, that shall he speak: and he will shew you things to come." John 16:12-13 (KJV)*

He is the truth-giving Spirit, Who guides you in every area of life. The Spirit of Truth knows all things and wants to give you knowledge. Many believers are destroyed for a lack of knowledge.

*"My people are destroyed for lack of knowledge: because
thou hast rejected knowledge, I will also reject thee, that
thou shalt be no priest to me: seeing thou hast forgotten
the law of thy God, I will also forget thy children." Hosea
4:6 (KJV)*

The Holy Spirit wants to make sure that you are never destroyed. If you engage the help of the Holy Spirit and submit to Him, He will show you things to come.

The Comforter reminds you of what you have been taught.

*"But the Comforter, which is the Holy Ghost, whom
the Father will send in my name, he shall teach you
all things, and bring all things to your remembrance,
whatsoever I have said unto you." John 14:26 (KJV)*

He will remind you of the Word that you have stored inside of you at the very time that you need it.

When you acknowledge Him, you will have a solution to every problem. You need the assistance and guidance of the Holy Spirit to experience fruitful increase in your life.

The Holy Spirit reproves the world of sin, righteousness and judgment. The Holy Spirit convicts you when you revert back to your old sinful nature.

You are empowered to walk in righteousness through the Holy Spirit's ministry. If you are still interested in ungodly or unhealthy things, ask the Holy Spirit to reprove you and empower you to walk in His righteousness.

*"And when he is come, he will reprove the world of sin,
and of righteousness, and of judgment:" John 16:8 (KJV)*

He establishes the judgment of the world through believers. You have
the authority to judge and condemn ungodly behavior.

*"No weapon that is formed against thee shall prosper;
and every tongue that shall rise against thee in judgment
thou shalt condemn. This is the heritage of the servants
of the LORD, and their righteousness is of me, saith the
LORD." Isaiah 54:17 (KJV)*

The Holy Spirit testifies to the truth.

*"But when the Comforter is come, whom I will send
unto you from the Father, even the Spirit of truth, which
proceedeth from the Father, he shall testify of me:" John
15:26 (KJV)*

The greatest testimony is seeing the Word established in your life.
Decree a thing with your mouth:

*"Thou shalt also decree a thing, and it shall be established
unto thee: and the light shall shine upon thy ways." Job
22:28 (KJV)*

When it shows up, that is the Holy Spirit giving testimony of it. There
can be no testimony without your giving a decree. You must have trust
and confidence that the Holy Spirit will make it a reality.

The Holy Spirit intercedes for the saints. To intercede means, "to go
on the behalf of another." The Spirit intercedes for you when you pray
in the Spirit.

"Likewise the Spirit also helpeth our infirmities: for we know not what we should pray for as we ought: but the Spirit itself maketh intercession for us with groanings which cannot be uttered. And he that searcheth the hearts knoweth what is the mind of the Spirit, because he maketh intercession for the saints according to the will of God. And we know that all things work together for good to them that love God, to them who are the called according to his purpose." Romans 8:26-28 (KJV)

The Holy Spirit will help the weaknesses of your flesh, which is your inability to always know what to pray. Since the Spirit of God knows everything, He intercedes and helps you to pray about the unknown; as a result, you always pray the perfect prayer. When you love God, you can be confident that everything concerning your prayer life will work together for your good.

The Holy Spirit is a real Person, and He ministers in the earth today. It is through Him that the kingdom of God system operates. Failure to develop a relationship with the Holy Spirit prevents you from benefiting from His presence. In these last days, it is crucial to acknowledge His presence in your life.

HOW TO BE LEAD BY THE HOLY SPIRIT

The Holy Spirit's main objective is to bring truth. God' people are destroyed, or cut off, due to a lack of knowledge.

"My people are destroyed for lack of knowledge: because thou hast rejected knowledge, I will also reject thee, that thou shalt be no priest to me: seeing thou hast forgotten the law of thy God, I will also forget thy children." Hosea 4:6 (KJV)

God's answer for you to receive knowledge was to send the Holy Spirit.

> *"I have yet many things to say unto you, but ye cannot bear them now. Howbeit when he, the Spirit of truth, is come, he will guide you into all truth: for he shall not speak of himself; but whatsoever he shall hear, that shall he speak: and he will shew you things to come." John 16:12-13 (KJV)*

Many times, instead of allowing the Holy Spirit to guide them, people allow circumstances to determine whether or not they are on the right path and doing so can lead to destruction. Ask the Holy Spirit to lead you in the areas which you need help.

Don't think that you haven't been saved long enough or that you won't be able to know when the Holy Spirit is speaking. Those who are born again have a right to recognize His guidance.

> *"For as many as are led by the Spirit of God, they are the sons of God." Romans 8:14 (KJV)*

He wants to show you things regarding your life by guiding you into all truth.

> *"Howbeit when he, the Spirit of truth, is come, he will guide you into all truth: for he shall not speak of himself; but whatsoever he shall hear, that shall he speak: and he will shew you things to come. He shall glorify me: for he shall receive of mine, and shall shew it unto you." John 16:13-14 (KJV)*

The Holy Spirit bears witness, or testifies, with your spirit.

> *"The Spirit itself beareth witness with our spirit, that we are the children of God:" Romans 8:16 (KJV)*

When your spirit and the Holy Spirit are in agreement, you will have peace about your situation.

Man is created in the image of God; he is a spirit. Man is a spirit and possesses a soul that lives in a physical body. When a person dies, his or her spirit separates from their physical body and continue to live on forever.

Proverbs 20:27 says that the spirit of man is the lamp, or candle, of the Lord, which searches the inward parts of the belly; if you follow your spirit, rivers of living water will flow out of you.

> *"He that believeth on me, as the scripture hath said, out of his belly shall flow rivers of living water." John 7:38 (KJV)*

Guidance comes through your spirit. Many times people try to be led by their mind, senses or by what others say, although these things do not line up with the Word of God. God made man in His image (Genesis 1:26-27); God is a spirit.

> *"God is a Spirit: and they that worship him must worship him in spirit and in truth." John 4:24 (KJV)*

Man is a tri-part being with a spirit, soul and body. (1 Thessalonians 5:23).

> *"And the very God of peace sanctify you wholly; and I pray God your whole __spirit__ and __soul__ and __body__ be preserved blameless unto the coming of our Lord Jesus Christ." 1 Thessalonians 5:23 (KJV)*

Many people confuse the spirit and soul as being the same thing when they are actually different. You are a spirit being who posses a soul which refers your mind, will and emotions and you live in a physical body. Paul was trying to decide if his spirit should stay in his body or go to be with Jesus.

> *"For I am in a strait betwixt two, having a desire to depart, and to be with Christ; which is far better:"*
> *Philippians 1:23 (KJV)*

The flaw in the human body is that it perishes and decays; the beauty of the inward man, your spirit, is that it is renewed daily.

> *"For which cause we faint not; but though our outward man perish, yet the inward man is renewed day by day."*
> *2 Corinthians 4:16 (KJV)*

Being born again does not take place through the flesh, but through your spirit.

> *"Jesus answered and said unto him, Verily, verily, I say unto thee, Except a man be born again, he cannot see the kingdom of God. Nicodemus saith unto him, How can a man be born when he is old? can he enter the second time into his mother's womb, and be born? Jesus answered, Verily, verily, I say unto thee, Except a man be born of water and of the Spirit, he cannot enter into the kingdom of God. That which is born of the flesh is flesh; and that which is born of the Spirit is spirit." John 3:3-6 (KJV)*

Man's spirit receives eternal life, God's nature and the life of God. Man's spirit is made a new creature in Christ.

We have to learn to hear His voice. The more time you spend in the Word, the easier it will be to recognize His voice. The New Testament uses heart and spirit interchangeably; the heart is defined as the center of man.

> *"But let it be the hidden man of the heart, in that which is not corruptible, even the ornament of a meek and quiet spirit, which is in the sight of God of great price."*
> *1 Peter 3:4 (KJV)*

Look at the word "heart" and you'll see the words: hear, ear, he and art. He is in the center of your heart so you can have an ear to hear Him.

Everything in your spirit becomes brand new when you are in Christ.

> *"Therefore if any man be in Christ, he is a new creature: old things are passed away; behold, all things are become new." 2 Corinthians 5:17 (KJV)*

You have received the Holy Spirit so that you will know and understand spiritual things.

> *"Now we have received, not the spirit of the world, but the spirit which is of God; that we might know the things that are freely given to us of God. Which things also we speak, not in the words which man's wisdom teacheth, but which the Holy Ghost teacheth; comparing spiritual things with spiritual. But the natural man receiveth not the things of the Spirit of God: for they are foolishness unto him: neither can he know them, because they are spiritually discerned. But he that is spiritual judgeth all things, yet he himself is judged of no man." 1 Corinthians 2:12-15 (KJV)*

A natural person can't understand spiritual things because his spirit isn't aligned with God's. Spiritual things will become more real to you the more spirit-conscious you become.

It is God's will for you to hear Him. Don't think that just because you've been "bad" He won't talk to you. He's a counselor and will speak to you even while you are doing "bad" things.

> "My sheep hear my voice, and I know them, and they follow me:" John 10:27 (KJV)

For your steps to be ordered, or established, by God, you must hear Him.

> "The steps of a good man are ordered by the LORD: and he delighteth in his way." Psalm 37:23 (KJV)

God wants to instruct, teach and direct your path.

> "I will instruct thee and teach thee in the way which thou shalt go: I will guide thee with mine eye." Psalm 32:8 (KJV)

> "Trust in the LORD with all thine heart; and lean not unto thine own understanding. In all thy ways acknowledge him, and he shall direct thy paths." Proverbs 3:5-6 (KJV)

When you are searching for something such as a house, a new job, a spouse, etc. allow the Holy Spirit to give your heart peace and to be a witness to your spirit.

> "And let the peace of God rule in your hearts, to the which also ye are called in one body; and be ye thankful." Colossians 3:15 (KJV)

Ask yourself five questions to see if what you are doing is in agreement with the Holy Spirit:

1. Does it go against the reasons and rationalizations of the world?
2. Does it require courage?
3. Does it require trusting and relying on God?
4. Does it line up with the Word of God?
5. Does peace rule in your heart?

The Holy Spirit has been sent to lead and guide us. He is known as the truth giver; the truth that He gives brings enlightenment. By listening and yielding to the Holy Spirit, you can avoid negative life experiences.

HOW TO BE LED BY THE HOLY SPIRIT, PART 2

The more spirit-conscious you are, the more spiritual things become real to you. You are a tri-part being; the Word distinguishes between your soul and spirit.

> *"For the word of God is quick, and powerful, and sharper than any twoedged sword, piercing even to the dividing asunder of soul and spirit, and of the joints and marrow, and is a discerner of the thoughts and intents of the heart." Hebrews 4:12 (KJV)*

You are a spirit, you possess a soul and you live in a physical body. Your spirit contacts the spiritual realm, your soul contacts the intellectual realm and your body contacts the physical realm.

God is a spirit being; you can only contact Him through your spirit.

The Holy Spirit is the truth giver.

"Howbeit when he, the Spirit of truth, is come, he will guide you into all truth: for he shall not speak of himself; but whatsoever he shall hear, that shall he speak: and he will shew you things to come. He shall glorify me: for he shall receive of mine, and shall shew it unto you."
John 16:13-14 (KJV)

The Holy Spirit imparts truth to your life. You must develop an awareness of your unseen Partner.

Your spirit man is the avenue through which God leads you.

"The spirit of man is the candle of the LORD, searching all the inward parts of the belly." Proverbs 20:27 (KJV)

God uses your spirit as a candle, or lamp, to provide guidance for your life. The leading of the Holy Spirit is governed by your born-again spirit. God will light the "candle" of your spirit to lead you.

"For thou wilt light my candle: the LORD my God will enlighten my darkness." Psalm 18:28 (KJV)

"For if I pray in an unknown tongue, my spirit prayeth, but my understanding is unfruitful." 1 Corinthians 14:14 (KJV)

"In the last day, that great day of the feast, Jesus stood and cried, saying, If any man thirst, let him come unto me, and drink. He that believeth on me, as the scripture hath said, out of his belly shall flow rivers of living water. (But this spake he of the Spirit, which they that believe on him should receive: for the Holy Ghost was not yet given;

because that Jesus was not yet glorified.)" John 7:37-39
(KJV)

Continuous rivers of wisdom, information and insight flow out of your spirit, because the Holy Spirit dwells in you once you become born again.

God desires to lead you to the place you're supposed to be.

> *"Come ye near unto me, hear ye this; I have not spoken in secret from the beginning; from the time that it was, there am I: and now the Lord GOD, and his Spirit, hath sent me. Thus saith the LORD, thy Redeemer, the Holy One of Israel; I am the LORD thy God which teacheth thee to profit, which leadeth thee by the way that thou shouldest go." Isaiah 48:16-17 (KJV)*

The inward witness is God's number-one way of leading people.

> *"The Spirit itself beareth witness with our spirit, that we are the children of God:" Romans 8:16 (KJV)*

You have the inward witness of the Spirit of God in you already.

> *"He that believeth on the Son of God hath the witness in himself: he that believeth not God hath made him a liar; because he believeth not the record that God gave of his Son." 1 John 5:10 (KJV)*

God lets you know you are His child by the inward witness. Trust the witness inside of you; don't ignore the "checks" in your spirit. You won't get the witness of the Spirit apart from the love of God.

The inward witness will show you how to love others.

When you believe you have the inward witness, you won't make haste.

> *"Therefore thus saith the Lord GOD, Behold, I lay in Zion for a foundation a stone, a tried stone, a precious corner stone, a sure foundation: he that believeth shall not make haste." Isaiah 28:16 (KJV)*

Being able to hear from and being led by the Holy Spirit are the keys to your success as a born-again believer. The Holy Spirit is the truth giver Who leads and guides you into profit. You have rivers of living water on the inside of you, giving you insight and wisdom to succeed in life.

"DOGS" AND "SWINE"

I want to tell everyone that I wanted to consider this my last Bible Study. I was reminded that we should not cast our pearls among swine. I was told, "Sometimes it's better that people learn the hard way. At least they learn, and maybe it will stay with them forever." I thought, "Great! This releases me of the responsibility for the knowledge that God gave me and that I can just quit! After all, I'm tired and why try to help believers who don't want to be helped?" As I prayerfully pondered this, God showed me what that scripture really refers to.

In Matthew 7:6, Jesus uses two examples to reveal a spiritual truth. "Dogs" and "swine" are both analogies that represent unbelievers in the Bible. "Pearls" and "that which is holy" represent precious biblical truths, principles, commandments of God, and directions, which God speaks to your heart. These precious things are not meant for the unbeliever. A spiritually dead man can't perceive the things of God (John 3:3, 1 Corinthians 2:14).

With this understanding, it doesn't release me from my responsibility to minister to my fellow believers. We are to be in a close relationship with God and sensitive the the leading of the Holy Spirit and do as He directs us to do. People have no problem accepting that God will judge us for wrong teachings and misdirecting our fellow believers; would we also, then, not be accountable for the knowledge and revelation given to us that we refused to share? Keeping everything that God reveals to you for yourself is selfish.

PREREQUISITES TO BEING LED BY THE SPIRIT OF GOD

The Spirit of God will only lead a person onto profitable paths.

As a result of allowing the Spirit of God to lead your life, you will enjoy four benefits:

1. Protection.
2. God's backing.
3. Ease.
4. The Devil rendered helpless against you.

It is vital that you learn to fellowship with the Holy Spirit and to follow His leading. The Holy Spirit sees your future and wants to lead you into all truth for your life. Success is the result of living a Spirit-led life. God leads you through your born-again spirit.

> *"The spirit of man is the candle of the LORD, searching all the inward parts of the belly." Proverbs 20:27 (KJV)*

Check with the Holy Spirit before you proceed to do anything in life.

There are prerequisites to hearing from God.

You must be born again. You must be a covenant child of God before He can lead you. A spiritually dead man can't perceive the things of God.

> *"Jesus answered and said unto him, Verily, verily, I say unto thee, Except a man be born again, he cannot see the kingdom of God." John 3:3 (KJV)*

Being a good person without having Jesus as your Lord and personal Savior is not enough to get you into heaven.

God can be speaking to you, but if you aren't born again, you will not hear Him.

> *"But the natural man receiveth not the things of the Spirit of God: for they are foolishness unto him: neither can he know them, because they are spiritually discerned." 1 Corinthians 2:14 (KJV)*

Divine direction is only the heritage of sons of God.

> *"For as many as are led by the Spirit of God, they are the sons of God." Romans 8:14 (KJV)*

Don't allow condemnation to hinder you from hearing from God. Stand in your righteousness.

You must bear the element of the fruit of the Spirit of meekness. Character is the key to hearing from God. God will guide the meek and teach them His ways.

> *"The meek will he guide in judgment: and the meek will he teach his way." Psalm 25:9 (KJV)*

The meek will inherit the earth.

> *"Blessed are the meek: for they shall inherit the earth."*
> *Matthew 5:5 (KJV)*

There is a three-fold definition of meekness.

1. self-controlled and slow to give or take offense.
2. Humble in spirit and lowly in mind.
3. Teachable.

Real humility is submitting yourself to the Word of God. An unteachable man will find an excuse to remain average. The meek man will do what's right even when he's being falsely accused.

When you are mistreated, hit the "pause button" and let God show you how to react His way.

Hearing from God is vital to living an abundant life of peace; however, many people are not in position to hear His voice. God speaks to everyone, but only those who are properly positioned will hear Him and be open to His leading.

PREREQUISITES TO BEING LED BY THE SPIRIT OF GOD, PART 2

You must have faith to hear from God.

> *"(For we walk by faith, not by sight:)"* 2 Corinthians
> 5:7 (KJV)

"We order our conduct daily by the Word of God that we have come to believe and embrace and not by what we see with our physical eyes:" 2 Corinthians 5:7 (Atarah)

Faith comes by the Word of God. Therefore, you must have the Word of God and continue in it, seeing that faith comes by hearing and hearing it.

"So then faith cometh by hearing, and hearing by the word of God." Romans 10:17 (KJV)

Faith comes by hearing the Word of God, analyzing and assimilating it into your way of thinking (hearing and hearing it over and over). What you think on consistently, you will come to believe, then you will act accordingly. (Proverbs 23:7)

Faith involves walking by the Word that has yet to be made manifest in your life. God cannot direct you if you are led by your physical senses. Emotions are unstable, and you cannot live by them. Your actions should be based on truth (the Word), which is stable. You cannot live by the unstable opinions of society, either. The Word of God, not your feelings, should determine your actions.

Worship God in Spirit and in truth.

"God is a Spirit: and they that worship him must worship him in spirit and in truth." John 4:24 (KJV)

God leads you through your born-again spirit.

"The spirit of man is the candle of the LORD, searching all the inward parts of the belly." Proverbs 20:27 (KJV)

Without faith (the Word of God from whence it comes), it is impossible to please God.

> "But without faith it is impossible to please him: for he that cometh to God must believe that he is, and that he is a rewarder of them that diligently seek him." Hebrews 11:6 (KJV)

To seek God means, "to research Him, inquire of Him and practice His presence."

Faith will cause you to seek Him. Divine direction is given to those who diligently seek God.

God will use peace to direct your life.

> "And let the peace of God rule in your hearts, to the which also ye are called in one body; and be ye thankful." Colossians 3:15 (KJV)

> "Let the peace of God lead you through the spirit within, to which also you are called in one body; and be thankful." Colossians 3:15 (Atarah)

You must spend time with God, His Word and the Holy Spirit to receive His divine direction.

You have an anointing to know all things.

> "But ye have an unction from the Holy One, and ye know all things." 1 John 2:20 (KJV)

When you fellowship with God, His Word and the Holy Spirit, He shares His knowledge with you and leads you into all truth.

Develop a consciousness of His presence by talking to Him. When you do, He will confirm His presence and will show you things to come. Your fellowship with Him gives you an advantage over the world.

A quiet spirit enhances your ability to hear from God. You cannot hear from God when your spirit is consumed by the cares of the world. Learn to cast your cares on Him. Worry is a sin, because it is a negative form of meditation. Spend time meditating on the Word.

> *"This book of the law shall not depart out of thy mouth; but thou shalt meditate therein day and night, that thou mayest observe to do according to all that is written therein: for then thou shalt make thy way prosperous, and then thou shalt have good success." Joshua 1:8 (KJV)*

Your quietness demonstrates your confidence in God's Word.

> *"For thus saith the Lord GOD, the Holy One of Israel; In returning and rest shall ye be saved; in quietness and in confidence shall be your strength: and ye would not." Isaiah 30:15 (KJV)*

Like Noah, you can hear from God in specific detail. Don't try to locate God in the "big" things. Instead, listen for His still, small voice.

> *"And he said, Go forth, and stand upon the mount before the LORD. And, behold, the LORD passed by, and a great and strong wind rent the mountains, and brake in pieces the rocks before the LORD; but the LORD was not in the wind: and after the wind an earthquake; but the LORD was not in the earthquake: And after the*

earthquake a fire; but the LORD was not in the fire: and
after the fire a still small voice." 1 Kings 19:11 (KJV)

A quiet spirit allows you to hear His voice in the midst of a noisy environment. Although a quiet environment is helpful, an inner quietness is more profitable. Get rid of the stress in your life; learn how to have fun. Laughter will help you to develop a quiet spirit.

You cannot expect to hear from God if you are not walking in love. To walk in love is to live without malice and anger. You must be free from "dis-ease" in your mind.

When you obey God's commandments, you demonstrate your love for Him. Nothing will work in your life if you don't love others. Don't allow past situations to ruin your ability to hear from God.

The Holy Spirit wants to lead and guide you through green pastures to still water. However, to hear from Him, certain prerequisites must be met. Once you hear His voice, your life will become directed instead of driven.

PREREQUISITES TO BEING LED BY
THE SPIRIT OF GOD, PART 3

God wants you to understand the importance of being led by the Spirit. Don't live by your emotions, because they are not stable. God created you with emotions, but not so that they would drive and direct your life.

Man is a tri-part being—he is a spirit being who has a soul and lives in a physical body. Through his spirit, he is able to contact God.

"The spirit of man is the candle of the LORD, searching all the inward parts of the belly." Proverbs 20:27 (KJV)

God will only guide you through your spirit, because He is a Spirit.

"But the hour cometh, and now is, when the true worshippers shall worship the Father in spirit and in truth: for the Father seeketh such to worship him. God is a Spirit: and they that worship him must worship him in spirit and in truth." John 4:23-24 (KJV)

Even though God speaks to your spirit, the flesh will override what He is saying if your spirit is underdeveloped and your flesh is strong. If you spend time in the Word, you'll be able to hear and trust the voice of your spirit (your conscience).

Many people wonder if the voice they heard giving directions was God's, the devil's or their own. The way to discern if God is speaking is by asking yourself several questions about what you hear:

1 Does it line up with the Word?

2 Does it require trusting and relying on God and His Word?

3 Does it require courage to do it?

4 Does it go against all the reasons and rationalizations of the world?

5 Do you have the peace of God about it?

"Mortify therefore your members which are upon the earth; fornication, uncleanness, inordinate affection, evil concupiscence, and covetousness, which is idolatry:" Colossians 3:5 (KJV)

Not everyone is in a position to hear God's voice and to be led by Him. God is always speaking, but there are three different types of receivers:

1. Those who can't hear because of the lives they live.
2. Those who hear, but choose to ignore what they've heard.
3. Those who hear and obey.

There are eight prerequisites to hearing the voice of God.

1) You must be born again.

> *"Jesus answered and said unto him, Verily, verily, I say unto thee, Except a man be born again, he cannot see the kingdom of God." John 3:3 (KJV)*

The natural man will think the things of God are foolish.

> *"But the natural man receiveth not the things of the Spirit of God: for they are foolishness unto him: neither can he know them, because they are spiritually discerned." 1 Corinthians 2:14 (KJV)*

Hearing from God is part of your divine heritage.

> *"For as many as are led by the Spirit of God, they are the sons of God." Romans 8:14 (KJV)*

2) You must be a person of meekness. God will teach and guide the meek.

> *"The meek will he guide in judgment: and the meek will he teach his way." Psalm 25:9 (KJV)*

Moses was the meekest man on the earth in his day, and God was able to use him mightily.

> *"He made known his ways unto Moses, his acts unto the children of Israel." Psalm 103:7 (KJV)*

A man who is meek will receive the leadership and guidance of the Holy Spirit. Meekness has three parts: 1) Self-control, or slowness to give or take offense. 2) Humility, or being humble in spirit and lowly in mind. 3) Teachability. Meekness is displayed when a person does not take offense when he suffers for being in the right.

3) You must display faithfulness. Don't let your senses guide you. Walk by faith (trusting the Word of God) and not by sight.

> *"(For we walk by faith, not by sight:)" 2 Corinthians 5:7 (KJV)*

> *"We order our conduct daily by the Word of God that we have come to believe and embrace and not by what we see with our physical eyes:" 2 Corinthians 5:7 (Atarah)*

4) You need to spend time in fellowship with the God, His Word and the Holy Spirit. Talk with and seek the advice of the Holy Spirit so that He can lead and guide you.

5) You must walk in "quietness." Don't listen to the cares of the world; give them to God to handle.

> *"Casting all your care upon him; for he careth for you." 1 Peter 5:7 (KJV)*

6) You must walk in love. You will be unable to hear from God when you walk in selfishness. When you are operating in selfishness,

you crown yourself "god" and lead yourself instead of consulting God for His direction. By not walking in love, you grieve the Holy Spirit and quench His fire through your disobedience.

> *"And grieve not the holy Spirit of God, whereby ye are sealed unto the day of redemption. Let all bitterness, and wrath, and anger, and clamour, and evil speaking, be put away from you, with all malice: And be ye kind one to another, tenderhearted, forgiving one another, even as God for Christ's sake hath forgiven you." Ephesians 4:30-32 (KJV)*

> *"Quench not the Spirit." 1 Thessalonians 5:19 (KJV)*

Walking in love means having a life without malice or entanglement.

7) You must be open to His direction. Don't be set in your ways; be open to hear what He has to say and then make the appropriate adjustments.

> *"And said, Verily I say unto you, Except ye be converted, and become as little children, ye shall not enter into the kingdom of heaven. Whosoever therefore shall humble himself as this little child, the same is greatest in the kingdom of heaven." Matthew 18:3-4 (KJV)*

Be willing to obey God's instructions, even if they contradict your desired actions. You must have a perfect heart, which is soft and pliable.

> *"For the eyes of the LORD run to and fro throughout the whole earth, to shew himself strong in the behalf of them whose heart is perfect toward him. Herein thou*

*hast done foolishly: therefore from henceforth thou shalt
have wars." 2 Chronicles 16:9 (KJV)*

You may try to make plans for your life, but God will direct your steps
if you have an open heart to hear Him. He will make those steps sure.

*"A man's heart deviseth his way: but the LORD directeth
his steps." Proverbs 16:9 (KJV)*

8) You must worship and praise. Because of the blood of Jesus, we
    have access to His presence and should give Him praise.

    *"Having therefore, brethren, boldness to enter into the
    holiest by the blood of Jesus," Hebrews 10:19 (KJV)*

God inhabits your praise.

*"But thou art holy, O thou that inhabitest the praises of
Israel." Psalm 22:3 (KJV)*

When situations arise, the first thing you should do is give Him
praise so that when He comes to help, He'll speak to you and you will
hear Him.

Many people follow their own lead, only to end up in the wrong
place. They find themselves with nothing working for them. The
Holy Spirit, Who is the truth giver, has been sent to you and I to bring
enlightenment. He wants to direct you on the correct path for your
life, but you must first learn how to listen to His voice.

FIVE HINDRANCES TO HEARING FROM GOD

The true sheep will hear the voice of the Shepherd and will be led by Him.

> *"Verily, verily, I say unto you, He that entereth not by the door into the sheepfold, but climbeth up some other way, the same is a thief and a robber. But he that entereth in by the door is the shepherd of the sheep. To him the porter openeth; and the sheep hear his voice: and he calleth his own sheep by name, and leadeth them out. And when he putteth forth his own sheep, he goeth before them, and the sheep follow him: for they know his voice. And a stranger will they not follow, but will flee from him: for they know not the voice of strangers." John 10:1-5 (KJV)*

True sheep will not follow a stranger's voice, only God's. When the Lord is your Shepherd, you will not lack.

> *"The LORD is my shepherd; I shall not want." Psalm 23:1 (KJV)*

God will speak to you in specific details, not just vague impressions. You must expect to hear God's voice and then follow it. You must know His voice to keep you from the dangers lurking in the world. God speaks to you every day; however, if your receiver is clogged up, you won't hear His instructions.

Unbelief hinders your ability to hear from God. Unbelief fosters a distrust of God, which causes you to waver and leads to doubt.

> *"He staggered not at the promise of God through unbelief; but was strong in faith, giving glory to God;" Romans 4:20 (KJV)*

An unbelieving heart turns you away from God and shuts you off from His promises.

> *"Take heed, brethren, lest there be in any of you an evil heart of unbelief, in departing from the living God."* Hebrews 3:12 (KJV)

> *"So we see that they could not enter in because of unbelief."* Hebrews 3:19 (KJV)

If you don't believe what God says, His Word won't work for you. You must trust God even if you can't see how His promises will come to pass or if they don't manifest in the way that you had planned.

An <u>undeveloped spirit</u> hinders your ability to hear from God. God leads and guides you through your spirit. Don't be more developed in your emotions than you are in your spirit, allowing them to take over and lead your life. God wants your spirit to be whole so that He can lead you; therefore, you must develop it.

> *"And the very God of peace sanctify you wholly; and I pray God your whole spirit and soul and body be preserved blameless unto the coming of our Lord Jesus Christ. Faithful is he that calleth you, who also will do it."* 1 Thessalonians 5:23-24 (KJV)

You develop your spirit by studying and obeying the Bible, praying in the Holy Spirit, worshiping God and then listening to His voice.

God's Word is the connection to manifestation; therefore, you must fill your spirit with the Word.

To be a successful born-again believer, you must know how to hear from God for yourself.

A spirit of deafness hinders your ability to hear from God. Having unforgiveness opens you up to torment. Your heart stops hearing when you focus on painful memories. Anger, jealousy, bitterness, resentment and malice grieve the Holy Spirit and block your ability to hear.

> "And grieve not the holy Spirit of God, whereby ye are sealed unto the day of redemption. Let all bitterness, and wrath, and anger, and clamour, and evil speaking, be put away from you, with all malice:" Ephesians 4:30-31 (KJV)

A calloused conscience hinders your ability to hear from God. You become insensitive when you constantly ignore your conscience to do what your flesh wants to do. Your conscience is the voice of your spirit, and God leads you through your spirit. Every time you disobey the Spirit of God, it becomes harder and harder to hear His voice when He speaks to you.

Neglect hinders your ability to hear from God. When you neglect prayer, Bible study and fellowship with God, it affects your thoughts, actions, habits, character and destiny, because you are no longer aligned with God and His Word. If you want to fulfill your destiny, you must ensure that your mindset and decisions line up with His Word.

Believers must learn to hear God's voice if they are ever going to realize their God-given purpose. To fulfill your destiny, you must be willing to remove anything that hinders you from hearing from God. Once you remove the barriers, God is free to lead you into abundant living.

THE ANOINTING: WHAT IT IS AND HOW IT WORKS

The anointing is the master key to accomplishment and fulfillment. The anointing removes burdens and destroys yokes and it is a "performance enhancer".

> "The Spirit of the Lord is upon me, because he hath anointed me to preach the gospel to the poor; he hath sent me to heal the brokenhearted, to preach deliverance to the captives, and recovering of sight to the blind, to set at liberty them that are bruised," Luke 4:18 (KJV)

> "And it shall come to pass in that day, that his burden shall be taken away from off thy shoulder, and his yoke from off thy neck, and the yoke shall be destroyed <u>because of the anointing</u>." Isaiah 10:27 (KJV)

The level of anointing you have determines your level of productivity. It is because of the anointing that you can be like God in the demonstration of power.

The anointing is an outflow of the Holy Spirit through a human vessel. When God is with you, you are anointed for a mission.

You must exercise the anointing in your life if you want to see it godly fruit and increase. Lack of use brings decay. Active use of the anointing increases maturity.

There are three different levels of the anointing.

The <u>first level</u> is the "well level" (John 4:1-14) and is the <u>level of the indwelling Holy Spirit in a person's life at the point of the new birth.</u>

The <u>second level</u> is the "river level" (John 7:37-39) and occurs at the point of the <u>Baptism of the Holy Spirit</u>. The Baptism of the Holy Spirit is the initiation into spiritual depth. It brings about identification with God.

Both rivers and wells are subject to "climatic" changes. With what and whom you associate and how much Word of God you are getting determines whether or not your "well" and "river" are full. There are certain activities that cannot take place in a well or a river without them being full of water—you must make sure that your well and river do not run dry.

Rivers make deposits along the way; likewise, you can't be at the river level and be selfish. The anointing is not for you, but for others. Increase can't happen in the life of a selfish person.

The <u>third level </u>is the "rain level." <u>Rain is the equivalent of the anointing</u>. If you want your well and river to be full, you must have rain. God promised to rain His power on His people; He promised a storm of anointing.

> *"Ask ye of the LORD rain in the time of the latter rain; so the LORD shall make bright clouds, and give them showers of rain, to every one grass in the field."*
> *Zechariah 10:1 (KJV)*

> *"Be glad then, ye children of Zion, and rejoice in the LORD your God: for he hath given you the former rain moderately, and he will cause to come down for you the rain, the former rain, and the latter rain in the first month. And the floors shall be full of wheat, and the fats shall overflow with wine and oil. And I will restore to you the years that the locust hath eaten, the cankerworm,*

*and the caterpiller, and the palmerworm, my great army
which I sent among you. And ye shall eat in plenty, and
be satisfied, and praise the name of the LORD your God,
that hath dealt wondrously with you: and my people
shall never be ashamed. And ye shall know that I am in
the midst of Israel, and that I am the LORD your God,
and none else: and my people shall never be ashamed."*
Joel 2:23-27 (KJV)

Rain is symbolic of the release of God's power; it makes performance possible. Ask God for rain and He will give it.

The anointing comes after the Baptism of the Holy Spirit occurs (Acts 4:8, 29-31). The disciples had already been baptized in the Holy Spirit and the power of God showed up afterward. The anointing is what fills the water levels in your life.

The anointing (divine enablement), removes burdens and destroys yokes and enables people to do better in life than they could without it. The anointing is a "performance enhancer" and is the master key to accomplishment and fulfillment in the life of a born-again believer.

FUNDAMENTALS TO OPERATING
IN THE ANOINTING

To operate in the anointing, you must love righteousness and hate wickedness.

*"Thy throne, O God, is for ever and ever: the sceptre of
thy kingdom is a right sceptre. Thou lovest righteousness,
and hatest wickedness: therefore God, thy God, hath
anointed thee with the oil of gladness above thy fellows."*
Psalm 45:6-7 (KJV)

Old Testament righteousness referred to righteous acts. Because Jesus loved righteousness and hated wickedness, He was anointed of God—and Jesus remained anointed throughout His earthly ministry.

New Testament righteousness—righteousness by faith —comes as a result of what Jesus has done. Through Jesus, you are declared righteous before you ever perform a righteous act. Do not be deceived into believing that because you are the righteousness of God, you do not have to do what is right.

> *"Little children, let no man deceive you: he that doeth righteousness is righteous, even as he is righteous." 1 John 3:7 (KJV)*

You must be willing to do what is necessary for God to anoint you with the ability to get results. There is a price to pay for the anointing that removes burdens and destroys yokes.

> *"And it shall come to pass in that day, that his burden shall be taken away from off thy shoulder, and his yoke from off thy neck, and the yoke shall be destroyed because of the anointing." Isaiah 10:27 (KJV)*

When you are tempted to sin, ask yourself, "What will it cost me where the anointing is concerned?"

Jesus, Who had the anointing without limits, lived a life without sin.

> *"For he hath made him to be sin for us, who knew no sin; that we might be made the righteousness of God in him."* 2 Corinthians 5:21 (KJV)

The apostle Paul who was also anointed behaved himself in a holy manner, just and unblameable in the sight of all that believed.

> *"Ye are witnesses, and God also, how holily and justly and unblameably we behaved ourselves among you that believe:"* 1 Thessalonians 2:10 (KJV)

To operate in the anointing, you must walk in love. Walking in love is walking in God. The fruit of love has been deposited in your born-again spirit.

> *"But the fruit of the Spirit is love, joy, peace, longsuffering, gentleness, goodness, faith, Meekness, temperance: against such there is no law."Galatians 5:22-23 (KJV)*

To demonstrate the power of the Spirit, you must walk in love. You cannot have more anointing than you have love. Spiritual gifts cannot compare to the more excellent way of love.

> *"But covet earnestly the best gifts: and yet shew I unto you a more excellent way."* 1 Corinthians 12:31 (KJV)

> *"Though I speak with the tongues of men and of angels, and have not charity, I am become as sounding brass, or a tinkling cymbal. And though I have the gift of prophecy, and understand all mysteries, and all knowledge; and though I have all faith, so that I could remove mountains, and have not charity, I am nothing. And though I bestow all my goods to feed the poor, and though I give my body to be burned, and have not charity, it profiteth me nothing."* 1 Corinthians 13:1-3 (KJV)

Don't allow the actions of others to cause you to lose the anointing. Strife, hatred, unforgiveness and bitterness prevent the anointing from operating in your life. When you walk in love and stay anointed, the negative situations in your life will melt away. Even when Jesus, who is our example, was dying on the cross He prayed for others because He was sill more concerned with their well-being than His own.

To operate in the anointing, you must live a life of praise. "Thank You, Lord." is always an appropriate response to every situation. A life void of praise and worship experiences the absence of the anointing. Begin thanking God for what He has already done in your life. Jesus gave thanks before the loaves of bread were multiplied.

Trouble is an opportunity to see the power of God at work in your life.

The anointing is not just reserved for pastors and those in ministry; it is available to all born-again believers. It is the power of God that flows out of the Holy Spirit into your born-again spirit. This power guarantees you the ability to get results. However, you must pay a price for it.

THE GATEWAY TO THIS POWER

What is the anointing and how does it work? The anointing is a divine enabling. It is God's ability on your ability to get the job done. It is required for results in a Believer's life in these last days.

With the anointing on your life, burdens are removed and yokes are destroyed.

> *"And it shall come to pass in that day, that his burden shall be taken away from off thy shoulder, and his yoke from off thy neck, and the yoke shall be destroyed because of the anointing." Isaiah 10:27 (KJV)*

To have the anointing operating in your life, you must: love righteousness, walk in love and live a life of praise.

Jesus, Who is our example, was anointed with the oil of gladness because He <u>loved righteousness</u> and hated wickedness. (Old Testament righteousness referred to righteous acts. New Testament righteousness—righteousness by faith —comes as a result of what Jesus has done. Through Jesus, you are declared righteous before you ever perform a righteous act. However, do not be deceived into believing that because you are the righteousness of God that you do not have to do what is right.)

> *"Thou lovest righteousness, and hatest wickedness: therefore God, thy God, hath anointed thee with the oil of gladness above thy fellows." Psalm 45:7 (KJV)*

Just as the Word of God carries the faith of God, the love of God carries the anointing of God. <u>We are to walk in love</u>.

<u>Live a life of praise</u>. The anointing doesn't operate in the lives of whiners and complainers.

Power is necessary to accomplish great things. Power isn't the spectacular, but the supernatural; it is the ability to get results.

If you aren't willing to do what the Word says, then you don't need the anointing.

The kingdom of God is based on power, not enticing words.

> *"For the kingdom of God is not in word, but in power." 1 Corinthians 4:20 (KJV)*

> *"For the kingdom of God (that is within a man) is not a matter of mere talk; it's an empowered life." 1 Corinthians 4:20 (Atarah)*

"And my speech and my preaching was not with enticing words of man's wisdom, but in demonstration of the Spirit and of power:" 1 Corinthians 2:4 (KJV)

The kingdom of God does not rely on church attendance, prayer, fasting or tithing. These are important, but if they don't culminate in power, then they are useless.

If you are a born again believer, God had endowed you with power.

"Behold, I give unto you power to tread on serpents and scorpions, and over all the power of the enemy: and nothing shall by any means hurt you." Luke 10:19 (KJV)

Power is the true identity of the saints.

"But as many as received him, to them gave he power to become the sons of God, evento them that believe on his name:" John 1:12 (KJV)

Power is not limited to miracles; instead, it is demonstrated in every area of your life. The mark of every born-again believer is the power of God on their life to get the job done.

The day will come when born-again believers will rule in the midst of their enemies.

"The LORD said unto my Lord, Sit thou at my right hand, until I make thine enemies thy footstool. The LORD shall send the rod of thy strength out of Zion: rule thou in the midst of thine enemies. Thy people shall be willing in the day of thy power, in the beauties of holiness

*from the womb of the morning: thou hast the dew of thy
youth." Psalm 110:1-3 (KJV)*

You must have a never-ending thirst for God and His Word. Thirst is
the gateway to power. It is an insistent desire or longing. King David
compared his thirst for the Word of God to a deer who pants after a
brook.

*"As the hart panteth after the water brooks, so panteth
my soul after thee, O God." Psalm 42:1 (KJV)*

Thirst is how you receive power. Thirst will buy you what you need.

*"Ho, <u>every one that thirsteth,</u> come ye to the waters, and
he that hath no money; come ye, buy, and eat; yea, come,
buy wine and milk without money and without price."
Isaiah 55:1 (KJV)*

God knows your level of thirst.

Many mighty men of God thirsted after Him.

Moses had experienced God many times, yet he prayed that he would
get to know Him better.

*"And Moses said unto the LORD, See, thou sayest unto
me, Bring up this people: and thou hast not let me know
whom thou wilt send with me. Yet thou hast said, I know
thee by name, and thou hast also found grace in my
sight. Now therefore, <u>I pray thee,</u> if I have found grace in
thy sight, shew me now thy way, <u>that I may know thee,</u>
that I may find grace in thy sight: and consider that this
nation is thy people." Exodus 33:12-13 (KJV)*

Paul, who was anointed, also wanted to know God better.

> *"That I may know him, and the power of his resurrection, and the fellowship of his sufferings, being made conformable unto his death;" Philippians 3:10 (KJV)*

Only a thirst for God and His Word gives us the ability to get results. Don't be satisfied with the small amount of the anointing that you have experienced or the first victory or answered prayer.

When you have a thirst, you will never be satisfied and complacent with where you are. Continually seek God; seek understanding and revelations of His Word. Ask yourself if you are thirsty or satisfied.

The anointing is not for those who don't plan to use it; instead, it is for those who want positive results in their lives. It is available to those who recognize that they need God and His Word every day, knowing that they are nothing without Him. You open the gate to the anointing with an insatiable thirst for God.

VICTORY THROUGH THE
KNOWLEDGE OF THE WORD

Your victory is more of a reality than the battles you may face. Emotions don't determine your victory; what is inside of you does.

> *"But the natural man receiveth not the things of the Spirit of God: for they are foolishness unto him: neither can he know them, because they are spiritually discerned." 1 Corinthians 2:14 (KJV)*

God is mighty in battle.

> *"Lift up your heads, O ye gates; and be ye lift up, ye everlasting doors; and the King of glory shall come in. Who is this King of glory? The LORD strong and mighty, the LORD mighty in battle." Psalm 24:7-8 (KJV)*

Might is "an anointing (ability) that enables you to do anything".

> *"And the spirit of the LORD shall rest upon him, the spirit of wisdom and understanding, the spirit of counsel and might, the spirit of knowledge and of the fear of the LORD;" Isaiah 11:2 (KJV)*

God will strengthen you through the spirit of might.

> *"Finally, my brethren, be strong in the Lord, and in the power of his might." Ephesians 6:10 (KJV)*

Wisdom is knowing what to do; might is the ability to carry it out.

You need knowledge before you can get the power to do things. Might enables the knowledge of God's Word to come to pass in your life.

When you have knowledge of God, nothing will be impossible for you. Those people who have an intimate fellowship with God and His Word will be strong and do exploits.

> *"And such as do wickedly against the covenant shall he corrupt by flatteries: but the people that do know their God shall be strong, and do exploits." Daniel 11:32 (KJV)*

Exploits are "those things which are humanly impossible". To perform exploits is to obtain what others have said couldn't be obtained.

God only does things for those who know Him. <u>The degree of what you know from the Word determines the degree to which you know God. The Holy Spirit came to reveal God; however, He is limited by the amount of Word that you have in your heart.</u>

> *"But as it is written, Eye hath not seen, nor ear heard, neither have entered into the heart of man, the things which God hath prepared for them that love him. But God hath revealed them unto us by his Spirit: for the Spirit searcheth all things, yea, the deep things of God. For what man knoweth the things of a man, save the spirit of man which is in him? even so the things of God knoweth no man, but the Spirit of God. Now we have received, not the spirit of the world, but the spirit which is of God; that we might know the things that are freely given to us of God." 1 Corinthians 2:9-12 (KJV)*

Knowledge of the Word produces strength.

God doesn't have love; He is love.

> *"Beloved, let us love one another: for love is of God; and every one that loveth is born of God, and knoweth God. He that loveth not knoweth not God; for God is love. In this was manifested the love of God toward us, because that God sent his only begotten Son into the world, that we might live through him. Herein is love, not that we loved God, but that he loved us, and sent his Son to be the propitiation for our sins. Beloved, if God so loved us, we ought also to love one another. No man hath seen*

God at any time. If we love one another, God dwelleth in us, and his love is perfected in us." 1 John 4:7-12 (KJV)

God is love, and He loves you. We know we are born of God by the fact that we love our brothers and sisters (1 John 4: 9-12).

God wants to manifest Himself to you, but He can't manifest Himself to someone who doesn't love Him; keep and attend to His Word.

"He that hath my commandments, and keepeth them, he it is that loveth me: and he that loveth me shall be loved of my Father, and I will love him, and will manifest myself to him." John 14:21 (KJV)

A revelation of God and His Word will causes you to win every battle or struggle that you face every time.

As a born-again believer, you will have battles in life; however, your victory is more of a reality than any battle you may face. Although the Holy Spirit came to reveal God to you, you must educate your spirit with the Word of God for Him to give you revelation knowledge of God. When you have an intimate knowledge of the Father and of the fact that He loves you, nothing will be too hard for you to overcome.

THE ANOINTING FOR BATTLE

Your victory is assured.

"Now thanks be unto God, which always causeth us to triumph in Christ, and maketh manifest the savour of his knowledge by us in every place." 2 Corinthians 2:14 (KJV)

The spirit of might shows up to assist you when you are faced with a battle.

> "Lift up your heads, O ye gates; and be ye lift up, ye everlasting doors; and the King of glory shall come in. Who is this King of glory? The LORD strong and mighty, the LORD mighty in battle." Psalm 24:7-8 (KJV)

A revelation of God will release the spirit of might.

God is love and He loves you. In fact, He wants you to be convinced of His love for you. The knowledge (or revelation) of Him will build your confidence and give you strength.

> "A wise man is strong; yea, a man of knowledge increaseth strength." Proverbs 24:5 (KJV)

This knowledge is available through the Holy Spirit. Knowledge produces strength and strength guarantees triumph.

The Holy Spirit can only act on the Word that is in you. It is crucial to regularly fill up on the Word of God. When you continue in the Word, you will know the truth (or the Word), and it will set you free.

> "Then said Jesus to those Jews which believed on him, <u>If ye continue in my word,</u> then are ye my disciples indeed; And ye shall know the truth, and the truth shall make you free." John 8:31-32 (KJV)

Your freedom comes from the revelation you receive from the truth that you know. The enemy cannot feed you lies when you have revelation knowledge. Nothing can stop you when you are possessed with revelation.

The first degree of truth is the written Word. God speaks through His written Word.

The second degree of truth is the prophetic (or rhema) Word. The prophetic Word comes as a result of diligently reading God's written Word. It is the prophetic Word that causes deliverance, results and manifestations.

Seek and you will find. To seek means "to research God and to inquire of Him.". When you are in the Word and the Word is in you, God will speak. To know what the Bible says is only the first level of knowledge of the Word. To experience the Word, you must spend time in it to hear the voice behind it.

You cannot overcome adversity if you neglect what the Lord has spoken to you. Your way of escape will come in the form of knowledge.

God is faithful to His love and His Word. Because God loves you, He will never allow you to be tested above your ability to win.

> *"There hath no temptation taken you but such as is common to man: but God is faithful, who will not suffer you to be tempted above that ye are able; but will with the temptation also make a way to escape, that ye may be able to bear it." 1 Corinthians 10:13 (KJV)*

God will say something in the midst of your trail and will show you what to do. Read the Bible, knowing that it is the way and that it will position you to receive the truth. The Word will give you boundaries so that you won't follow the wrong voice.

Please note that sin will prevent you from hearing God's voice.

The root of every issue in your life is found in your love walk. The ultimate way of escape is a revelation of love between you and the Father, and between you and your neighbors.

To win the battles of life, you must have the anointing of might, which is "the ability to accomplish anything." Knowledge of the Word is the switch that will "turn on" the spirit of might. The Holy Spirit will cause you to triumph over your enemies because of the Word of God that is at work inside of you.

CONFIDENCE IN THE WORD OF GOD

To turn on the spirit of might, you must have a revelation of God's Word; God is love and He loves you.

Allow it to go beyond simple head knowledge.

> *"Now thanks be unto God, which always causeth us to triumph in Christ, and maketh manifest the savour of his knowledge by us in every place."* 2 Corinthians 2:14 *(KJV)*

> *"Now thanks be to God, Who in Christ always leads us in triumph (as trophies of Christ's victory) and makes evident the fragrance of the knowledge of God everywhere,"* 2 Corinthians 2:14 (Atarah)

Knowing the Word of God and His love causes all of the principles in the Bible to work for you.

As you study the Word, be open to hear from God. The rhema Word you receive will cause your deliverance, results and manifestations. It is the revelation knowledge of God and His Word that gives you power and builds your confidence.

Jesus said that those who love God and their neighbors would be loved by the Father, and He would manifest Himself to them.

> *"He that hath my commandments, and keepeth them, he it is that loveth me: and he that loveth me shall be loved of my Father, and I will love him, and will manifest myself to him." John 14:21 (KJV)*

Knowledge produces confidence.

The enemy will try to cause you to doubt God's Word. He uses doubt to rob you of your victory.

> *"But call to remembrance the former days, in which, after ye were illuminated, ye endured a great fight of afflictions; Partly, whilst ye were made a gazingstock both by reproaches and afflictions; and partly, whilst ye became companions of them that were so used. For ye had compassion of me in my bonds, and took joyfully the spoiling of your goods, knowing in yourselves that ye have in heaven a better and an enduring substance. Cast not away therefore your confidence, which hath great recompence of reward. For ye have need of patience, that, after ye have done the will of God, ye might receive the promise." Hebrews 10:32-36 (KJV)*

While you are under attack, take joy in what you know from the Word of God! Opposition always melts away when you put up a good fight and stay your course.

Your knowledge will build confidence in God and His Word and bring great reward.

Never think when things don't go according to your plans that God doesn't love you. This is God saying that He has something else planned for you; He is changing your direction.

Place your confidence in God, not in yourself. Don't be moved by your circumstances or allow anything to separate you from the love of God.

"They that trust in the LORD shall be as mount Zion, which cannot be removed, but abideth for ever." Psalm 125:1 (KJV)

"He only is my rock and my salvation: he is my defence; I shall not be moved." Psalm 62:6 (KJV)

"Likewise the Spirit also helpeth our infirmities: for we know not what we should pray for as we ought: but the Spirit itself maketh intercession for us with groanings which cannot be uttered. And he that searcheth the hearts knoweth what is the mind of the Spirit, because he maketh intercession for the saints according to the will of God. And we know that all things work together for good to them that love God, to them who are the called according to his purpose. For whom he did foreknow, he also did predestinate to be conformed to the image of his Son, that he might be the firstborn among many brethren. Moreover whom he did predestinate, them he also called: and whom he called, them he also justified: and whom he justified, them he also glorified. What shall we then say to these things? If God be for us, who can be against us? He that spared not his own Son, but

delivered him up for us all, how shall he not with him also freely give us all things? Who shall lay any thing to the charge of God's elect? It is God that justifieth. Who is he that condemneth? It is Christ that died, yea rather, that is risen again, who is even at the right hand of God, who also maketh intercession for us. Who shall separate us from the love of Christ? shall tribulation, or distress, or persecution, or famine, or nakedness, or peril, or sword? As it is written, For thy sake we are killed all the day long; we are accounted as sheep for the slaughter. Nay, in all these things we are more than conquerors through him that loved us. For I am persuaded, that neither death, nor life, nor angels, nor principalities, nor powers, nor things present, nor things to come, Nor height, nor depth, nor any other creature, shall be able to separate us from the love of God, which is in Christ Jesus our Lord." Romans 8:26-39 (KJV)

To build your confidence in God, look at what He has already done for you. Meditate on Acts 20:24 and Philippians 1:28.

"But none of these things move me, neither count I my life dear unto myself, so that I might finish my course with joy, and the ministry, which I have received of the Lord Jesus, to testify the gospel of the grace of God." Acts 20:24 (KJV)

"And in nothing terrified by your adversaries: which is to them an evident token of perdition, but to you of salvation, and that of God." Philippians 1:28 (KJV)

The knowledge of God's Word concerning you will produce your confidence in Him. It's important that you develop a revelation of His

Word and His love for you. The enemy will try his best to cause you to doubt God's Word; however, don't be swayed from your belief in what God has said in His Word.

CONFIDENCE: AN ANOINTING CONNECTOR

There will never be any deliverance, results or manifestations in the lives of people who don't hear a Word from God. Until you spend enough time fellowshipping in the Word to hear the voice behind the Word, you'll never be a candidate for deliverance, results or manifestations. Don't be satisfied with a mental assent of the Word, because you'll never be successful if you can't hear from God.

None of the miracles in the Bible took place without someone having first heard a Word from God. When you hear a Word from God, no devil in hell can stop you. You are made strong and mighty, and you will not quit.

Your confidence and trust in the Word of God and His love for you is the first area the enemy will attack.

If you don't believe God and His Word, you don't have a leg to stand on when an attack comes. You must meditate on the Word of God and the truth that God loves you, because the enemy will try to bring guilt and condemnation to defeat you.

God knew you would always come up short, so He sent Jesus to make up the difference. Remember every time you doubt God, you doubt His love.

Don't allow past sins to escort you into your future. As it is written, Satan, not God, is the accuser of the brethren. God won't mention past sins or even recall them.

> *"In that day it shall be said to Jerusalem, Fear thou not:*
> *and to Zion, Let not thine hands be slack. The LORD*
> *thy God in the midst of thee is mighty; he will save, he*
> *will rejoice over thee with joy; he will rest in his love,*
> *he will joy over thee with singing." Zephaniah 3:16-17*
> *(KJV)*

God rejoices and sings over you because He sees what you will become through the blood of Jesus. Whenever disappointment comes your way, have a mental attitude that says, "I cannot be defeated, and I will not quit."

Your trust and confidence in the Word of God is your strength, and that's what the enemy is after.

> *"For thus saith the Lord GOD, the Holy One of Israel;*
> *In returning and rest shall ye be saved; in quietness and*
> *in confidence shall be your strength: and ye would not."*
> *Isaiah 30:15 (KJV)*

Condemnation and guilt are indicators that you have lost confidence in God.

> *"Beloved, if our heart condemn us not, then have we*
> *confidence toward God." 1 John 3:21 (KJV)*

God did not start loving you when you became born again; He loved you while you were in sin. It was that love that drew you to Him. How much more does God love you now that you are born again? He's in love with you!

Your confidence should be in God's Word and in His love for you, not in yourself. You must trust and have confidence in God with all your heart, instead of relying on your own insight and understanding.

> *"Trust in the LORD with all thine heart; and lean not unto thine own understanding." Proverbs 3:5 (KJV)*

Don't allow what you know or don't know in the natural to overshadow the all-knowing God; there is nothing He can't do. He'll work things out in your favor. When you trust in God and His Word you build confidence; knowing He "has your back." Confidence in God and His love, not your prayer technique, will produce manifestation in your life.

> *"And this is the confidence that we have in him, that, if we ask any thing according to his will, he heareth us:" 1 John 5:14 (KJV)*

Prayer isn't like casting a spell. You must have confidence in the One to Whom you pray.

Biblical principles won't work if you don't believe the Word of God and believe that God loves you.

> *"He that hath my commandments, and keepeth them, he it is that loveth me: and he that loveth me shall be loved of my Father, and I will love him, and will manifest myself to him." John 14:21 (KJV)*

Manifestation is a result of God's love for you and your love for Him – if you love God you will keep His Word. The word "keep" means so much more than "holding on to something"; it mean to attend to or to know well. For example, as a mother I attend to my toddler so well that I can anticipate her next move. I know her so well that I can tell you what she wants without her even speaking.

If you want manifestation in your life, you must have confidence in God's Word, keep and attend to it. Believe the Word and have confidence in His love for you. If you doubt His Word, you hinder your manifestation.

You can't walk around expecting manifestation when you don't know and attend to His Word – You can't believe in something that you don't even know about and you certainly can't have any confidence in it!

Manifestation is attached to His Word and His love for you.

You must do more than say, "I love you.". You must manifest actions that show your love. As it is written, *"He that hath my commandments, and keepeth them, he it is that loveth me..."* John 14:21.

Think about it: you expect your spouse to manifest their love for you by bearing gifts, spending time with you, romancing you and so on. As parents, we should manifest our love through gifts, time, affection and so on to show our children that they are loved. Should we give God any less?

Hard times will hit the earth, but those who are confident in God's Word and His love for them won't even know it. God's kingdom will always supply what you need, regardless of what's going on in the world's system. When you know and believe the Word of God concerning His love for you, you have confidence that He'll supply whatever you need; therefore, you won't be stressed when situations come up.

Be careful of how you respond to circumstances, because your response indicates your level of confidence. Even when you don't see how things will work, know that God is faithful to His Word and His love for you. He will manifest Himself on your behalf.

You must hold fast to your confidence until you see the deliverance, results and manifestations of what God has said in His Word.

> *"But Christ as a son over his own house; whose house are we, if we hold fast the confidence and the rejoicing of the hope firm unto the end." Hebrews 3:6 (KJV)*

> *"For we are made partakers of Christ, if we hold the beginning of our confidence stedfast unto the end;" Hebrews 3:14 (KJV)*

Payday will come because of the confidence you have in God.

> *"Cast not away therefore your confidence, which hath great recompence of reward." Hebrews 10:35 (KJV)*

When you trust in the Lord (and His Word), you are like a mountain that cannot be moved.

> *"They that trust in the LORD shall be as mount Zion, which cannot be removed, but abideth for ever." Psalm 125:1 (KJV)*

The enemy will try to do everything he can to demonstrate to you that God's Word won't work for you and that God doesn't love you. The enemy will try to get you to blame God for the mess in your life instead of accepting responsibility for your part.

Nothing that the enemy does should move you. Do not be terrified by anything he throws at you.

> *"But none of these things move me, neither count I my life dear unto myself, so that I might finish my course with joy, and the ministry, which I have received of the Lord Jesus, to testify the gospel of the grace of God." Acts 20:24 (KJV)*

> *"And in nothing terrified by your adversaries: which is to them an evident token of perdition, but to you of salvation, and that of God." Philippians 1:28 (KJV)*

Even in hard times, you must have confidence in God's Word and His love for you. It is in revelation of God's Word and His love concerning you that will produce the might you need to win every battle. When you are confident of His Word and His love, that love will manifest everything you need to be victorious in this life.

MAINTAINING YOUR CONFIDENCE
THROUGH RIGHTEOUSNESS

Confidence is your connection to the anointing.

> *"Cast not away therefore your confidence, which hath great recompence of reward." Hebrews 10:35 (KJV)*

Confidence, for the believer, is assurance, trust and a firm belief in God's Word. Because of your love for God, keeping God's Word will bring manifest of Himself to you.

> *"He that hath my commandments, and keepeth them, he it is that loveth me: and he that loveth me shall be*

loved of my Father, and I will love him, and will manifest myself to him." John 14:21 (KJV)

The number one fear of born-again believers is that the God's Word won't come to pass. Confidence is the enemy's first area of attack; if he can get you to doubt God's Word concerning you, he can prevent you from receiving God's promises.

Understanding the free gift of righteousness is a root to your confidence in God. The moment you doubt your righteousness because of sin-consciousness, your confidence in God will be out of place. Righteousness cannot be earned; it is a free gift that is given by God's grace. All of mankind are born into sin because of Adam's high treason in the Garden of Eden and all men are made righteous through Jesus Christ.

"Wherefore, as by one man sin entered into the world, and death by sin; and so death passed upon all men, for that all have sinned: (For until the law sin was in the world: but sin is not imputed when there is no law. Nevertheless death reigned from Adam to Moses, even over them that had not sinned after the similitude of Adam's transgression, who is the figure of him that was to come. But not as the offence, so also is the free gift. For if through the offence of one many be dead, much more the grace of God, and the gift by grace, which is by one man, Jesus Christ, hath abounded unto many. And not as it was by one that sinned, so is the gift: for the judgment was by one to condemnation, but the free gift is of many offences unto justification. For if by one man's offence death reigned by one; much more they which receive abundance of grace and of the gift of righteousness shall reign in life by one, Jesus Christ.)

> *Therefore as by the offence of one judgment came upon*
> *all men to condemnation; even so by the righteousness of*
> *one the free gift came upon all men unto justification of*
> *life. For as by one man's disobedience many were made*
> *sinners, so by the obedience of one shall many be made*
> *righteous. Moreover the law entered, that the offence*
> *might abound. But where sin abounded, grace did much*
> *more abound: That as sin hath reigned unto death, even*
> *so might grace reign through righteousness unto eternal*
> *life by Jesus Christ our Lord." Romans 5:12-21 (KJV)*

The only thing you need to do to become a sinner is to be born, and the only thing you need to do to be made righteous is to be born again.

God enables you to rule in life through the free gift of righteousness. If you don't receive the gift of righteousness, you will not rule and reign in life. Righteousness, however, is not a license to sin.

> *"What shall we say then? Shall we continue in sin, that*
> *grace may abound? God forbid. How shall we, that are*
> *dead to sin, live any longer therein?" Romans 6:1-2*
> *(KJV)*

Your good works won't make you righteous, only Jesus can.

> *"Therefore by the deeds of the law there shall no flesh be*
> *justified in his sight: for by the law is the knowledge of*
> *sin. But now the righteousness of God without the law is*
> *manifested, being witnessed by the law and the prophets;*
> *Even the righteousness of God which is by faith of Jesus*
> *Christ unto all and upon all them that believe: for there*
> *is no difference: For all have sinned, and come short*
> *of the glory of God; Being justified freely by his grace*

through the redemption that is in Christ Jesus." Romans 3:20-24 (KJV)

"And enter not into judgment with thy servant: for in thy sight shall no man living be justified." Psalm 143:2 (KJV)

"Knowing that a man is not justified by the works of the law, but by the faith of Jesus Christ, even we have believed in Jesus Christ, that we might be justified by the faith of Christ, and not by the works of the law: for by the works of the law shall no flesh be justified." Galatians 2:16 (KJV)

Righteousness is available to all, in the same way that sin is available to all.

The only thing you have to do to receive righteousness is to believe.

"For if Abraham were justified by works, he hath whereof to glory; but not before God. For what saith the scripture? Abraham believed God, and it was counted unto him for righteousness. Now to him that worketh is the reward not reckoned of grace, but of debt. But to him that worketh not, but believeth on him that justifieth the ungodly, his faith is counted for righteousness." Romans 4:2-5 (KJV)

When you try to achieve righteousness by yourself, guilt and condemnation will set in when you sin or miss the mark. Only righteousness-conscious people will be able to stand in the face of battle. To say that you are unworthy is to say that Jesus' blood didn't get the job done. Righteousness will produce boldness in your life.

"The wicked flee when no man pursueth: but the righteous are bold as a lion." Proverbs 28:1 (KJV)

Because you are the righteousness of God, when you sin and ask forgiveness, God forgets your sin.

"If thou, LORD, shouldest mark iniquities, O Lord, who shall stand?" Psalm 130:3 (KJV)

Confidence in God's Word connects you to the anointing. The number one fear of born-again believers is that the God's Word won't come to pass. When you don't have a firm grasp on your righteousness, your confidence in God's ability to manifest Himself in your life will be diminished.

CONFIDENCE IN THE VOICE OF GOD

The voice of the Lord breaks the strongholds in your life.

"Give unto the LORD, O ye mighty, give unto the LORD glory and strength. Give unto the LORD the glory due unto his name; worship the LORD in the beauty of holiness. The voice of the LORD is upon the waters: the God of glory thundereth: the LORD is upon many waters. The voice of the LORD is powerful; the voice of the LORD is full of majesty. The voice of the LORD breaketh the cedars; yea, the LORD breaketh the cedars of Lebanon." Psalm 29:1-5 (KJV)

When you hear and obey the voice of God, there are no obstacles that can stand in your way. The Bible is God's Word that came from His voice. You must know God's written Word in order to understand

His spoken Word. What He speaks will always line up with what is written.

Reading the Bible alone won't bring deliverance, results or manifestations. The Bible is the door that leads you into the secret things of God. When you meditate on the Word, God will speak. Deliverance, results and manifestations comes when you hear the voice behind the Word (a Rhema word).

Faith comes by hearing.

> *"So then faith cometh by hearing, and hearing by the word of God." Romans 10:17 (KJV)*

Faith, which is the Word of God, is substance. Faith comes two ways: through the reading of the written Word and hearing a Rhema word.

Paul saw the light and heard the voice of God on the road to Damascus.

> *"And it came to pass, that, as I made my journey, and was come nigh unto Damascus about noon, suddenly there shone from heaven a great light round about me. And I fell unto the ground, and heard a voice saying unto me, Saul, Saul, why persecutest thou me?"*
> *Acts 22:6-7 (KJV)*

Those traveling with Him only saw the light. You can see the words written in the Bible, but can you hear the voice behind them?

Your ability to hear from God is crucial to experiencing success, deliverance, results and manifestations. Therefore, you must have confidence in the voice of God and be quick to obey. When He speaks, the anointing to get results is released.

THE VOICE BEHIND THE WORD

You must hear the Word of God from God in order to achieve the highest level of success. You must know God intimately and not be casually acquainted with Him to recognize His voice. Hearing God speak directly to you will bring revelation or confirmation about what is in His Word and will transform your life. Jesus' mother advised the servants to do whatever Jesus told them to do. When they obeyed, transformation took place, and Jesus turned water into wine (John 2:1-11).

Being able to hear what God tells you is the key to life's success. The Holy Spirit was sent to lead and guide you into all truth, but He can't lead you if you can't hear Him. You can't hear Him unless you read the Bible—you can't be faithful to the spoken Word if you aren't faithful to the written Word.

The wisdom of God is given to you by the Holy Spirit.

> *"Howbeit we speak wisdom among them that are perfect: yet not the wisdom of this world, nor of the princes of this world, that come to nought: But we speak the wisdom of God in a mystery, even the hidden wisdom, which God ordained before the world unto our glory: Which none of the princes of this world knew: for had they known it, they would not have crucified the Lord of glory. But as it is written, Eye hath not seen, nor ear heard, neither have entered into the heart of man, the things which God hath prepared for them that love him. But God hath revealed them unto us by his Spirit: for the Spirit searcheth all things, yea, the deep things of God." 1 Corinthians 2:6-10 (KJV)*

Wisdom is not knowledge; it is the ability to use knowledge. Wisdom is knowing what to do when you don't know what to do. The Holy Spirit reveals hidden wisdom, so it is important for you to have a relationship with God, His Word and His Spirit.

God knows all secrets—He has the secret to every situation in your life. When God's secrets are revealed to you by the Holy Spirit, they belong to you and your children.

> "The secret things belong unto the LORD our God: but those things which are revealed belong unto us and to our children for ever, that we may do all the words of this law." Deuteronomy 29:29 (KJV)

The key to your victory is the inside information that God's Spirit reveals to you. God wants to show you some things. If you open yourself up to receive revelation knowledge from God, you will never have to live an average life. You have to decide what kind of believer you want to be: one who doesn't hear from God and remains average, or one who reaches the ultimate level of success because he hears from God.

You must position yourself to receive revelation knowledge. The more time you spend in the Word and praying, the clearer your hearing becomes.

It's never a waste of time to spend time praying. Meditating on the Word positions you to hear from God. When you read a teaching (like these devotionals) several times, more will be revealed to you each time you hear it. When God says it and you see it, might and strength come into your life.

Colossians 1:9-11 is the foundation for the following prayer, which will position you to hear from God: "Lord, I thank You that I am filled with the knowledge of Your will in all wisdom and spiritual understanding, so that I might walk worthy of You, Lord, being pleasing and fruitful in every good work, increasing in the knowledge of God and strengthened with all might, according to Your glorious power."

Hearing from God involves using more than your physical ears; you must also use the ears of your heart. You have an "ear" in the center of your "heart" or in the center of your spirit, and He speaks to that ear so you can hear Him. Hearing from God is the art of being a born-again believer. God spoke to Noah in specific details when He told him to build an ark, so you also should not be satisfied with only vague impressions from God.

As a result of your getting revelation knowledge, you'll be strengthened with all might (the ability to do anything). Matthew 16:13-18 illustrates how revelation knowledge occurs and how you are strengthened with might once you receive it. Jesus asked His disciples who people thought He was, as well as who they thought He was. Simon Peter answered that Jesus was the Christ, an answer that was given to him through revelation knowledge (vv. 16-17). As a result of the revelation knowledge that Simon Peter received, Jesus called him "Peter," which means "a piece of the rock." Jesus then said that God would build His church (His believers) on the rock of revealed knowledge, and nothing would ever be able to stand against it (v. 18).

Once God reveals something to you, it strengthens you with might and empowers you to prosper. Nothing can prevail against a believer who has received revelation knowledge.

In order to achieve breakout success in life, you must hear the Word of God directly from God. He is always speaking, but if you want to receive revelation knowledge (the secret things of God revealed to you by His Spirit), you must position yourself to hear God's voice. Praying and meditating on the Word will position you to hear directly from Him.

THE ANOINTING FOR CONQUEST

You are more than a conqueror, even in the middle of hard situations.

> *"Nay, in all these things we are more than conquerors through him that loved us."*
> *Romans 8:37 (KJV)*

A conqueror is someone who consistently wins battles. Paul went through many trials, and he conquered them all.

> *"Who shall separate us from the love of Christ? shall tribulation, or distress, or persecution, or famine, or nakedness, or peril, or sword? As it is written, For thy sake we are killed all the day long; we are accounted as sheep for the slaughter. Nay, in all these things we are more than conquerors through him that loved us."*
> *Romans 8:35-37 (KJV)*

You must be possessed with a winning attitude and know that you will win every battle you face. Consistent conquest has its roots in God. Conquerors are not man-made, they are made by God. God has your back and is your guarantee to win every time.

Conquerors are Believers with the hand of the Lord upon them. The hand of the Lord, or the Spirit of God, is the anointing.

Every time something awesome happened in the Bible, it was because the hand of the Lord came upon a man or a woman. You must position yourself so that the anointing can rest on you. The hand of the Lord on your life will propel you. It will increase your strength, wisdom and your know-how. In these last days, you must have the hand of the Lord on your life if you want to get results.

David was a conquering king who never lost a battle or sustained bodily injury during war. David didn't look like "king" material; but he was chosen and appointed by God, and the anointing rested on him.

His days as a shepherd were training for his destiny. Don't get upset about where you are right now. You may be in training for the position that God is getting ready to put you in. God often allows you to be trained by the Word to be used for kingdom purposes. God won't promote you unless you're trained and ready. You may have to go through certain things in preparation for your new position. You must allow God's power to operate through you to get consistent results. The key to David's success was the anointing on his life.

> *"Then Samuel took the horn of oil, and anointed him in the midst of his brethren: and the Spirit of the LORD came upon David from that day forward. So Samuel rose up, and went to Ramah." 1 Samuel 16:13 (KJV)*

The anointing always produces proven results. As my Pastor always says, "it is better to be a 'sent' one than a 'went' one." Those who are sent by God have an anointing to get the job done. David was sent by God to defeat the Philistines (1 Samuel 17:17-54). Because of the anointing, he defeated Goliath with a single effort.

If the anointing isn't producing consistent results in your life, you may be doing something God didn't intend for you to do.

David was confident in his battle against Goliath because his mind was already trained to win. With God's help, he had already killed a lion and a bear. He had proven experience.

God loves to use the weak and the foolish to confound the wise and the strong. Don't be so quick to say what you can't do. You can do all things through Christ.

Your decision to obey the call of God should not be based on your natural abilities or age—do what God commands. If God tells you to do something, His hand will be on your life; you'll accomplish things you never dreamed you could do. If you are born again, you have a covenant with God to back you up; but until you begin consciously reminding yourself of the covenant you have with God, you will be defeated by the giants in your life.

A covenant man never begs God; He knows God will deliver him and he places a demand on God based on the Word. The battle is the Lord's, so turn your battles over to Him. If you remain covenant-minded, the enemies that now confront you will see the power of God on your life and flee from you.

David encouraged himself in the Lord in the middle of a battle and so should you (1 Samuel 30:1-19).

David always sought the Lord before going after any of his enemies. He never assumed which course of action he should take. The key to victory in battle is in hearing God's directions and obeying them.

Think about others when you're going through problems. Even in the middle of your battles you must take the time to help others. By doing so, you will find the key to your victory.

As a Believer, you need to know how to win in life. An anointing designed for conquering is available to you; but in order to tap into it, you must know that you have a right to dominate every situation you encounter.

CONQUERING THE SPIRIT OF FEAR

God did not give you a spirit of fear.

> *"Wherefore I put thee in remembrance that thou stir up the gift of God, which is in thee by the putting on of my hands. For God hath not given us the spirit of fear; but of power, and of love, and of a sound mind." 2 Timothy 1:6 (KJV)*

God gave you the gift of love, which casts out fear.

> *"There is no fear in love; but perfect love casteth out fear: because fear hath torment. He that feareth is not made perfect in love." 1 John 4:18 (KJV)*

You must stir up the gift inside of you. When you walk in the love of God, you walk in His power.

Fear is the spirit of Satan, who used fear to trick Eve in the Garden of Eden (Genesis 3:1-6). Eve feared that God was withholding something from them. Immediately after they sinned, Adam and his wife became fearful.

The root of all fear is in the belief that God's Word won't come to pass. You must make a decision to believe the Word of God.

Do not be deceived into believing that fear is a good motivator. There is torment in fear. Satan is motivated by fear. God is motivated by the Word of God that you have come to believe and embrace (faith).

The fearful and the unbeliever arrive at the same destructive end.

> *"But the fearful, and unbelieving, and the abominable, and murderers, and whoremongers, and sorcerers, and idolaters, and all liars, shall have their part in the lake which burneth with fire and brimstone: which is the second death." Revelation 21:8 (KJV)*

Unbelief is made wicked because of the presence of fear. Job's fear connected his household to destruction.

> *"For the thing which I greatly feared is come upon me, and that which I was afraid of is come unto me." Job 3:25 (KJV)*

Fear and faith operate by the same principles and are both spiritual connectors. Faith comes by hearing God's Word while fear comes by hearing Satan's words.

In these last days, men's hearts will fail because of fear.

> *"Men's hearts failing them for fear, and for looking after those things which are coming on the earth: for the powers of heaven shall be shaken." Luke 21:26 (KJV)*

Jesus has delivered you from the fear of death.

> *"Forasmuch then as the children are partakers of flesh and blood, he also himself likewise took part of the same; that through death he might destroy him that had the*

> *power of death, that is, the devil; And deliver them who*
> *through fear of death were all their lifetime subject to*
> *bondage." Hebrews 2:14-15 (KJV)*

Satan no longer has the power of death. Jesus rose with all power in His hands.

One of the reasons conquerors win every battle is because they are fearless. As a result, they are able to perform great exploits. On the other hand, people who walk in fear are slaves and are powerless against Satan. Fear is a spirit that must be resisted.

FAITH VS. FEAR

Live a life that is free from fear. You must be ready for Jesus' return and be found free from fear.

> *"Wherefore, beloved, seeing that ye look for such things,*
> *be diligent that ye may be found of him in peace, without*
> *spot, and blameless." 2 Peter 3:14 (KJV)*

You have to decide if you are going to let your life be ruled by the devil or by God. If you do not choose, you have already chosen to let the devil rule your life.

If fear is present, Satan has access to your life. If faith is present, God has access to your life.

A little bit of fear is not okay. Where there is fear, there is unbelief. You can't believe in the Word and have fear at the same time.

Understand that "nothing just happens." Nothing happens by accident. There is a reason behind everything that happens. Don't be quick to blame the devil for the things that happen to you.

There are fundamental laws that govern life. A law is an established principle. For example:

There is a <u>Law of seedtime and harvest</u> ...

> *"While the earth remaineth, seedtime and harvest, and cold and heat, and summer and winter, and day and night shall not cease." Genesis 8:22 (KJV)*

There is a <u>Law of kindness</u> ...

> *"She openeth her mouth with wisdom; and in her tongue is the <u>law of kindness</u>." Proverbs 31:26 (KJV)*

There is a Law of faith ...

> *"Where is boasting then? It is excluded. By what law? of works? Nay: but by the law of faith." Romans 3:27 (KJV)*

There is a Law of the anointing ...

> *"Bear ye one another's burdens, and so fulfil the law of Christ." Galatians 6:2 (KJV)*

There are two major laws that govern life: the law of the Spirit of life in Christ Jesus and the law of sin and death.

> *"There is therefore now no condemnation to them which are in Christ Jesus, who walk not after the flesh, but after the Spirit. For the law of the Spirit of life in Christ Jesus hath made me free from the law of sin and death." Romans 8:1-2 (KJV)*

Your lifestyle will determine which law you are under. You will experience condemnation when you walk in the flesh, which is a mindset that opposes the Word of God. You are in line with Christ when you get into the Word and aline your thinking with it.

The law of reciprocals applies to fear and faith. A reciprocal is "a corresponding but reversed or inverted action."

The reciprocal of fear is faith. The law of sin and death is the reciprocal of the law of the Spirit of life in Christ Jesus. Everything that the enemy tries to use to defeat you has a reciprocal in the law of the Spirit of life in Christ Jesus.

There are two great forces that influence your life. Faith and fear operate by the same principles.

In the same way that it is impossible to please God without faith, it is impossible to please the devil without fear.

> "But without faith it is impossible to please him: for he that cometh to God must believe that he is, and that he is a rewarder of them that diligently seek him." Hebrews 11:6 (KJV)

Fear's objective is for you not to trust in the Word. For example, the enemy doesn't want you to think that God will supply all of your needs.

> "But my God shall supply all your need according to his riches in glory by Christ Jesus." Philippians 4:19 (KJV)

Unlike faith, fear makes you rely on your senses (what you can see, touch and hear) to determine what you believe.

> "(For we walk by faith, not by sight:)" 2 Corinthians 5:7 (KJV)

Fear and faith both come by hearing.

> "So then faith cometh by hearing, and hearing by the word of God." Romans 10:17 (KJV)

Faith comes by hearing God's words and fear comes by hearing other words.

The world diligently drives fear into your thinking. Faith and fear are both spiritual connectors; they connect you to the physical manifestations that you speak, hear, think and/or do. The law of receiving says that whatever you say, hear, see and do in abundance will get into your heart. Out of your heart flow the issues of life.

> *"Keep thy heart with all diligence; for out of it are the issues of life." Proverbs 4:23 (KJV)*

Words are important because they are the seeds that shape your life. Where you are right now is the sum total of what you have allowed yourself to see, hear, say and/or do.

You turn on laws with your words.

Death and life are in the power of your tongue.

> *"Death and life are in the power of the tongue: and they that love it shall eat the fruit thereof." Proverbs 18:21 (KJV)*

You must carefully choose the words that come out of your mouth. Your mouth will guide the direction of your life like a bit guides a horse. Stop saying, "I'm afraid," "I love him to death," "I'm sick and tired of things," or "You tickle me to death." Say what you mean.

> *"But above all things, my brethren, swear not, neither by heaven, neither by the earth, neither by any other oath: but let your yea be yea; and your nay, nay; lest ye fall into condemnation." James 5:12 (KJV)*

The tongue may be small but it can cause a lot of trouble.

> *"Even so the tongue is a little member, and boasteth great things. Behold, how great a matter a little fire kindleth! And the tongue is a fire, a world of iniquity:*

> *so is the tongue among our members, that it defileth the*
> *whole body, and setteth on fire the course of nature; and*
> *it is set on fire of hell." James 3:5-6 (KJV)*

Don't allow your mouth to get you off course and away from your destination. The law of sin and death will govern your life until you repent and correct what you said. What Job feared the most came to pass.

> *"For the thing which I greatly feared is come upon me,*
> *and that which I was afraid of is come unto me." Job*
> *3:25 (KJV)*

The words that you speak may take time to produce that which you need or desire, but the manifestation is on its way, good or bad. Call those things that be not as though they were.

> *"(As it is written, I have made thee a father of many*
> *nations,) before him whom he believed, even God, who*
> *quickeneth the dead, and calleth those things which be*
> *not as though they were." Romans 4:17 (KJV)*

<u>Don't try to stop wrong actions with right actions. Change the way you think and your actions will begin to line up with the Word</u>.

Faith will connect you to everything that is under the law of the Spirit of life in Christ Jesus, such as health, prosperity, deliverance and eternal life (Hebrews 11).

Eradicate fear from your life. Where there is fear, there is no faith. Fear contaminates faith.

> *"And he saith unto them, <u>Why are ye fearful, O ye of</u>*
> *<u>little faith</u>? Then he arose, and rebuked the winds and*

the sea; and there was a great calm." Matthew 8:26 (KJV)

"And he said unto them, <u>Why are ye so fearful? how is it that ye have no faith</u>?"
Mark 4:40 (KJV)

"And he said unto them, <u>Where is your faith? And they being afraid wondered</u>, saying one to another, What manner of man is this! for he commandeth even the winds and water, and they obey him." Luke 8:25 (KJV)

Believers cannot operate effectively living in fear. Fear is not a good motivator. A small amount of fear will become haunting and tormenting and even a little fear will open the door to the enemy.

Fearing others will cause a person to fall into a trap, but those who put their trust in God will be safe.

"The fear of man bringeth a snare: but whoso putteth his trust in the LORD shall be safe." Proverbs 29:25 (KJV)

You can't be a conqueror if you have fear. "Fear not," "Be not afraid" and "Thou shall not fear" are three paramount commands for the soldiers in the army of God. There is no place in heaven for a fearful person. Fear is the root to all sin such as being an unbeliever, a degenerate, a murderer, a whoremonger, a sorcerer and an idolater or a liar, which all lead to eternity in hell.

"But the fearful, and unbelieving, and the abominable, and murderers, and whoremongers, and sorcerers, and idolaters, and all liars, shall have their part in the lake

which burneth with fire and brimstone: which is the
second death." Revelation 21:8 (KJV)

There is an old belief that a little bit of fear is good for a person. But any type of fear that is tolerated will contaminate your faith. Though fear and faith operate by the same principles, they are still very different. Learn to identify which one is operating in your life.

TITHING?

God blesses you to be a blessing to others. God has established a way for you to receive a perpetual flow of blessings in your life so that you can be a blessing to others in need.

Abraham, the father of our faith, is our example of how to be established in the blessings of God. Abraham had to change his mindset to receive God's blessings. In Genesis 12:1-3, God dealt with Abraham's way of thinking.

> *"Now the Lord said to Abram, "Get out of your land,*
> *and get away from your kinfolk, and get away from your*
> *father's house and go to a land that I will show you: I*
> *will make of you a great people, and I will bless you with*
> *abundant increase of favors and I will make your name*
> *famous and distinguished, and you will be a blessing,*
> *dispensing good to others. I will bless them that bless you,*
> *and he is cursed that curses you: through you all families*
> *of the earth will be blessed." Genesis 12:1-3 (Atarah)*

God told Abraham to get away from his relatives because they negatively influenced his mindset. If your mindset is wrong, your motives will also be wrong. Even if you read the Word, your traditions will make the Word of God of no effect.

The blessings you receive should be used to bless others. Being a blessing means dispensing good to others (v. 2). You can't dispense good to others if you don't have enough for yourself, or if you have just enough for yourself. It is only when you have an overflow that you can dispense good into somebody's life.

To receive God's blessings, you should bless those whom God blesses (v. 3). You will be blessed by sowing into the life of someone whom God has blessed. Always be sure to sow your seed into good ground.

Because the blessing was on Abraham, he overflowed in riches.

> *"And Abram was very rich in cattle, in silver, and in gold." Genesis 13:2 (KJV)*

Abraham was very rich; the spiritual blessing on his life caused physical riches to manifest. Abraham's obedience in departing from his old ways was rewarded by God.

Being obedient to God's voice along the way establishes you in God's promises.

> *"Melchizedek, the king of Salem, brought out bread and wine. He was the priest of the most high God. He blessed him by saying, "Blessed be Abram of the most high God, possessor of heaven and earth. Blessed be the most high God, who handed your enemies over to you." <u>Abram gave him a tenth of everything</u>. The king of Sodom said to Abram, "Give me the people, and keep the goods for yourself." But Abram answered the king of Sodom, "I have raised my hand in an oath to the Lord, the most high God, the possessor of heaven and earth, That I will not take so much as a thread or a sandal thong of*

anything that is yours: so that you won't be able to say, 'I made Abram rich.'" Genesis 14:18-23 (Atarah)

Tithing this ten percent must have been revealed by God, since this law had not yet been established and Abram was obedient and tithed when he gave Melchizedek (the High Priest of the Most High God) 10 percent of all the spoils of war.

"For this Melchisedec, king of Salem, priest of the most high God, who met Abraham returning from the slaughter of the kings, and blessed him; To whom also Abraham gave a tenth part of all; first being by interpretation King of righteousness, and after that also King of Salem, which is, King of peace; Without father, without mother, without descent, having neither beginning of days, nor end of life; but made like unto the Son of God; abideth a priest continually. Now consider how great this man was, unto whom even the patriarch Abraham gave the tenth of the spoils. And verily they that are of the sons of Levi, who receive the office of the priesthood, have a commandment to take tithes of the people according to the law, that is, of their brethren, though they come out of the loins of Abraham: But he whose descent is not counted from them received tithes of Abraham, and blessed him that had the promises. And without all contradiction the less is blessed of the better." Hebrews 7:1-7 (KJV)

Melchizedek was made like the Son of God, Jesus. His appearance to Abraham is one of the appearances of Jesus Christ in the Old Testament. Jesus existed from the beginning; that's why God said in Genesis 1:26, "Let Us" make man in Our image.

Melchizedek blessed Abraham when Abraham was obedient and gave the tithe.

Tithing is not the same as "giving." The tithe is a systematic release of the tenth of all of your increase to God.

> *"And all the tithe of the land, whether of the seed of the land, or of the fruit of the tree, is the LORD'S: it is holy unto the LORD." Leviticus 27:30 (KJV)*

Under the New Covenant, we have already been blessed with all spiritual blessings. We do not give for the windows of heaven to be opened up as it was under the Old Covenant.

> *"Blessed be the God and Father of our Lord Jesus Christ, who hath blessed us with all spiritual blessings in heavenly places in Christ:" Ephesians 1:3 (KJV)*

We now tithe out of our love and reverence for the Lord and because He have <u>already</u> blessed us! The Lord required 10% of one's increase, the result of his or her efforts to provide for the needs of the family, were to be given to the Lord, since the Lord was the superior of a covenant between Himself and the descendents of Abraham.

Because of our love, reverence and desire to tithe, I will tell you where you should tithe: under the Covenant of Moses, people gave to the Levites, or priests, who ministered to the Lord on their behalf. The practical application of the principle is that you should give your tithe in that place where you have your primary spiritual allegiance, where you are fed spiritually, where you are prayed for and where you are sustained, comforted and supported.

One may ask, "My spouse does not attend services and objects to my tithing. What should I do?"

Do not press the issue. Do not take anything I've said about tithing or finances and give your spouse or any member of your family any reason to suspect that you are trying to extract money which they are reluctant to give. Tithes and offerings should be given only out of your love, reverence and a willing, cheerful, and open heart before the Lord.

Born-again believers have a covenant with God and are supposed to be wealthy. In the last days, God will use the wealth of His servants to impact the lives of people around the world. You must be permanently established in the blessings of God to arrive at the place He ordained for you. The blessings of God give you the ability to have success in every area of your life. When God's blessings rest on you, they will transform your "average" existence into a life of overflow.

Under the old covenant, people gave a tithe because they were supposed to. Under the new covenant, we should tithe like Abraham did- out of love and appreciation for what the Lord has already done.

TAKING AUTHORITY OVER YOUR EMOTIONS
PART 1

We are emotional beings. We all have emotions. The question is: Do your emotions have you? Both men and women have emotions, but they deal with them differently. Most women verbalize, while most men internalize.

Emotions are "feelings caused by pain or pleasure that try to move you in a certain direction." If your emotions are in charge of your life, they will determine the direction of your life. When you are in charge of your life and you believe the Word of God above anything and everything, your emotions will line up with God and His Word. Emotions come from your thoughts (soul).

> *"Beloved, I wish above all things that thou mayest prosper and be in health, even as thy soul prospereth."*
> 3 John 1:2 (KJV)

As your soul (thoughts, feeling and emotions) go, your life will follow.

God created us to dominate; however, we were not designed to dominate people. People who try to control others don't have control over their own emotions.

Mastering your emotions doesn't mean that you can no longer express them. God designed us to express passion and emotion. Sin, the devil and the curse that resulted from Adam's disobedience in the garden perverted emotions.

People who are not born again are controlled by their feelings and emotions and are under the curse.

Adam and Eve were controlled by their emotions when they took in the evil thoughts and acted on those thoughts. Their disobedience brought the curse of the law into place.

You must not be ruled by your emotions because they can constantly change. Emotions are designed to take you somewhere. Ask yourself: Where are my emotions taking me?

It is important that you allow the Word of God to control your emotions and decisions. When your thoughts line up with the Word, your emotions will fall in line, and you will have peace and security.

Learn to control your thoughts, because your emotions will follow your most dominate thoughts.

If you can control your feelings and emotions, you can do anything.

> "He that is slow to anger is better than the mighty; and he that ruleth his spirit than he that taketh a city."
> Proverbs 16:32 (KJV)

> "He that is slow to anger is more valuable than the mighty; and he that rules his thoughts and emotions more valuable than an army that takes a city." Proverbs 16:32 (Atarah)

A person who can control his emotions is more powerful than an army that can take a city.

Here are some points to remember:

- You *can* take control over your emotions.
- Self-control is a godly force that God uses to direct your life where He has designed it to go.
- Uncontrolled or unyielding emotions lead to controlling people.

Jesus had emotions, but His emotions did not have control over Him. Jesus understands our weaknesses and temptations; He experienced them also.

> "For we have not an high priest which cannot be touched with the feeling of our infirmities; but was in all points tempted like as we are, yet without sin." Hebrews 4:15 (KJV)

Jesus' emotions tried to move Him out of the will of God.

> *"And they came to a place which was named Gethsemane: and he saith to his disciples, Sit ye here, while I shall pray. And he taketh with him Peter and James and John, and began to be sore amazed, and to be **very heavy**; And saith unto them, <u>My soul is exceeding sorrowful unto death</u>: tarry ye here, and watch. And **he went forward** a little, and <u>fell on the ground</u>, **and prayed** that, if it were possible, the hour might pass from him." Mark 14:32-35 (KJV)*

Jesus' emotions were apparent—He was struck with terror and amazement. He was deeply troubled and depressed, and His soul was exceeding sorrowful to the point that it almost killed Him. He was attacked in His emotions, just like we are.

> We have to find the balance between the Word of God that we say we believe and our emotions. Jesus did not allow His emotions to dictate His decisions. Don't allow your decisions to be based on how you feel. The world has a saying, "If it feels good, then it must be right.", but as a born-again believer, you have to follow the Word of God.

Even though Jesus' emotions were trying to lead Him away from the cross, He:

1. went forward—He didn't stop going in the direction that God called Him to.
2. continued to pray—you have to pray through the situation.

How you deal with your feelings and emotions will determine whether you experience a blessing or the curse.

Don't make decisions based on emotions, but on the Word of God and His guidance.

Don't allow things that look good to the eye to move you. The fruit was appealing to Adam and Eve. In the beginning, Adam and Eve based their decision to sin on the thoughts, the appearance and their emotions.

There are three factors in making successful decisions vs. emotional decisions:

1. Accurate knowledge.

   "My people are destroyed for lack of knowledge: because thou hast rejected knowledge, I will also reject thee, that thou shalt be no priest to me: seeing thou hast forgotten the law of thy God, I will also forget thy children." Hosea 4:6 (KJV)

2. Wisdom and wise counsel.
3. Understanding the process to reach the desired goals.

Many problems that people face are based on their emotions.

The degree to which you gain control of your emotions is the degree to which you will walk free from the dictates of sin.

Everybody has emotions. They are a part of who God made us to be and a part of our spiritual makeup. It is important that we acknowledge our emotions and learn how to align them with the Word of God. It's time to take charge over our emotions!

THE ROOT TO NEGATIVE EMOTIONS

Feelings are designed to move you in a certain direction—either toward or away from the will of God for your life and are a part of your soul.

> *"Beloved, I wish above all things that thou mayest prosper and be in health, even as thy soul prospereth."*
> 3 John 1:2 (KJV)

It is okay to have emotions, but your emotions should not control you.

Jesus had emotions, but instead of yielding to them He prayed and kept moving forward in God's plan for His life. In the Garden of Gethsemane, He was overwhelmed with sorrow and depression, but He continued on in the will of God for His life, which meant going to the cross.

The root to every negative emotion is a sense of powerlessness.

There are three areas that Satan wants you to believe that you cannot change:

1. Your circumstances.
2. Your personality.
3. Your weaknesses.

You have the God-given authority to change your circumstances, personality and weaknesses. You have been given two gifts: seed and dominion. Jesus has endowed you with His authority.

> *"And Jesus came and spake unto them, saying, All power is given unto me in heaven and in earth." Matthew 28:18 (KJV)*

You have authority over every attack of the enemy, including attacks on your mind and emotions.

> *"Behold, I give unto you power to tread on serpents and scorpions, and over all the power of the enemy: and nothing shall by any means hurt you." Luke 10:19 (KJV)*

Take authority over mental and emotional attacks in the name of Jesus. Nothing can hurt the person who believes he has authority over the devil.

As a born-again believer, you are "authorized" to determine what happens on the earth. Prayer is the Believer's authority to put into motion and approve the requisitions for God to get involved in any area of your life. If you don't allow God to get involved in your life, He can't – God is bound by His own Word.

Satan will test you to see if you know your authority.

> *"Then certain of the vagabond Jews, exorcists, took upon them to call over them which had evil spirits the name of the Lord Jesus, saying, We adjure you by Jesus whom Paul preacheth. And there were seven sons of one Sceva, a Jew, and chief of the priests, which did so. And the evil spirit answered and said, Jesus I know, and Paul I know; but who are ye?" Acts 19:13-15 (KJV)*

When you know who you are and Whose you are, you don't have to prove anything; all you have to do is speak the Word.

> *"Then was Jesus led up of the Spirit into the wilderness to be tempted of the devil. And when he had fasted forty*

days and forty nights, he was afterward an hungred. And when the tempter came to him, he said, If thou be the Son of God, command that these stones be made bread. But he answered and said, It is written, Man shall not live by bread alone, but by every word that proceedeth out of the mouth of God. Then the devil taketh him up into the holy city, and setteth him on a pinnacle of the temple, And saith unto him, If thou be the Son of God, cast thyself down: for it is written, He shall give his angels charge concerning thee: and in their hands they shall bear thee up, lest at any time thou dash thy foot against a stone. Jesus said unto him, It is written again, Thou shalt not tempt the Lord thy God. Again, the devil taketh him up into an exceeding high mountain, and sheweth him all the kingdoms of the world, and the glory of them; And saith unto him, All these things will I give thee, if thou wilt fall down and worship me. Then saith Jesus unto him, Get thee hence, Satan: for it is written, Thou shalt worship the Lord thy God, and him only shalt thou serve." Matthew 4:1-10 (KJV)

When you allow negative emotions to rule your life, it is because you feel powerless to change your situation or circumstance. However, God has given you authority over your emotions. You can rule over them rather than allowing your emotions to rule over you and govern your decisions. By using your God-given authority, you can walk in complete dominion over negative emotions to the point that nothing can hurt you.

TAKING CONTROL OVER YOUR EMOTIONS
PART 2

God created you to have emotions. Man is a tri-part being—he is a spirit, he lives in a physical body and possesses a soul. Your soul is made up of three parts: your thoughts, your decisions and the way you feel. The way you think determines what type of emotions you have. If you think in line with the Word, you will experience life and peace. If you don't, you'll experience emotional turmoil. As a free moral agent, God has equipped you with the right to make decisions (Deuteronomy 30:19).

God wants your soul to be in good health.

> *"Beloved, I wish above all things that thou mayest prosper and be in health, even as thy soul prospereth."*
> *3 John 1:2 (KJV)*

Emotions are feelings on the inside caused by pain or pleasure that will direct your life to a certain place. If you allow your emotions or feelings to direct your life, Satan will be able to move you away from the will of God for your life.

God gave you emotions, but He did not intend for your emotions to rule your life. God wants you to take control over your emotions. Having an understanding of the Word and allowing your life to be governed by the Word will enable you to control your emotions. If you don't have control over your emotions, you will try to control others, which is not God's will. A person who can control his or her emotions can accomplish anything in life.

Jesus had emotions, but He was in control of them regardless of the situation. Jesus is able to understand and sympathize with our weaknesses and the feelings of our infirmities because He was also tempted.

> *"For we have not an high priest which cannot be touched with the feeling of our infirmities; but was in all points tempted like as we are, yet without sin." Hebrews 4:15 (KJV)*

Mark 14:32-36 shows Jesus' emotions attacking Him in the Garden of Gethsemane, but He didn't cave in or quit. He followed the will of God for His life. Ask yourself: Am I allowing my emotions and feelings to move me away from the will of God for my life?

Take control over your emotions. People often make emotional decisions when trying to protect their feelings. When they do so, they are not thinking about their future.

The root to negative emotions is a sense of powerlessness. Satan tries to negatively convince you that:

1. You can't change your circumstances.
2. You can't change your personality.
3. You are weak.

The truth is that God has given you the control and ability to change everything.

God gave His authority to Adam. Adam then gave away his authority to Satan, but Jesus returned the authority and control to the Believer by taking it from Satan.

> *"Behold, I give unto you power to tread on serpents and scorpions, and over all the power of the enemy: and nothing shall by any means hurt you." Luke 10:19 (KJV)*

You have authority over the earth and are able to call those things that are not as though they were, so speak your health, wisdom, wealth and prosperity no matter what it looks like.

Know your authority. In Acts 19:13-16, the sons of Sceva tried to use the authority found in Jesus' name to cast out demons, without having a revelation of His power. As a result, the demons were able to defeat them. If you don't believe that you have authority, you will put up with sickness, depression, lack, powerlessness and bondage. Knowing your authority gives you power over everything.

Satan will test you to see if you know who you are in Christ and if you know your authority. Adam and Eve did not know their authority and gave it away (Genesis 3:1-6). Jesus knew His authority and put Satan in his place (Matthew 4:1-11).

You have the authority to hire heaven or hire hell to work on your behalf. Which will you choose?

It is time to get rid of hurt. Hurt is designed to keep you away from the blessings of God in your life. Hurt keeps you where you are and stops you from moving forward. God is committed to healing those who are hurt.

> *"He healeth the broken in heart, and bindeth up their wounds." Psalm 147:3 (KJV)*

A broken and hurt person will not be able to stand up under pressure.

> *"The spirit of a man will sustain his infirmity; but a wounded spirit who can bear?" Proverbs 18:14 (KJV)*

Throw out the old saying, "Sticks and stones may break my bones, but words will never hurt me.", because the truth is that words hurt. Harsh words can pierce like a sword, but the words of the wise bring healing.

"There is that speaketh like the piercings of a sword: but the tongue of the wise is health." Proverbs 12:18 (KJV)

Locate your hurt and get rid of it. Don't build a foundation on it or use it as a crutch. Hurt will distort your view and make you bitter toward others; it will stop you from moving forward in life.

To stop hurt from happening, you have to stop finding your point of reference in past pains and relating those pains to every situation. Even though it hurts, you must dismiss what people have done to you and forgive them. Stop exposing your wounds to everyone and let them heal.

There are three things that you will notice when you are around hurt people:

1. They are unpleasant to be around. They talk about their past often. They prompt you to ask them what is wrong. They wear their feelings on their sleeves and seek sympathy.
2. They become angry, which can turn inward. They lose initiative to fight against the hurt, allowing depression to set in.
3. They seldom make good decisions. Hurt people make decisions to protect their feelings, not their future.

Understand that life is a series of decisions that must be governed by the Word of God to live an abundant and prosperous life.

God gave us authority over everything on the earth, including our emotions. Unfortunately, most people allow their emotions to rule their lives. When emotions dominate you, they will lead you away from the will of God for your life. Living an emotional life leads to hurt, depression, sickness, lack and no thought concerning your future. It is time for born-again believers to take authority over their emotions.

TAKING CONTROL OVER OUR EMOTIONS

God desires your soul to prosper, which includes your emotions.

> *"Beloved, I wish above all things that thou mayest prosper and be in health, even as thy soul prospereth."*
> 3 John 1:2 (KJV)

Your soul is made up of your mind, will and emotions. Emotions are feelings on the inside, caused by pleasure or pain, that try to get you to move in a certain direction.

It is God's will for you to master your emotions. When you are not mastering your emotions, they are mastering you. When you take control of your thoughts by lining them up with the Word, your emotions will fall in line with your thinking.

> Your emotions should not lead your life. Self-control is a godly force – *"He that is slow to anger is more valuable than the mighty; and he that rules his thoughts and emotions more valuable than an army that takes a city."* Proverbs 16:32 (Atarah)

> *"He that is slow to anger is better than the mighty; and he that ruleth his spirit than he that taketh a city."* Proverbs 16:32 (KJV)

The root cause of every negative emotion is a sense of powerlessness.

Jesus had emotions, but He didn't let His emotions control Him.

> *"Seeing then that we have a great high priest, that is passed into the heavens, Jesus the Son of God, let us hold fast our profession." Hebrews 4:14 (KJV)*

Jesus experienced every feeling that we experience. He understands our emotions when we go through things, but we must follow His example.

You don't give authority to feelings just because they show up.

Satan tried to move Jesus away from the will of God for His life by attacking His emotions in the Garden of Gethsemane.

> *"And they came to a place which was named Gethsemane: and he saith to his disciples, Sit ye here, while I shall pray. And he taketh with him Peter and James and John, and began to be <u>sore amazed</u>, and to be **very heavy**; And saith unto them, <u>My soul is exceeding sorrowful unto death</u>: tarry ye here, and watch. And **he went forward** a little, and <u>fell on the ground,</u> **and prayed** that, if it were possible, the hour might pass from him. " Mark 14:32-35 (KJV)*

No matter what you face emotionally, go forward and pray through it as Jesus did.

There are three areas in which the devil wants to convince you that you can't change:

1. Your personality.
2. Your circumstances.
3. Your weaknesses.

God has given you authority over all the power of the enemy.

> *"Behold, I give unto you power to tread on serpents*
> *and scorpions, and over all the power of the enemy:*
> *and nothing shall by any means hurt you." Luke 10:19*
> *(KJV)*

The devil can't force you to do anything; he can only make suggestions. He tries to hurt you emotionally so that you are vulnerable to his attacks. When you are hurt, your emotions are pumped up and cause you to make emotional decisions, which move you out of the will of God for your life. When you put up defenses to protect your feelings, you are also protecting Satan's access points into your life. Hurt is designed to stop you from moving forward. You can make a firm decision and be determined to never be hurt another day in your life. You can be emotionally invincible. You must dismiss what people have done to you.

When you get angry and depressed, you lose the ability to fight off negative feelings. Hurt people make bad decisions.

There is a right and a wrong way to get over hurt.

The seven steps to being delivered from hurt are:

1. Take up the shield of faith, which is the Word of God (Ephesians 6:16). It is what God says that matters, not what others say.
2. Forgive others as an act of obedience to the Word of God that you say you believe. Forgiveness is a decision, not something that is done according to how you feel or how another person treats you. Your forgiveness should never be for sale

by expecting others to do something or change before you forgive them.

3. Stop reliving the situation.
4. Stop making excuses for why you are so easily hurt. Get out of your past (Philippians 3:13).
5. Stop wearing your emotions on your sleeve.
6. Stop trying to get even with people who have hurt you.
7. Take the cares of the situation to Jesus and trust Him - lean and depend on Him. Rest assured in God.

When you have been hurt, don't:

1. Try to get back at someone by hurting him or her.
2. Pretend you are not hurt.
3. Decide not to trust anymore.
4. Harden your heart.

God created you with emotions, but He never intended for your emotions to control you. It is possible to completely master your emotions. By taking authority over hurt and unruly emotions, you can become emotionally invincible.

TRUST

Trusting God leads to peace and it opens the door to blessings. Trust God with your whole heart and do not lean on your own understanding. (Proverbs 3:5).

> *"Trust in the LORD with all thine heart; and lean not unto thine own understanding."*
> *Proverbs 3:5 (KJV)*

In every situation, there will be things we do not understand in the natural and can only be understood through the Word of God. Leaning on our own understanding makes us double-minded.

God keeps us in perfect peace when our mind is fixed on Him, because we trust in Him.

> *"Thou wilt keep him in perfect peace, whose mind is stayed on thee: because he trusteth in thee." Isaiah 26:3 (KJV)*

Keeping our mind on the Word is especially important when it is under attack. This is easier when we find something from the Word of God that we can verbally confess when the enemy hits.

David wrote of his trust in God and that his times were in God's hand. He verbally confessed that God was his God.

> *"But I trusted in thee, O LORD: I said, Thou art my God. My times are in thy hand: deliver me from the hand of mine enemies, and from them that persecute me." Psalm 31:14 -15 (KJV)*

We must be careful what we verbally confess, and avoid religious declarations that go against the Word.

When we trust God and commit our way to Him, He will bring to pass the desires of our heart.

> *"Commit thy way unto the LORD; trust also in him; and he shall bring it to pass."*
> *Psalm 37:5 (KJV)*

If we trust God, it will show in our lives.

Certain things will be evident in our lives of we fully trust God.

Whoever makes God his trust and does not respect the proud or turn aside to lies will be blessed.

> *"Blessed is that man that maketh the LORD his trust, and respecteth not the proud, nor such as turn aside to lies." Psalm 40:4 (KJV)*

We are empowered to prosper when we resist the temptation to be moved by the things of the world, and trust God instead.

> *"Let us labour therefore to enter into that rest, lest any man fall after the same example of unbelief." Hebrews 4:11 (KJV)*

Here, "rest" is defined as trust and a confident reliance on God. Our trust and rest will apprehend our manifestations in life such as healing, deliverance, and success. For example, if your car breaks down on the side of the road and you call your spouse to come and get you, you trust and have confidence that they are on their way. Someone else may offer to help you while you wait and your confidence in your spouse will determine whether or not you trust they'll be there or begin to doubt.

There are seven things will be evident on our lives if we are trusting and leaning on God.

1. Not being depend on ourselves.
2. Crying out to God. In all your ways acknowledge God, and He will direct your paths (Proverbs 3:6). That the closeness (intimacy) that you have with the Word of God that you have come to embrace by analyzing and assimilating it into your

way of thinking – *in doing these things,* you produce results by the acknowledging of every good thing that is in you in Christ Jesus (the Anointed One and His Anointing) (Philemon 1:6). When we pray and cry out loud to God at all times, He will hear us (Psalm 55:17).

3. Avoiding evil. Do not be wise in your own eyes, fear God, and depart from evil (Proverbs 3:7). Flee youthful lusts. Follow righteousness, faith, love, and peace with those who call on God with a pure heart (2 Timothy 2:22).

4. Putting God first in our lives.

5. Checking ourselves by His Word.

6. Listening to the Holy Spirit which is the inward voice within; our conscience. (When you are a born-again believer who has been meditating on the Word of God, you can trust your conscience).

7. Learning how to rest in God's love.

When we strike a balance between the Word of God that we have heard and come to believe and grace (the unmerited love, favor and empowerment), we learn that trust brings the manifestations from the kingdom of God. This trust teaches us that God is faithful, and He will do exactly what He says He will do. When we examine the word "trust," it must go beyond the simple cliché most people utter when they say they trust God. For many, this is just a word, but it actually boils down to what we practice beyond the cliché. As Believers, we must take the steps to ensure we are leaning on Him.

TRUST
PART 2

When we trust God instead of ourselves, supernatural things begin to happen.

> *"Trust in the LORD with all thine heart; and lean not unto thine own understanding. In all thy ways acknowledge him, and he shall direct thy paths."*
> *Proverbs 3:5-6 (KJV)*

To trust Him is to rely or lean on Him, having confidence in His integrity, strength, ability and surety. It is a confident expectation of something. For example, if your car breaks down on the side of the road and you call your spouse to come and get you, you trust and have confidence that they are on their way. Someone else may offer to help you while you wait but your confidence in your spouse will cause you to turn away someone else's help.

We verify our trust when we refuse to rely on what we understand about the situation, relying instead on the promises God made.

God keeps in perfect peace those who fix their mind on Him because they trust Him.

> *"Thou wilt keep him in perfect peace, whose mind is stayed on thee: because he trusteth in thee." Isaiah 26:3 (KJV)*

We keep our mind on Him by keeping it in the Word.

We trust in God when we verbally confess He is our God. Our times are in His hand, and He will deliver us.

"But I trusted in thee, O LORD: I said, Thou art my God. My times are in thy hand: deliver me from the hand of mine enemies, and from them that persecute me." Psalm 31:14-15 (KJV)

What we say and do will verify whether or not we trust Him.

When we commit our way to God and trust Him, He will bring manifestations to pass.

"Commit thy way unto the LORD; trust also in him; and he shall bring it to pass." Psalm 37:5 (KJV)

This promise is based on trust, not on what we do. What we do and say is a result of what we believe and trust.

Learning to trust God is work, but we are commanded to do so.

The person who makes the Lord his trust and does not turn aside to lies, is blessed.

"Blessed is that man that maketh the LORD his trust, and respecteth not the proud, nor such as turn aside to lies." Psalm 40:4 (KJV)

Being blessed means being empowered to have success in every area of life.

We must labor to enter into God's rest, lest anyone fall after the example of unbelief.

"Let us labour therefore to enter into that rest, lest any man fall after the same example of unbelief." Hebrews 4:11 (KJV)

If we labor to rest, our blessings will include manifestations such as healing, success, deliverance and wholeness.

Jesus' sheep know His voice and follow Him. He gives them eternal life, and no one can pluck them out of God's hand.

> *"Jesus answered them, I told you, and ye believed not: the works that I do in my Father's name, they bear witness of me. But ye believe not, because ye are not of my sheep, as I said unto you. My sheep hear my voice, and I know them, and they follow me: And I give unto them eternal life; and they shall never perish, neither shall any man pluck them out of my hand. My Father, which gave them me, is greater than all; and no man is able to pluck them out of my Father's hand. I and my Father are one." John 10:25-30 (KJV)*

Sheep follow their shepherd because they trust and depend on him.

In the book of Numbers, we read that the people complained against God and Moses because of a lack of bread and water. God allowed the serpents to bite the people and many died. God told Moses to make a brass serpent and put it on a pole so that all who looked upon the serpent would live.

"And the people complained and spoke against God and against Moses, saying, "Why have you brought us out of Egypt to die here in the wilderness? There is nothing to eat or drink here. And we hate this horrible manna (bread)!" Then the Lord loosed the poisonous serpents that were held-back from the people; and they bit the people, and many Israelites died. The people came to

Moses and said, "We sinned by speaking against the LORD and against you. Pray to the LORD that he rid us of these snakes." Moses prayed for the people, The Lord said to Moses, "Make a fiery serpent and set it on a pole; and everyone who is bitten, when he looks at it, shall live." Moses made a serpent of bronze and put it on a pole, and if a serpent had bitten any one, when they looked to the serpent of bronze (attentively and expectantly), they lived." Numbers 21:5-9

We live when we look upon God instead of the situation.

There are seven steps to follow to ensure we are leaning on God.

1. Do not depend on yourself.
2. Cry out to God. Evening, morning, and noontime I will pray and cry aloud. (Psalm 55:17).
3. Run from evil. Do not be wise in your own eyes, fear God, and depart from evil (Proverbs 3:7-8). Run away from youthful lust (childish ways). Follow righteousness, the Word of God that you have heard and come to believe, follow love in peace and fellowship with all believers, who call upon the Lord out of a pure heart. (2 Timothy 2:22).
4. Put God first in your life. Honor God with the first fruits of your increase (Proverbs 3:9-10).
5. Evaluate yourself by His Word.
6. Listen to the Holy Spirit (the inner voice inside; your conscience).
7. Rest in God's love.

All Believers know the importance of trusting God, but how do we really know we are truly trusting in Him? "I trust God" must be more than simply a cliché or a religious saying. We know for sure that the enemy will attack our minds to make us question whether or not we are relying on God, but as born-again believers, there are certain things we can do to verify we are actually depending on Him. Every manifestation we see in our lives is a result of trust. To know for sure that we truly trust God, there is a practical side to trust that we can use to gauge how much we really lean and depend on Him.

THE UNDENIABLE LAWS OF PROSPERITY

Faith comes by hearing the Word.

> *"So then faith cometh by hearing, and hearing by the word of God." Romans 10:17 (KJV)*

Belief in the Word comes by hearing the Word of God, analyzing and assimilating it into your way of thinking (hearing it over and over). *What you think on consistently, you will come to believe, then you will act accordingly. (Proverbs 23:7)*

When you believe and act on what you see in the Word, faith will come.

No Word, no faith.

Truth is only found in God's Word.

> *"Sanctify them through thy truth: thy word is truth." John 17:17 (KJV)*

There is a difference between truth and fact. The diagnosis you receive from a doctor is a fact but the Word of God contains the truth regarding your health. Truth can change the facts and set you free.

What makes something true or false depends on what God has to say about it. To understand the truth about prosperity, you must read the Word.

> *"Beloved, I wish above all things that thou mayest prosper and be in health, even as thy soul prospereth. For I rejoiced greatly, when the brethren came and testified of the truth that is in thee, even as thou walkest in the truth. I have no greater joy than to hear that my children walk in truth."* 3 John 1:2 (KJV)

Many preachers teach that prosperity is evil and ungodly but you have to ask, "What is their definition of prosperity?", because God desires for you to prosper. Therefore, prosperity cannot be evil.

> *"Beloved, I wish <u>above all things that thou mayest prosper</u> and be in health, even as thy soul prospereth."* 3 John 1:2 (KJV)

> *"Beloved, follow not that which is evil, but that which is good. He that doeth good is of God: but he that doeth evil hath not seen God."* 3 John 1:11 (KJV)

God doesn't want you to follow that which is evil, only that which is good. Prosperity is good in and of itself.

Prosperity is translated from the Hebrew word "shalom", which means, "peace, well-being, wholeness, nothing missing and nothing broken."

You can be made whole in your spirit, soul and body.

> *"And the very God of peace sanctify you wholly; and I pray God your whole spirit and soul and body be*

preserved blameless unto the coming of our Lord Jesus Christ. Faithful is he that calleth you, who also will do it." 1 Thessalonians 5:23-24 (KJV)

God takes pleasure in your prosperity.

"Let them shout for joy, and be glad, that favour my righteous cause: yea, let them say continually, Let the LORD be magnified, <u>which hath pleasure in the prosperity of his servant</u>." Psalm 35:27 (KJV)

We have allowed the world to define prosperity instead of reading the Word and finding out what God's definition is.

Another misconception that has been taught to Believers is that "money is the root of all evil". Money is neither good nor bad; it depends on who has it. It is written that the **love of money** is the root of all evil.

"For the <u>love of money is the root of all evil</u>: which while some coveted after, they have erred from the faith, and pierced themselves through with many sorrows." 1 Timothy 6:10 (KJV)

The love of money is the root of all evil: it is through this craving that some have been led astray and have wandered from the Word of God that they came to believe, and they live to regret it bitterly ever after.

Having a wrong relationship with material things is the root to all evil. Money makes a lousy god but an excellent servant.

Materialism is when you try to resolve a spiritual need with a physical solution. For example, you try to resolve depression by shopping.

Prosperity covers much more than finances. People who think prosperity means money are not incorrect, but they are incomplete.

You are a spirit being that has a soul and lives in a physical body.

To prosper in your soul means that you control your mind, will and emotions. You must cast down thoughts that go against the Word of God.

> *"Casting down imaginations, and every high thing that exalteth itself against the knowledge of God, and bringing into captivity every thought to the obedience of Christ;" 2 Corinthians 10:5 (KJV)*

To prosper in your body means that you are healthy. Your degree of soul prosperity determines how well you prosper in other areas of life. If your soul is not fed the truth, it will decrease in its prosperity, as well as in other areas of your life.

Let's read it again...

> *"Beloved, I wish above all things that thou mayest prosper and be in health, even as thy soul prospereth." 3 John 1:2 (KJV)*

The Word of God is the highway to the world of wealth. It brings prosperity to the spirit, soul and body.

When you walk in the Word of God, you will prosper and be in health.

> *"For the word of God is quick, and powerful, and sharper than any twoedged sword, piercing even to the dividing asunder of soul and spirit, and of the joints and*

marrow, and is a discerner of the thoughts and intents of the heart." Hebrews 4:12 (KJV)

Jesus was anointed to preach the Gospel (Good News) to the poor.

"The Spirit of the Lord is upon me, because he hath anointed me <u>to preach the gospel to the</u> <u>poor</u>; he hath sent me to heal the brokenhearted, to preach deliverance to the captives, and recovering of sight to the blind, to set at liberty them that are bruised," Luke 4:18 (KJV)

It is interesting that the solution for the poor is to have the Gospel preached to them! Here we read Jesus said it again ...

"Now when John had heard in the prison the works of Christ, he sent two of his disciples, And said unto him, Art thou he that should come, or do we look for another? Jesus answered and said unto them, Go and shew John again those things which ye do hear and see: The blind receive their sight, and the lame walk, the lepers are cleansed, and the deaf hear, the dead are raised up, <u>and the poor have the gospel preached to them</u>." Matthew 11:2 (KJV)

Why didn't Jesus say that He gives money to the poor instead of preaching to the poor? How is preaching going to help a poor person? Only the Word of God triumphs over the spirit of poverty. For example, I know someone who was dirt poor and living in poverty; they were given money and placed in a nice home. I went to visit them later and noticed that poverty followed them. The money is gone, they are sick and the nice home now is trashed and the neighbors were complaining. This is when I came to the realization that you can take a person out of poverty but you can't take poverty out of the person – only the Word of God can do that!

If you are going to live in the kingdom of God system, you must have a relationship with the King. A higher system of operation is at work in God's kingdom. The anointing operates in the kingdom of God. Satan doesn't want you to believe that there is something more powerful than the anointing. When you have the anointing, you have wisdom (the ability to use knowledge), and the finances will come.

A law is an established principal that always works the same way for anyone who gets involved in it. Spiritual laws govern prosperity. When most people hear the word "prosperity," however, they mistakenly think it only refers to money. Money cannot adequately define prosperity. If you want to experience prosperity in every area of life, you must do so through the Word of God.

THE UNDENIABLE LAWS OF PROSPERITY (CONT'D)

Prosperity is more than money. The word prosperity comes from the word "shalom", which means "peace; well-being; wholeness; having nothing missing or broken.".

Prosperity is having the ability to meet the needs of mankind no matter what those needs are. God desires for you to have total life prosperity.

> "Beloved, I wish above all things that thou mayest prosper and be in health, even as thy soul prospereth."
> 3 John 1:2 (KJV)

Soul prosperity is when your mind is yielded to the Word of God. There is no true prosperity apart from the Word.

The Law of the Spirit of life in Christ Jesus governs prosperity and supersedes the law of sin and death.

> *"For the law of the Spirit of life in Christ Jesus hath made me free from the law of sin and death." Romans 8:2 (KJV)*

When you don't obey laws, you can get hurt. For example, if you step off of the top of a building, the law of gravity dictates that you will fall to the ground. The force of gravity makes the law of gravity work.

To get out from under laws that are working against you, you must begin to operate under a law that is greater. The laws of thrust and lift supersede the law of gravity.

Depression, sickness, poverty, lack and bondage cannot override the Law of the Spirit of life in Christ Jesus. You have to learn how to operate on a higher level of existence.

Everyone can be prosperous, but not everyone will be prosperous.

People don't go to hell for being bad; they go to hell for rejecting Jesus and not accepting their deliverance. We have examples of great men and women of God who did exploits and were blessed because they accepted their deliverance.

> *"By faith the harlot Rahab perished not with them that believed not, when she had received the spies with peace. And what shall I more say? for the time would fail me to tell of Gedeon, and of Barak, and of Samson, and of Jephthae; of David also, and Samuel, and of the prophets: Who through faith subdued kingdoms, wrought righteousness, obtained promises, stopped the*

mouths of lions, Quenched the violence of fire, escaped the edge of the sword, out of weakness were made strong, waxed valiant in fight, turned to flight the armies of the aliens. Women received their dead raised to life again: and others were tortured, not accepting deliverance; that they might obtain a better resurrection." Hebrews 11:31-35 (KJV)

You have to accept prosperity as yours in order to be prosperous.

"Wealth and riches shall be in his house: and his righteousness endureth for ever." Psalm 112:3 (KJV)

God has promised you days of heaven on earth.

Faith (the Word of God that you have heard and come to believe) causes every law to function. The Word must be your base. Spiritual laws will work when they are put to work.

Satan's goal is to convince you that God's Word won't come to pass. He causes you to doubt, which causes your faith to stop working. Jump-start your faith by getting back in the Word of God.

God has already done everything He is going to do; He has put laws in place that will propel you in the corresponding direction of your decisions.

Jesus came so that you could experience the abundant life.

"The thief cometh not, but for to steal, and to kill, and to destroy: I am come that they might have life, and that they might have it more abundantly." John 10:10 (KJV)

The devil comes to steal, kill and destroy. God wants you to enjoy life and experience the overflow of His goodness.

God wants you to prosper in every way, but prosperity, like anything else in the kingdom of God, is governed by certain spiritual laws. There is no prosperity apart from the Word of God, so the Word must be the basis of your prosperity. The Law of the Spirit of life in Christ Jesus governs prosperity and overrides the law of sin and death.

HOW TO OVERCOME THE SPIRIT OF JEALOUSY

There are negative consequences associated with jealousy. Jealousy causes hopelessness and depression. As born-again a Believer, you should never be jealous or envious.

> *"Let not thine heart envy sinners: but be thou in the fear of the LORD all the day long. For surely there is an end; and thine expectation shall not be cut off." Proverbs 23:17-18 (KJV)*

There is a future and a reward for Believers. Be grateful for what God is doing in your life.

Jealousy makes you mean and cruel.

> *"Set me as a seal upon thine heart, as a seal upon thine arm: for love is strong as death; <u>jealousy is cruel as the grave</u>: the coals thereof are coals of fire, which hath a most vehement flame." Song of Solomon 8:6 (KJV)*

Envy and jealousy are more detrimental than wrath or anger.

"Wrath is cruel, and anger is outrageous; but who is able to stand before envy?" Proverbs 27:4 (KJV)

When you walk in jealousy, you have limited power.

Unwise comparisons open the door to envy and jealousy.

"For we dare not make ourselves of the number, or compare ourselves with some that commend themselves: but they measuring themselves by themselves, and <u>comparing themselves among themselves, are not wise.</u>" 2 Corinthians 10:12 (KJV)

People who compare themselves with others are without understanding. To compare is to belittle what God has done in your life. You can receive more from God by being grateful.

Jealous people are not spiritual and are walking in the flesh.

"For ye are yet carnal: for whereas there is among you envying, and strife, and divisions, are ye not carnal, and walk as men?" 1 Corinthians 3:3 (KJV)

Walking in the flesh is a way of thinking that opposes the Word of God and there is no profit to walking in the flesh. God has not called you to walk as mere men.

Jealousy makes you bitter, and where jealousy exists there is disorder and the potential for every evil work.

"But if ye have bitter envying and strife in your hearts, glory not, and lie not against the truth." James 3:14 (KJV)

If you have strife, jealousy (bitter envy) and selfish ambitions in your hearts, do not pride yourselves on it (trying to look better than others) or make yourself sound wise and thus be in resistance of and false to the Truth.

The spirit of jealousy will lead you down a path that could ultimately destroy your life.

Jealousy brings confusion. Wherever there is envy, there is disorder and every evil work (James 3:16).

Jealousy is feeling as though your needs will not be met. Jealousy is doubting your self-worth and whether you have what it takes to succeed in life. It is also feelings of powerlessness and insecurity.

How we get free from jealousy:

1) Realize the power you have in the Holy Spirit.

> "But ye shall receive power, after that the Holy Ghost is come upon you: and ye shall be witnesses unto me both in Jerusalem, and in all Judaea, and in Samaria, and unto the uttermost part of the earth." Acts 1:8 (KJV)

The same power that raised Jesus from the dead dwells inside of you and is capable of raising you up from any emotional attack.

> "But if the Spirit of him that raised up Jesus from the dead dwell in you, he that raised up Christ from the dead shall also quicken your mortal bodies by his Spirit that dwelleth in you." Romans 8:11 (KJV)

2) You have been given power over the enemy and nothing can hurt you.

"Behold, I give unto you power to tread on serpents and scorpions, and over all the power of the enemy: and nothing shall by any means hurt you." Luke 10:19 (KJV)

3) You possess the power to destroy harassing and oppressing thoughts about others.

"How God anointed Jesus of Nazareth with the Holy Ghost and with power: who went about doing good, <u>and healing all that were oppressed of the devil</u>; for God was with him." Acts 10:38 (KJV)

4) You have the power to get wealth; therefore, you have no reason to feel threatened by someone else's financial success.

"But thou shalt remember the LORD thy God: for it is he that giveth thee power to get wealth, that he may establish his covenant which he sware unto thy fathers, as it is this day." Deuteronomy 8:18 (KJV)

5) There is power in your seed. Plant good seeds – you reap what you sow! Whenever there is a need, plant a seed. Need more love – show more love.

"Be not deceived; God is not mocked: for whatsoever a man soweth, that shall he also reap." Galatians 6:7 (KJV)

6) Be content. When you are content, you don't have to be jealous.

"Not that I speak in respect of want: for I have learned, in whatsoever state I am, therewith to be content. I know both how to be abased, and I know how to abound: every

where and in all things I am instructed both to be full and
to be hungry, both to abound and to suffer need. I can
do all things through Christ which strengtheneth me."
Philippians 4:11-13 (KJV)

Contentment is not an acceptance of how things are, or settling for less; it is the confidence that God is your Source and He will supply all your needs.

The Apostle Paul learned the secret of contentment, which is to rely on God and let Him strengthen you. Trust God! It is not under your own strength or ability that you will overcome envy and jealousy.

Jealousy is a feeling of discontentment and inadequacy. Jealous people view someone else's success as a threat to their own success. Envy is proof that the spirit of jealousy is present in your life; and as a result, you will experience many negative consequences.

WALKING FREE FROM THE
DESTRUCTIVE FORCE OF STRESS

You have to attack the root of stress in order to deal with the fruit of it.

Some of the fruits of stress are:

1. Forgetfulness
2. Temper
3. Chronic fatigue
4. Cynicism (distrusting or disparaging the motives of others)
5. A sense of helplessness
6. Never having a sense of accomplishment
7. Feeling like a failure
8. Constant illness

9. Headaches/Migraines
10. High blood pressure
11. Heart disease

Emotional problems that aren't dealt with will translate into physical problems.

Don't willingly submit to stressful situations; go in the opposite direction.

> *"Surely in vain the net is spread in the sight of any bird."*
> *Proverbs 1:17 (KJV)*

It is useless to set a trap in the sight of a bird, because if a bird sees a trap being set, it knows to stay away. Likewise, stay away from stressful situations!

Learn the value of living a stress-free lifestyle. Train yourself to not let things bother you. Develop a "whatever" attitude.

You will have trouble in life, but that doesn't mean that you have to be stressed out.

> *"We are troubled on every side, yet not distressed; we are*
> *perplexed, but not in despair;" 2 Corinthians 4:8 (KJV)*

It is your responsibility to not let your heart be troubled, not God's.

> *"Let not your heart be troubled: ye believe in God, believe*
> *also in me." John 14:1 (KJV)*

Do not be troubled (distressed or agitated).You have to choose peace rather than be stressed out, and believe God in the midst of turmoil.

> *"And ye shall hear of wars and rumours of wars: <u>see that ye be not troubled</u>: for all these things must come to pass, but the end is not yet." Matthew 24:6 (KJV)*

The way to get peace is to get into God's Word. Be of good cheer—get happy!

> *"<u>These things I have spoken unto you, that in me ye might have peace.</u> In the world ye shall have tribulation: but <u>be of good cheer</u>; I have overcome the world." John 16:33 (KJV)*

<u>Jesus has said to us that in Him we may have perfect peace and confidence</u>. In the world we have tribulation, trials, distress and frustration; <u>but we are to be of good cheer and take courage</u>! Jesus has overcome the world; He has deprived it of power to harm us and has conquered it for us.

Respond to stress through the Word of God. If you believe God, there is no room for fear in your life. Focus on the Good News, rather than the bad news of the world.

Many are the afflictions of the righteous, but God delivers you out of them all.

> *"Many are the afflictions of the righteous: but the LORD delivereth him out of them all." Psalm 34:19 (KJV)*

Any time affliction shows up in your life, tell yourself, "The power of God is working for me right now."

Here are some practical causes of stress.

1. Uncertainty, or not being certain about life.
   Take control of the seeds you sow and you can be certain of the harvest you will receive.
   The Word gives absolute certainty of your future.
   Having certainty delivers you from stress.
   Don't carry unnecessary pressures.

2. Unresolved conflict.
   Resolve conflicts in your life; conflict should not sit in your life week after week.
   Carrying conflict around wears you out.
   Be at peace with all men. (Ephesians 4:26).

3. Unrealistic comparisons.
   Don't ever compare yourself to other people.
   Comparison may lead you to belittling what God has done in your life.
   Refuse to compare.
   It is not wise to compare; you are without understanding when you compare yourself with others (2 Corinthians 10:12).

4. Unconfessed sin.
   God will cleanse you of all unrighteousness when you confess your sin (1 John 1:9).
   Judge yourself and confess your sins to God.
   Use wisdom when confessing your sins to others (James 5:16).
   If you bury sin and fail to deal with it, it will bury you (Psalm 32:3).

5. Unusual financial pressure.
    Stop spending more than what you earn.
    Buying things that you cannot afford is false
    prosperity.
    Learn how to save and invest.

You have been designed by God to withstand a certain amount of
stress. The problem comes when you allow stress to go beyond the
level you were created to withstand. If you don't learn to deal with
stress and get rid of it, it will kill you.

THE LAW OF ABUNDANCE

> *"The thief cometh not, but for to steal, and to kill, and
> to destroy: I am come that they might have life, and that
> they might have it more abundantly." John 10:10 (KJV)*

The Greek translation of the word "life" is zoe, which means, "absolute
fullness of life; the life of God."

Jesus wants you to live in the fullness of life. Your life should overflow
to the point that not only are your needs meet, but you are also able
to meet the needs of others. You should be able to give away what you
have because you have more than enough.

Under the Old Covenant, it was always God's will for His chosen
people to have more than enough if they obeyed His commandments.
It was part of the blessings.

> *"And all these blessings shall come on thee, and overtake
> thee, if thou shalt hearken unto the voice of the LORD
> thy God." Deuteronomy 28:2 (KJV)*

"The LORD shall command the blessing upon thee in thy storehouses, and in all that thou settest thine hand unto; and he shall bless thee in the land which the LORD thy God giveth thee." Deuteronomy 28:8 (KJV)

"<u>And the LORD shall make thee plenteous in goods,</u> in the fruit of thy body, and in the fruit of thy cattle, and in the fruit of thy ground, in the land which the LORD sware unto thy fathers to give thee." Deuteronomy 28:11 (KJV)

"Keep therefore the words of this covenant, and do them, that ye may prosper in all that ye do." Deuteronomy 29:9 (KJV)

They were to have so much that they were supposed to lend to many nations and never need to borrow. Lending money to an entire nation is a large sum of money.

"The LORD shall open unto thee his good treasure, the heaven to give the rain unto thy land in his season, and to bless all the work of thine hand: and <u>thou shalt lend unto many nations</u>, and <u>thou shalt not borrow</u>." Deuteronomy 28:12 (KJV)

They were to have so much that a tenth of what they had would be more than enough for strangers, orphans and widows in their city.

"When thou hast made an end of tithing all the tithes of thine increase the third year, which is the year of tithing, and hast given it unto the Levite, the stranger, the fatherless, and the widow, that they may eat within thy gates, and be filled;" Deuteronomy 26:12 (KJV)

Spiritual laws supersede natural laws. The law of abundance will work for anyone who gets involved with it. Spiritual laws will change natural laws. For example: Jesus walked on water. Water also came out of a rock to quench the thirst of the children of Israel.

Prosperity can be defined as, "to excel to the highest place; to go up to something desirable."

Money is only worth something when it is turned into goods and services. Money should be used to love people and to worship God. Money and material things should be used to bless people. People should never be used to obtain things or money.

The law of faith;

> *"Where is boasting then? It is excluded. By what law? of works? Nay: but by the law of faith." Romans 3:27 (KJV)*

Where is boasting then? It is excluded. By what law? Of works? No: but by the Law of the Word of God that we have believed and embraced. The Law of the Word of God (faith) will activate spiritual laws that will ultimately set you free.

The law of the Spirit of life in Christ Jesus will deliver a person from the law of sin and death once he or she makes the decision to switch laws.

> *"For I delight in the law of God after the inward man: But I see another law in my members, warring against the law of my mind, and bringing me into captivity to the law of sin which is in my members. O wretched man that I am! who shall deliver me from the body of this death? I*

*thank God through Jesus Christ our Lord. So then with
the mind I myself serve the law of God; but with the flesh
the law of sin." Romans 7:22-25 (KJV)*

*"There is therefore now no condemnation to them which
are in Christ Jesus, who walk not after the flesh, but
after the Spirit. For the law of the Spirit of life in Christ
Jesus hath made me free from the law of sin and death."
Romans 8:1-2 (KJV)*

You are no longer subject to the law of sin and death because Jesus
destroyed Satan, who had the power of death.

*"Forasmuch then as the children are partakers of flesh
and blood, he also himself likewise took part of the same;
that through death he might destroy him that had the
power of death, that is, the devil;" Hebrews 2:14 (KJV)*

The condition of your heart is the key to living an abundant life. The
law of abundance includes all areas of your life (See Deuteronomy
26:1-29:9). Money isn't always the answer to everything in life.

Abundance is available to every Believer. God wants you to live in the
overflow so you can consider the needs of your neighbor and be in a
position to prevent misfortune in his or her life.

*"And God is able to make all grace abound toward
you; that ye, always having all sufficiency in all things,
may abound to every good work: (As it is written,
He hath dispersed abroad; he hath given to the poor:
his righteousness remaineth for ever. Now he that
ministereth seed to the sower both minister bread for
your food, and multiply your seed sown, and increase*

the fruits of your righteousness;) <u>Being enriched in</u>
<u>*every thing to all bountifulness, which causeth through*</u>
<u>*us thanksgiving to God.*</u>*" 2 Corinthians 9:8-11 (KJV)*

Those who are opposed to abundance are generally selfish people who are only concerned with themselves and their households.

The condition of your heart determines where your treasure is. When the rich young ruler went to Jesus to find out how he could have eternal life, Jesus searched his heart to find out where his treasure was.

"And when he was gone forth into the way, there came one running, and kneeled to him, and asked him, Good Master, what shall I do that I may inherit eternal life? And Jesus said unto him, Why callest thou me good? there is none good but one, that is, God. Thou knowest the commandments, Do not commit adultery, Do not kill, Do not steal, Do not bear false witness, Defraud not, Honour thy father and mother. And he answered and said unto him, Master, all these have I observed from my youth. Then Jesus beholding him loved him, and said unto him, <u>One thing thou lackest</u>: go thy way, sell whatsoever thou hast, and give to the poor, and thou shalt have treasure in heaven: and come, take up the cross, and follow me. And he was sad at that saying, and went away grieved: for he had great possessions." Mark 10:17-22 (KJV)

Though the ruler was wealthy, he didn't have complete prosperity; his money didn't answer all of his problems.

The answer to having an everlasting, abundant life is to love God with all of your heart, soul, strength and mind, and to love your neighbor as yourself.

> *"Hear, O Israel: The LORD our God is one LORD: And thou shalt love the LORD thy God with all thine heart, and with all thy soul, and with all thy might. "* Deuteronomy 6:4-6(KJV)

> *"And he answering said, Thou shalt love the Lord thy God with all thy heart, and with all thy soul, and with all thy strength, and with all thy mind; and thy neighbour as thyself."* Luke 10:27 (KJV)

This is the law of abundance. When you love God, you love Him with your treasure (money) and things that are of great value to you, because where your heart is, so is your treasure.

> *"For where your treasure is, there will your heart be also."* Matthew 6:21 (KJV)

Religious tradition has taught that worshipping God is only lifting up your hands and praising His name, but worshipping God requires your heart being involved. You can't worship God without your heart, because He has attached your treasure to your heart.

Worshipping God involves sacrifice. Abraham told his servants that he and the lad (the sacrifice that was most dear to him) were going to worship God (Genesis 22:2, 5).

> *"And he said, Take now thy son, thine only son Isaac, whom thou lovest, and get thee into the land of Moriah;*

and offer him there for a burnt offering upon one of the mountains which I will tell thee of." Genesis 22:2 (KJV)

"And Abraham said unto his young men, Abide ye here with the ass; and I and the lad will go yonder and worship, and come again to you." Genesis 22:5 (KJV)

You can't worship God without obedience. If you want to glorify God, you have to bring an offering and come into His courts and worship Him.

"Give unto the LORD the glory due unto his name: bring an offering, and come into his courts. O worship the LORD in the beauty of holiness: <u>fear</u> before him, all the earth." Psalm 96:8 -9 (KJV)

Give to the Lord the glory and honor due to His name: bring an offering, and come into His presence, worship the Lord in the beauty of holiness. All the earth, be devoted with reverence and respect to Him.

You have to be rooted and grounded in love so you can be filled with the fullness of God.

"For this cause I bow my knees unto the Father of our Lord Jesus Christ, Of whom the whole family in heaven and earth is named, That he would grant you, according to the riches of his glory, to be strengthened with might by his Spirit in the inner man; That Christ may dwell in your hearts by faith; that ye, being rooted and grounded in love, May be able to comprehend with all saints what is the breadth, and length, and depth, and height; And to know the love of Christ, which passeth knowledge,

that ye might be filled with all the fulness of God. Now
unto him that is able to do exceeding abundantly above
all that we ask or think, according to the power that
worketh in us," Ephesians 3:14-20 (KJV)

The degree by which you demonstrate love will determine the degree of abundance that you will experience. If you don't learn how to get along with people, walk in love, worship God in obedience and control your emotions, then you will never experience abundance.

Everything (abundance, prosperity, healing, etc.) is activated through the law of love. When you keep the law of love, God will manifest Himself to you.

Under the Old Covenant, to walk in the Law of abundance they had to activate that Law by obedience. Today, we still activate the Law of abundance through obedience by walking in love as God instructed us to do.

The world teaches us that prosperity primarily involves money. While this is not incorrect, it is incomplete. Money by itself can't define prosperity. True prosperity is having wholeness in every area of your life. The principles of total life prosperity fall under the law of abundance.

THE DELIVERING POWER OF HUMILITY

True humility means to comply with, obey and submit to God's Word and will for your life. We are to humble ourselves before God.

"Wherewith shall I come before the LORD, and bow myself
before the high God? shall I come before him with burnt
offerings, with calves of a year old? Will the LORD be

pleased with thousands of rams, or with ten thousands of rivers of oil? shall I give my firstborn for my transgression, the fruit of my body for the sin of my soul? He hath shewed thee, O man, what is good; and what doth the LORD require of thee, but to do justly, and to love mercy, and to walk humbly with thy God?" Micah 6:6-8 (KJV)

Walking in humility means to be submissive and compliant. Humility reduces the power of independence and ensures dependence on God.

True success is fulfilling God's will for your life. God isn't going to tell you to do something that's going to hurt you.

"For I know the thoughts that I think toward you, saith the LORD, thoughts of peace, and not of evil, to give you an expected end." Jeremiah 29:11 (KJV)

God's plans for you are designed to prosper you. God will give you the desire to do what He has called you to do. God won't make you do something that will destroy you or that is unfulfilling.

Trust that God's plan for your life is the best plan and will bring enjoyment.

Humility can be likened to an obedient child submitting to the plans of his or her parent. When you are born again, you are to become like a little child.

"And said, Verily I say unto you, Except ye be converted, and become as little children, ye shall not enter into the kingdom of heaven. Whosoever therefore shall humble himself as this little child, the same is greatest in the kingdom of heaven." Matthew 18:3-4 (KJV)

Put yourself in a position to depend on God by being willing to do whatever He says. Ask yourself, "Am I depending on God for everything?"

Humility will make you great (Matthew 18:4).

Don't let your years of experience as a Christian keep you from being humble (1 Kings 3:7). You are nothing without God.

> *"And now, O LORD my God, thou hast made thy servant king instead of David my father: and I am but a little child: I know not how to go out or come in." 1 Kings 3:7 (KJV)*

God wants to be your very present help in times of trouble.

> *"God is our refuge and strength, a very present help in trouble." Psalm 46:1 (KJV)*

Humble yourself the way Jesus did.

> *"And being found in fashion as a man, he humbled himself, and became obedient unto death, even the death of the cross." Philippians 2:8 (KJV)*

The way up is down. You can "look" humble. False humility is an outward display without real submission to God. Being "religious" is false humility.

> *"Having a form of godliness, but denying the power thereof: from such turn away." 2 Timothy 3:5 (KJV)*

True Bible humility can't always be seen. It is on the inside and comes from your heart.

True humility is demonstrated by lying at the feet of Jesus. When Jesus fed the four thousand, there were many of the multitudes who were lame, blind and had all types of sickness. They would kneel down at Jesus' feet to be healed.

> "And great multitudes came unto him, having with them those that were lame, blind, dumb, maimed, and many others, and cast them down at Jesus' feet; and he healed them:" Matthew 15:30 (KJV)

Jairus' daughter was healed when he fell down and submitted himself at Jesus' feet (Mark 5:22-23).

Because of her faith, belief in Jesus and what she had heard of Him, a woman's young daughter was healed of demonic oppression when the woman cast herself down at Jesus' feet (Mark 7:25-30).

A woman washed Jesus' feet with her tears and dried them with her hair. She anointed His feet with precious oil. Jesus forgave her of her sin. (Luke 7:37-50).

A man was delivered of demons at Jesus' feet (Luke 8:35).

Martha's sister, Mary, sat at the feet of Jesus to hear the Word (Luke 10:39). Jesus raised Mary's brother Lazarus from the dead after she fell down at Jesus' feet (John 11:32-44).

John received a supernatural vision of end time events after he fell at the feet of Jesus (Revelation 1:17).

You cannot be successful by yourself. Nothing will ever go right without Jesus. It's not too late to acknowledge Jesus and He'll lift you up. Thirst and hunger for God and His plan is what you need to advance spiritually. Your intelligence and abilities shouldn't be exalted over your relationship with God. Freedom comes from knowing you don't have to play political games to get ahead in life. God has a better way for you to be exalted. Your way may seem faster but God's way is the more sure way.

There are many reasons to humble yourself but two of the most important are:

1. So that God will lift you up (James 4:10).
2. So that you can experience God's grace in your life.

True humility requires you to submit to God's Word and His plan for your life rather than your own words and plans. Trust Him for everything you need. When you submit your will to God's will, you will experience lasting success and honor.

THE LAWS THAT GOVERN POVERTY

A person will become rich or poor by applying the law of prosperity or the law of poverty. Laziness activates the law of poverty.

> *"I went by the field of the slothful, and by the vineyard of the man void of understanding; And, lo, it was all grown over with thorns, and nettles had covered the face thereof, and the stone wall thereof was broken down."*
> *Proverbs 24:30-31 (KJV)*

If you are lazy or do not understand your task, your efforts will not produce abundance.

If you are diligent and able to work without supervision, God's bountiful supply will be evident in your life.

"Go to the ant, thou sluggard; consider her ways, and be wise: Which having no guide, overseer, or ruler, Provideth her meat in the summer, and gathereth her food in the harvest." Proverbs 6:6-8 (KJV)

"There is that scattereth, and yet increaseth; and there is that withholdeth more than is meet, but it tendeth to poverty. The liberal soul shall be made fat: and he that watereth shall be watered also himself." Proverbs 11:24-25 (KJV)

Poverty is a curse and brings destruction.

"The rich man's wealth is his strong city: the destruction of the poor is their poverty." Proverbs 10:15 (KJV)

Since the devil's objective is to destroy, poverty is not God's agenda.

The person who trusts in their riches are wicked and will experience destruction.

"Lo, this is the man that made not God his strength; but trusted in the abundance of his riches, and strengthened himself in his wickedness." Psalm 52:7 (KJV)

God commands the wealthy man not to trust in his riches, because riches are uncertain.

"Charge them that are rich in this world, that they be not highminded, nor trust in uncertain riches, but in the living God, who giveth us richly all things to enjoy;" 1 Timothy 6:17 (KJV)

Trust God and not your money; wealth and riches come from Him. If God tells you to give your material possessions away but you can't do it, know that you trust in riches more than in God.

Enjoy what God gives you. If He tells you to give it away, obey Him quickly. When you are truly prosperous, you will never fear that you will run out of something. Instead, your trust in the Word of God will cause you to overflow in possessions, health, etc.

There are seven laws that govern poverty:

1. Laziness. (Proverbs 23:21)
2. Not obeying God by ignoring or not knowing His wisdom in what to do with your money. (Jer 18:10, Pro 3:5, Jer 42:6, Hos 4:6)
3. Hating correction and instruction. (Proverbs 13:18)
4. Loving sleep. (Proverbs 20:13)
5. Addictive behaviors and lack of temperance. (Proverbs 23:21)
6. Following worthless people and pursuits. (Proverbs 28:19)
7. Hastening to be rich at any cost. (Proverbs 28:22)

Everything that happens on the earth happens as a result of a spiritual law. These laws are established principles that, when applied, work for anyone who becomes involved with them. Prosperity is more than money. It also encompasses health, wealth, family and marriage. In the same way that the laws governing prosperity cause you to become rich, the spiritual laws that govern poverty cause you to become poor.

THE LAW OF HONOR

Honor comes from your heart.

> "This people draweth nigh unto me with their mouth, and honoureth me with their lips; but their heart is far from me." Matthew 15:8 (KJV)

Mere "lip service" doesn't honor God. God is honored when your decisions and actions are solely based on His Word. You cannot make Scripture "big" or "meaningful" in your life if you do not read your Bible and meditate on the Word. Ignorance of the Word prevents you from honoring God.

God is your Father, and the first commandment with promise is to honor your father and mother.

> "Honour thy father and mother; (which is the first commandment with promise;) That it may be well with thee, and thou mayest live long on the earth." Ephesians 6:2-3 (KJV)

Your parent's words should mean more to you than the words of other people. It should be the same with God your Father.

> "Render therefore to all their dues: tribute to whom tribute is due; custom to whom custom; fear to whom fear; honour to whom honour." Romans 13:7 (KJV)

God will honor those who honor Him.

> "Wherefore the LORD God of Israel saith, I said indeed that thy house, and the house of thy father, should walk before me for ever: but now the LORD saith, Be it far

from me; <u>for them</u> <u>that honour me I will honour,</u> and
they that despise me shall be lightly esteemed."
1 Samuel 2:30 (KJV)

When you allow God's Word to have value and meaning in your life, your prayers and declarations will have value with Him.

For example: When God's Word has value then you will not allow what others say about you to bother you. Their words will run off you like water off a duck's back, because what God says about you means more to you than what other people say and you act accordingly.

Ask yourself: what type of value does God's Word hold in my life?

No one can honor God without honoring His Son.

"That all men should honour the Son, even as they
honour the Father. He that honoureth not the Son
honoureth not the Father which hath sent him." John
5:23 (KJV)

You do not honor with words only, but also with your treasure.

To honor means to "to have meaning and value." You honor God when you value His Word in your life enough that nothing and no one can sway you away from the Word.

THE LAW OF LISTENING

If yo only hear and do not do according to the Word, you deceive yourself. A forgetful hearer is a person who hears but does not do the Word and is also a hypocrite. After you hear the Word, tests will come.

If you forget the information, you will fail the test. When hearing the Word, take notes with a plan to implement what you have learned.

If you do not obey Jesus, then it makes no sense to call Him "Lord." If Jesus is Lord of your life, your only response to the Word is to accept it and do what it says. Hypocrisy and secret sin are always eventually revealed. Jesus expects simple, child-like obedience. The Word of God is not optional, and until it becomes real to you, its promises will not become realities.

> *"And he said unto them, Set your hearts unto all the words which I testify among you this day, which ye shall command your children to observe to do, all the words of this law. For it is not a vain thing for you; because it is your life: and through this thing ye shall prolong your days ...." Deuteronomy 32:46 - 47 (KJV)*

In other words he is saying, "Make these Words valuable to you; keep them in the forefront of your thinking, all of my testimony today, so that you can use them in pleading with your children to be careful to obey all the Words of this Law. This is not a small matter for you; on the contrary, it is your life! Through it you will live long."

A man who hears and obeys the Word is wise. Jesus states that whoever hears and does the Word shall be likened to a wise man who builds his house upon a rock.

> *"Therefore whosoever heareth these sayings of mine, and doeth them, I will liken him unto a wise man, which built his house upon a rock:" Matthew 7:24 (KJV)*

How you handle the Word determines whether or not you are wise or foolish. Wise men know how to handle the Word, while foolish men disregard it. Do not act out on things without hearing God's Word on them first.

The Word of God is wisdom. The Word of God is life and health. The Word of God produces riches, honor and supernatural results. Hearing plus Doing = Transformation.

The written Word of God opens the door for you to hear a Word directly from God. If you don't pay attention to the written Word, you will not be able to hear Him when He speaks directly to you. The small voice from within (that spoken Word of God) includes specific details for success. For example: the Word instructs us to forgive and walk in love. When you hear the Word and decide to keep it, a test will always come, and I can attest to this personally. I recently had somebody try to bring up a very hurtful situation. Because I had been meditating on the Word of God, a small voice from within kept reminding me to just let it go, and no matter how many times they tried to bring it back up, I would not go there with them. I said I wasn't go to visit the issue again, and with the help of God, I haven't.

Our lives are the way they are either because of the way we hear and do the Word of God or because we hear and don't do the Word. Hear the Word. Do the Word. Enjoy life.

Disobedience to the written Word hardens your heart to the voice of God. Foolish men commonly disobey the Word by continuing in old behavior patterns, like murmuring and complaining, returning evil for evil, fornicating, not walking in love and failing to sow good seeds.

Doing the Word will produce supernatural results.

Your prosperity often depends on what you do with the instructions God gives you. It is important to do specifically what God says.

"And the third day there was a marriage in Cana of Galilee; and the mother of Jesus was there: And both Jesus was called, and his disciples, to the marriage. And when they wanted wine, the mother of Jesus saith unto him, They have no wine. Jesus saith unto her, Woman, what have I to do with thee? mine hour is not yet come. His mother saith unto the servants, Whatsoever he saith unto you, do it. And there were set there six waterpots of stone, after the manner of the purifying of the Jews, containing two or three firkins apiece. Jesus saith unto them, Fill the waterpots with water. And they filled them up to the brim. And he saith unto them, Draw out now, and bear unto the governor of the feast. And they bare it. When the ruler of the feast had tasted the water that was made wine, and knew not whence it was: (but the servants which drew the water knew;) the governor of the feast called the bridegroom, And saith unto him, Every man at the beginning doth set forth good wine; and when men have well drunk, then that which is worse: but thou hast kept the good wine until now." John 2:1-9 (KJV)

The manifestation may not be immediately apparent, but God's Word never fails. Obedience changes circumstances in the midst of you obeying God. When you sow obedience, you reap manifestation of God's promises.

People who hear the Word but don't act on it live foolishly, deceiving themselves and experiencing defeat in every area. The Word is the wisdom of God. The written wisdom of God will open you up to hear a Word directly from God. Hearing and obeying God's Word enables you to have success in every area of life.

THE LAW OF SEEDTIME AND HARVEST

The Bible holds 66 books worth of seeds that will produce a harvest for any area of your life whether it is spiritually, emotionally, physically or financially. The principle of seedtime and harvest will last as long as the earth remains.

> *"While the earth remaineth, seedtime and harvest, and cold and heat, and summer and winter, and day and night shall not cease." Genesis 8:22 (KJV)*

God's kingdom is a system of casting seeds into the ground.

> *"And he said, So is the kingdom of God, as if a man should cast seed into the ground; And should sleep, and rise night and day, and the seed should spring and grow up, he knoweth not how. For the earth bringeth forth fruit of herself; first the blade, then the ear, after that the full corn in the ear. But when the fruit is brought forth, immediately he putteth in the sickle, because the harvest is come. And he said, Whereunto shall we liken the kingdom of God? or with what comparison shall we compare it? It is like a grain of mustard seed, which, when it is sown in the earth, is less than all the seeds that be in the earth: But when it is sown, it groweth up, and becometh greater than all herbs, and shooteth out great branches; so that the fowls of the air may lodge under the shadow of it." Mark 4:26-32 (KJV)*

The Word is incorruptible seed that comes from God; it will never fail. The seeds that you sow determine what you get in return. For example, if you sow evil and strife, you'll receive evil and strife. If you sow forgiveness, you'll receive forgiveness. If you give, it will be given to you.

> *"Be ye therefore merciful, as your Father also is merciful. Judge not, and ye shall not be judged: condemn not, and ye shall not be condemned: forgive, and ye shall be forgiven: Give, and it shall be given unto you; good measure, pressed down, and shaken together, and running over, shall men give into your bosom. For with the same measure that ye mete withal it shall be measured to you again." Luke 6:36-38 (KJV)*

There is a promise in God's Word that will meet every need that you have.

> *"But my God shall supply all your need according to his riches in glory by Christ Jesus." Philippians 4:19 (KJV)*

When you decide what kind of harvest you want, you can find out what kind of seed you need to sow based on the Word of God.

Your heart is a garden and so is your life. God formed you from the soil of the ground; therefore, your heart is ground for sowing.

> *"And the LORD God formed man of the dust of the ground, and breathed into his nostrils the breath of life; and man became a living soul." Genesis 2:7 (KJV)*

You are not where you are in life for no reason. Your life is a sum total of the seeds you have sown. When you seek God first, read His Word and allow it to be rooted in your heart, you will discover the answers to the issues of life.

"But seek ye first the kingdom of God, and his righteousness; and all these things shall be added unto you." Matthew 6:33 (KJV)

Sow the seed by putting God's Word into your heart. Find scriptures on whatever issue you are dealing with (Psalm 34:10; Jeremiah 1:12).

"The young lions do lack, and suffer hunger: but they that seek the LORD shall not want any good thing." Psalm 34:10 (KJV)

"Then said the LORD unto me, Thou hast well seen: for I will hasten my word to perform it." Jeremiah 1:12 (KJV)

Make sure you water the seed; read the scripture over and over, write it down, confess it, speak it to others, dream about it, and out of your garden (your heart) will come your harvest.

Sowing and reaping are foundational principles that will never go away. Seedtime and harvest refer to every area of life. Seeds that are sown into the ground determine what type of crops will grow. For example, if a farmer sows corn seeds into the ground, he is sure to receive a harvest of corn. Likewise, when you sow God's Word into your heart, it is inevitable for you to reap His promises.

UNDERSTANDING SALVATION

The word salvation comes from the Greek word soteria, which means "deliverance, preservation and safety." It primarily involves deliverance from the bondage of sin.

> *"Stand fast therefore in the liberty wherewith Christ hath made us free, and be not entangled again with the yoke of bondage." Galatians 5:1 (KJV)*

Salvation also includes deliverance from our enemies.

> *"That we should be saved from our enemies, and from the hand of all that hate us;" Luke 1:71 (KJV)*

> *"Surely he hath borne our griefs, and carried our sorrows: yet we did esteem him stricken, smitten of God, and afflicted. But he was wounded for our transgressions, he was bruised for our iniquities: the chastisement of our peace was upon him; and with his stripes we are healed." Isaiah 53:4-5 (KJV)*

> *"That it might be fulfilled which was spoken by Esaias the prophet, saying, Himself took our infirmities, and bare our sicknesses." Matthew 8:17 (KJV)*

"Who his own self bare our sins in his own body on the tree, that we, being dead to sins, should live unto righteousness: by whose stripes ye were healed." 1 Peter 2:24 (KJV)

Salvation is a gift made available to those who believe that Jesus is Lord and that He died and rose from the dead to save mankind.

"Neither is there salvation in any other: for there is none other name under heaven given among men, whereby we must be saved." Acts 4:12 (KJV)

"And they said, Believe on the Lord Jesus Christ, and thou shalt be saved, and thy house." Acts 16:31 (KJV)

"That if thou shalt confess with thy mouth the Lord Jesus, and shalt believe in thine heart that God hath raised him from the dead, thou shalt be saved. For with the heart man believeth unto righteousness; and with the mouth confession is made unto salvation." Romans 10:9-10 (KJV)

The gift cannot be earned through good deeds or by simply being a "good person".

"For by grace are ye saved through faith; and that not of yourselves: it is the gift of God: Not of works, lest any man should boast." Ephesians 2:8 (KJV)

It is a matter of acting out on what you have come to believe according to God's Word concerning salvation. Furthermore, salvation involves a process that will not only guarantee you entrance into heaven, but will also position you to experience a complete life on earth.

PRAYER OF SALVATION

If you would like to enter into a relationship with Jesus, simply pray the prayer below:

"God, I know I am a sinner and I am sorry for the sins I have committed. I know my sins put distance between us and I know I cannot save myself. Only Your Son, Jesus, can save me and eliminate the distance between us. I believe He is Your Son, who died on the executioner's stake for my sins and rose from the dead. I receive Him as my Savior and accept Your offer of forgiveness and everlasting life. Thank you, Father. In Jesus' name I pray. Amen."

Printed in the United States
By Bookmasters